# Seven Myths of Africa
in World History

MYTHS OF HISTORY: A HACKETT SERIES

# Seven Myths of Africa in World History

by David Northrup

Series Editors
Alfred J. Andrea and Andrew Holt

Hackett Publishing Company, Inc.
Indianapolis/Cambridge

20  19  18  17     1  2  3  4  5  6  7

For further information, please address
   Hackett Publishing Company, Inc.
   P.O. Box 44937
   Indianapolis, Indiana 46244-0937

   www.hackettpublishing.com

Cover design by Rick Todhunter and Brian Rak
Interior design by Elizabeth L. Wilson
Composition by Aptara, Inc.

**Library of Congress Cataloging-in-Publication Data**

Names: Northrup, David, 1941– author.
Title: Seven myths of Africa in world history / by David Northrup.
Other titles: Myths of history.
Description: Indianapolis ; Cambridge : Hackett Publishing Company, 2017. | Series:
   Myths of history | Includes bibliographical references and index.
Identifiers: LCCN 2017009573 | ISBN 9781624666391 (pbk.) | ISBN 9781624666407
   (cloth)
Subjects: LCSH: Africa—History—Errors, inventions, etc. | Africa—Commerce—
   History. | Africa—Civilization.
Classification: LCC DT20 .N67 2017 | DDC 960—dc23
LC record available at https://lccn.loc.gov/2017009573

# CONTENTS

# Series Editors' Foreword

The series editors take great pride in presenting David Northrup's important contribution to Hackett Publishing Company's Myths of History Series, *Seven Myths of Africa in World History*. Arguably no other continent has been more enshrouded in myths, misconceptions, and stereotypes than Africa, especially sub-Saharan Africa, and that has been true in the West since the days of Greco-Roman antiquity.

As Northrup points out in his Introduction, many of the West's mistaken notions about Africa south of the Sahara were canonized in the first century CE by the Roman encyclopedist Pliny the Elder in his massive *Naturalis historia* (Natural History). A fair portion of Pliny's information, which included numerous half-truths, erroneous notions, and baseless legends, was passed on to medieval Europe by later, less-gifted compilers. Chief among them was Saint Isidore of Seville (ca. 560–636), whom Pope John Paul II, perhaps appropriately, nominated as patron saint of the Internet. Drawing on Pliny, Isidore described in the following manner the land that Greeks and Romans knew as Aethiopia, namely the vast region that lay south of the ancient kingdom of Kush (today the nation of Sudan):

> Aethiopia receives its name from the color of [its] people, who are scorched due to the sun's proximity. To be sure, the color of the people is a witness to the sun's intensity, for the broiling heat is never-ending there. . . . It has a great number of peoples of various appearance, who are fear-inspiring because they look so monstrous. It is filled to capacity with a multitude of wild beasts and serpents. There, in fact, are such beasts as the rhinoceros, the giraffe, the basilisk, [and] monstrous dragons, from whose brain gems are extracted.[1]

If you have failed to see a basilisk at your local zoo, count yourself fortunate. This "little king" is a serpent that kills simply by its gaze. As for extracting gems from a dragon's brain, Isidore (and Pliny before him) noted that the gems had to be taken from a living dragon. For that reason, bold individuals cut them out from sleeping dragons.[2] Aethiopia was, indeed, a fabulous land of wonder, mystery, menace, and potential riches.

To be sure, many centuries after Isidore's day, vague information filtered into medieval Europe regarding the rich kingdoms and empires of Africa's Western Sudan, a land that lies north of West Africa's tropical rain forest belt. In Chapter 3, Northrup

---

1. Isidorus Hispalensis, *Etymologiarum siue Originum libri XX*, Book 14, chapter 5, par. 14, http://clt.brepolis.net/llta/pages/Toc.aspx. Translated by A. J. Andrea, © 2017. All rights reserved.

2. Ibid., Book 16, chapter 14, par. 7.

sums up the state of current scholarly knowledge of these Sudanic polities. But what did late-medieval Europeans know or think they knew of them? The best surviving evidence of that knowledge is the *Catalan Atlas* of 1375, which is credited to the workshop of Abraham Cresques, a Jewish master mapmaker of Majorca.

The map, which lavishly illustrates all of the known and imagined regions of Afro-Eurasia that were part of the worldview of certain educated, late-fourteenth-century Europeans, depicts the West African, sub-Saharan trading empire of Mali and its fabled monarch Mansa Musa (Emperor Moses), who reigned from ca. 1312 to about 1337. Regarding the emperor and his empire, the mapmaker wrote:

> This black Lord is called Musse Melly and is the sovereign of the land of the negroes of Gineva [Ghana, or Guinea]. This king is the richest and noblest of all these lands due to the abundance of gold that is extracted from his lands.[3]

To represent the emperor's wealth and the amount of gold that flowed north out of Mali, the mapmaker portrayed Mansa Musa seated on a throne, wearing a crown embossed in gold leaf, and offering a golden nugget (also made of gold leaf) to a Tuareg merchant, who approaches riding on a dromedary (single-humped camel). Flanking the throne are two of the most prosperous and important cities of his empire and the entire Western Sudan, Timbuktu (Tenbuch) and Gao (Geugeu). Strangely, the emperor holds a scepter that is topped by, of all things, a fleur-de-lis. One explanation for the curious interjection of a French royal symbol into this scene is that the atlas was cataloged among the possessions of King Charles V of France in 1380. Possibly the king had either directly commissioned the map or, more likely, King Peter IV of Aragon sent it as a gift to King Charles, with whom he was allied. Whatever the reason, that fleur-de-lis is a prime example of the propensity of outsiders to project their attitudes, perspectives, and values onto an Africa that they barely knew and poorly understood.

It is no surprise that word of Mansa Musa had reached fourteenth-century Europe. His hajj of 1324/1325 had caught the attention of the Muslim world of North Africa, especially Egypt, where his lavish generosity is reputed to have had a profoundly negative effect on the value of gold in and around Cairo. Venetian and other Italian merchants who resided in Egypt's major cities and in other trading sites across North Africa could not have failed to take notice.

Indeed, word of a River of Gold (the Senegal), from which native peoples extracted that precious metal, had been filtering into Europe for some time. Driven by a desire to find the river, in 1346 a Catalan sailor, Jaume (or Jaime) Ferrer, set sail from Majorca and traveled down the west coast of Africa. He and his crew disappeared, but Cresques immortalized this failed expedition by depicting Ferrer, three of his crew, and his ship sailing along the northwest coast of Africa.

---

3. Gabriel Llompart and Jaume Riera, trans., *The Cresques Project, Catalan Atlas* Legends, Panel III, http://www.cresquesproject.net.

The *Catalan Atlas* of 1375, attributed to Abraham Cresques (1325–1387). Mansa Musa of Mali, a Tuareg merchant mounted on a dromedary, the cities of Timbuktu and Gao, and the River of Gold. Source: Wikimedia Commons, PD-US.

In the atlas, the River of Gold flows beneath Mansa Musa's feet, and as the eye moves eastward, or to the right, one sees a black person whipping a dromedary and the seated king of Organa (Golden Guinea) holding a scimitar. The caption next to him reads, "Here rules the King of Organa, a Saracen that constantly battles with the Saracens of the coast and with other Arabs."[4] Organa was the name that Europeans gave to the powerful central African empire of Kanem-Bornu, which Northrup also describes in Chapter 3. Other than the name, this presumed hostility with other Muslims, and the mistaken notion that Organa's royal banner was a Western-style heraldic standard depicting a green palm tree flanked by two yellow, downward-pointing keys on a white background, the West "knew" essentially nothing about Kanem-Bornu.[5] Note that the *Catalan Atlas* depicts two fortifications next to the king of Organa, each of which flies a white banner with a green palm tree.

Farther east there is an elephant with a castle-like enclosure on its back. But note that it is a small-eared Asian elephant. The same elephant and a similar cargo appear

---

4. Ibid., *Catalan Atlas* Legends, Panel IV, http://www.cresquesproject.net.

5. See the mid-fourteenth-century Castilian *Book of Knowledge of All Kingdoms*, trans. Clements R. Markham (London: Hakluyt Society, 1912), 31.

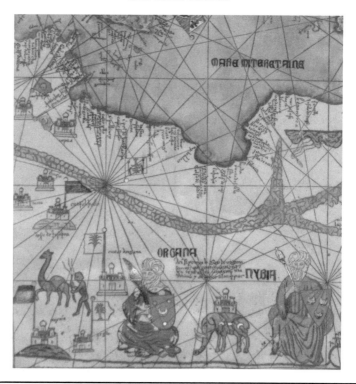

The *Catalan Atlas*. The River of Gold (with a fortified island), a black with a dromedary, the king of Organa, an Asian elephant, the king of Nubia. Source: Wikimedia Commons, PD-US.

in the atlas' depiction of the sub-continent of India. The confusion of elephant types aside, the mapmaker noted in his initial introduction to the African continent that "in these regions there is a lot of ivory due to the great amount of elephants."[6] True enough, but that statement suggests another truth as well. They who looked at Africa from the outside were primarily interested in it as a source of wealth, be it gold, ivory, or slaves, and exotica, especially its wild beasts. They had precious little knowledge of or concern for its rich variety of complex cultures, and that agnosticism persisted well into modern times.

Finally, one comes to Nubia and reads: "The king of Nubia is always at war with the Christians of Nubia who are under the dominion of the emperor of Ethiopia and the land of Prester John."[7] Having failed to find Prester John in Asia, Western Christians were now starting to think that he resided in Christian Ethiopia, as readers of this book will discover in Chapter 2.

---

6. Llompart and Riera, *Cresques Project, Catalan Atlas* Legends, Panel III, http://www.cresquesproject.net.

7. Ibid., *Catalan Atlas* Legends, Panel IV, http://www.cresquesproject.net.

The rest of Africa—namely that which lay to the south—does not appear on the map. It was unknown land. Moreover, as far as we know, no fourteenth-century Westerner had yet traveled along the caravan routes that led from North Africa to Mali and returned to report on it. Only a small handful of Europeans had seen the Swahili Coast of East Africa in this same century, and an even smaller handful of Dominican missionaries and European merchants had penetrated Nubia (the present-day nation of Sudan) and Ethiopia. Consequently, European knowledge of sub-Saharan Africa was derivative at best and vague in the extreme in the fourteenth century.

Europeans would not, however, forget the riches and opportunities of Africa south of the Sahara. A half century after the *Catalan Atlas* was produced, Portuguese sailors were progressing southward along Africa's west coast, with greater luck than the ill-fated voyage of Jaume Ferrer. As David Northrup points out, when the Portuguese opened up avenues of direct contact with the kingdoms of West Africa that lay south of Cape Bojador, Europeans finally had the opportunity to acquire a more direct knowledge of certain areas of sub-Saharan Africa. The bulk of the interior, however, was still a mysterious "Dark Continent," as far as these Westerners were concerned, and it remained such well into the nineteenth century. Consequently, ignorance bred even more myths, many of which have continued down to our day.

As Northrup further notes, "Ignorance has not been the only cause of mythmaking. Prejudice is another factor." That prejudice, buttressed by racist pseudo-science, is a well-known and well-documented phenomenon that, unhappily, is still with us today, despite the social and political advances of the last half century.

As readers of this book will discover, ignorance and prejudice have not been the only factors at work. The myths, distortions, exaggerations, untruths, misconceptions, wildly off-the-mark stereotypes, and overly simplistic analyses that have combined to distort our understanding of Africa's rich and variegated history have many origins.

In Chapter 1, Northrup takes on and demolishes in detail the myth that Africa, especially sub-Saharan Africa, had no history before the modern era, that is, before the coming of Europeans into the Dark Continent. Apart from its patent cultural blindness and Eurocentrism, this myth is predicated on a racist interpretation of human history that is worse than just ignorant or wrongheaded.

Ethiopia, one of the world's oldest Christian states and cultures, has fascinated Westerners and other outsiders for centuries, even millennia. Fascination, however, often carries with it more than a touch of the fantastic and even a smidgen of the enchanted. Chapter 2 takes Ethiopia out of the mythic world of the mystical and examines it with the sober scrutiny of historical scholarship. The Ethiopia that emerges from Northrup's examination is no less interesting and no less captivating than "mystical Ethiopia."

Chapter 3 examines the charge that Western trade with Africa was, from the beginning, imbalanced in favor of the newcomers and that it wound up impoverishing the continent, especially sub-Saharan Africa. Northrup's examination of the evidence shows that such a simplistic analysis is unsatisfactory on several levels.

No investigation of African interchange with the outside world is complete without confronting head-on the slave trade. Yet no single historical issue is more fraught with erroneous assumptions, both great and small, and more overlain with myths and misconceptions. As he must, in Chapter 4, Northrup tackles the difficult task of examining the impact that the Atlantic slave trade had on both Africa and the Americas. The results of his analysis will surprise many readers.

Chapter 5 examines the balance between continuity and change that Africans have struck since the early nineteenth century. Although, as Northrup shows, there are deep continuities throughout the many cultures of contemporary Africa, "the notion of unchanging African identities is a myth." Apparently Aristotle was correct when he asserted over 2,300 years ago that "there is always something new coming out of Africa."[8] Although "something new" meant for Aristotle the wonders, especially the animals, that were constantly emerging from this largely mysterious continent, the phrase, which became a Greco-Roman proverb, is more valid today than ever before. African responses to the challenges of the past two centuries have, indeed, resulted in much that is new.

In Chapter 6, Northrup, who is not intimidated by the heat of controversial issues, examines the proposition that Islam is better suited to the indigenous cultures of sub-Saharan Africa than the Western-style forms of Christianity introduced from across the waters. Here too, his conclusions, based on a careful analysis of the data, will surprise many. Readers will also find illuminating Ibn Battuta's mid-fourteenth-century commentary on the customs and practices of the Muslim inhabitants of the kingdom of Mali.

Finally, in Chapter 7, Northrup examines the polar opposite myths of contemporary Africa: the utopian myth that independence from colonial rule would solve all problems and the fashionable, dystopian myth of an Africa from where the news is always bad. Read the chapter and find out if this land of so many different cultures, histories, polities, and economies is making progress or failing.

Any serious student of history can and will benefit from this book. For anyone at all interested in the history of Africa, it is almost mandatory reading. With that in mind, we, the editors, commend it to your careful attention.

Alfred J. Andrea
Andrew Holt

8. Harvey M. Feinberg and Joseph B. Solodow, "Out of Africa," *Journal of African History* 43 (2002): 255–61.

# PREFACE

In 2003, my former departmental colleague Matthew Restall published *Seven Myths of the Spanish Conquest* with Oxford University Press, in which he refuted common myths, or misrepresentations, regarding the Spanish conquest of the Americas that were generated both by the participants and by latter-day historians. Restall's incisive refutation of these long-circulated beliefs inspired historians Andrew Holt and Alfred J. Andrea to oversee a team of authors in writing *Seven Myths of the Crusades* (Indianapolis/Cambridge: Hackett Publishing, 2015). The two editors convinced Hackett to launch a series of books on "myths of history," and they persuaded me to undertake this volume on Africa. My use of "seven myths" as a device for structuring my volume is also in homage to Restall's pioneering achievement.

Myths of history may be constructed consciously or unconsciously, but, as they pass from person to person, any initial uncertainty tends to disappear. A speculative hypothesis becomes a fixed belief. Myths have great power, but in understanding the past their power gets in the way of rigorous analysis based on fact and logic. African history is no exception. Myths about Africa seem to have sprung into existence with the first recorded writings about the continent, and new ones have been appearing ever since. Critiquing and refuting historical distortions is of the essence of what professional historians do in seeking to make sense of evidence left by the past. However, the debates and disputes among historians less commonly make it to the classroom, where a textbook may present events as much more certain and uncontested than professional historians know them to be. This series seeks to raise the level of historical discourse above the level of the textbook by taking a more confrontational approach.

This volume takes on the task of subjecting popular myths about African history to critical examination. Refuting or modifying a particular myth involves exposing the reasons why it exists, and testing its claims against the best interpretation of the evidence. Of course, there are more than seven myths about African history and more conflicting interpretations than can possibly be included in a brief book. At best, this volume takes some steps in the right direction and provokes critical thinking. It does not claim to have the full and final answer.

Unlike a standard textbook, this volume examines large themes in deep time perspective. The book may be read on its own or used as a stimulating supplement in courses in world, African, or Atlantic history. Not only do most of the chapters cover periods of several centuries, but they also argue comparatively. History has long benefited from looking at how patterns evolved in the long term and by comparing patterns in different places. It is temptingly easy to change one's standards when looking at different places or periods. Asking the same questions of different times and places is more difficult but more rigorous. One chapter probes whether Indian Ocean trade was similar to Atlantic Ocean trade or different. Another compares the trades in slaves to Muslim lands and to the Americas. A third chapter compares identity formation among communities in Africa and among Africans abroad. A fourth compares the spread of Islam and Christianity in Africa.

Africa is not a country; it is the second largest continent. Africans have a longer history than the people of any other continent and exhibit the greatest diversity (genetic, linguistic, and cultural) of any comparable part of the earth. Writing about so diverse a continent is a big challenge. But because most outside observers tend to see Africa as a place, it is right to take up the challenge so as to locate Africa in its rightful place in world history.

The study of history is a continuous dialogue between the present and the past. Knowledge of the present can be helpful in looking for the historical roots of contemporary circumstances. Present-day concerns may also construct distorting myths and impose inappropriate categories on past events. Though living in the present, historians must listen carefully to the historical record in order to craft a nuanced understanding that also speaks to the present. Too much emphasis on the past may risk losing the attention of contemporary young people. Too much emphasis on contemporary concerns may obscure the complexity of the historical past. Balance and sensitivity are needed.

Writing these chapters has been both a fulfilling and a humbling experience. It has been fulfilling because I have been able to draw upon many decades of study, teaching, writing, and reflecting about Africa. When I first went to teach in a rural Nigerian secondary school in 1965, I did not imagine that a decade later I would become a professor of African history, nor that a half century later I would be writing yet another book about Africa. The experience of living in a village in the rain forest and teaching eager students in a newly independent African country set me on a lifelong quest to discover and make sense of African history. This book was not in my plans when I retired from teaching a few years ago, but writing the essays in this book has allowed me to revisit some topics I had written about earlier as well as to extend my knowledge in new directions.

Writing these essays has also been a humbling experience. Again and again I have wondered whether, in pointing out the flaws in others' "myths," I was not perhaps inviting critiques of my own shortcomings. These essays are not intended to settle old scores or ridicule others' honest efforts to make sense of the African experience. Nor can I expect that these essays will be the last word on these topics. Rather, my hope is that they will stimulate thinking, discussion, and debate about important issues. I have tried to be fair and gentle in my demythologizing and hope those who take issue with my conclusions will be fair and gentle with me.

I wish to thank the series editors, Alfred J. Andrea and Andrew Holt, as well as the anonymous outside readers, for their careful reviews of the entire manuscript and for their suggestions and comments. I am also grateful to Professors Ibrahim Sundiata and Matteo Salvadore for suggestions on individual chapters.

# INTRODUCTION

> So geographers, in Afric maps,
> With savage pictures fill their gaps,
> And o'er uninhabitable downs
> Place elephants for want of towns.[1]
> —*Jonathan Swift, eighteenth-century Anglo-Irish satirist*

When Jonathan Swift wrote of filling empty spaces on African maps with elephants and savage pictures, he was not satirizing a new custom. As will be detailed later in this Introduction, even before geographers knew the shape of the continent, ancient Greek and Roman writers were inhabiting Africa with a mixture of factual and imaginary beings. Today the shape of the continent is well known, its rivers and mountains accurately mapped, its wildlife counted and classified by species. African history, once deemed non-existent or not worth knowing, has been too carefully reconstructed for any world history textbook to dream of omitting coverage of the continent once held to be shrouded in darkness. Indeed, Africa is where human history begins. Nevertheless, modern writers continue to inhabit the continent with new versions of Swift's imaginary beasts and beings. In news media and classrooms, distorted interpretations and ideas may obscure African realities.

This book seeks to identify and correct some of the most pervasive of these distorted images (or "myths") of Africa's past and present. Some myths are complete falsehoods, while others involve half-truths or suffer from misplaced emphases. Some myths have been around a long time; others are of recent origin. Whether or not readers are already aware of these myths, the author believes challenging these distorted ideas provides an engaging way to explore important topics in African history.

Each of the chapters explores a particular myth or cluster of myths. The chapters follow a rough chronological order, starting with events as far back as 50,000 BCE and concluding with information from contemporary times. Except for last one, each chapter spans several centuries. Overall, the chapters explore a range of cultural, economic, social, and political topics. The book tries to include all parts of the continent, but consideration of North Africa is curtailed by the fact that most of the myths concern Africa south of the Sahara. Taken together the chapters constitute a thematic introduction to African history.

In addition to discussing African history this book also seeks to place African experiences in a larger global context. This seems a natural and necessary approach for

---

1. "On Poetry: A Rhapsody," 1733, *The Literature Network*, http://www.online-literature.com.

two major reasons. First, Africans have always interacted with people outside their continent. Second, many of the myths about the African past originated outside the continent.

Too often people imagine Africa as lying in isolation from the rest of the world until discovered and explored by Europeans in modern times. The historical record does not support this misconception. African interaction with outsiders dates from ancient and medieval times: North Africans crossed the Sahara; southwestern and southeastern Asians sailed to Africa's Indian Ocean coast to trade. Africans became early members of both of the world religions that arose nearby, first Christianity and then Islam. Even more important is the fact that early Africans initiated outside links. All of the other continents were settled by people whose ancestors came from Africa. In medieval times some West African Muslims made the pilgrimage to Mecca, and delegations from Christian Ethiopia reached southern Europe well before the first Europeans laid eyes on sub-Saharan Africa. Other Africans were taken as slaves to Asia, Europe, and, in greatest numbers after 1650, to the Americas. By choice, chance, or misadventure Africans were participants in world history.

Although Africans devised some of the myths about their continent, most myths originated elsewhere. Some of the myths that are explored in this volume began in Europe, whether due to ignorance, prejudice, or overactive imaginations. Other myths arose in the African diaspora in the Americas that the Atlantic slave trade created. Seeking to reconnect to a homeland remembered only hazily, if at all, some in the diaspora were led to mis-imagine or oversimplify the motherland. Thus, it is impossible to understand the myths of African history without including the far-flung mythmakers.

## Where Do Myths Come From?

A good place to begin the quest to discover what circumstances generated myths about Africa is with an ancient text by an illustrious Roman scholar. The *Natural History* of the man commonly known as Pliny the Elder (23–79 CE) is one of the largest research works surviving from Roman times. In summarizing all that was known about life on earth, Pliny's account of black Africans differs little from what the Greek historian Herodotus (484–425 BCE) wrote five centuries earlier. Both Pliny and Herodotus call the vast lands south of Egypt "Ethiopia" and identify as its capital the city of Meroë, located along the Nile south of Egypt. But Pliny adds accounts of improbably deformed people in Africa below the Sahara, accounts already old when he wrote and that would be repeated for many centuries to come. Pliny's credulity appears to come from his belief in myths about dark skin and tropical heat. He derives the name Ethiopia from Ethiops, the son of the god of fire and blacksmithing whom the Romans called Vulcan. The connection becomes clearer if one knows that *ethiops* in Greek means having a burnt or blackened face. Pliny seems to be suggesting that

black people were darkened by the heat of the sun the way Ethiops' face had been darkened by the heat of his father's forge, but he goes on to suggest that the intensity of the sun in tropical African had caused humans there to exhibit numerous extraordinary deformities. "It is not at all surprising" he writes, "that towards the extremity of this region the men and animals assume a monstrous form, when we consider the changeableness and volubility of fire, the heat of which is the great agent in imparting various forms and shapes to bodies." Pliny gives examples of people who have no noses and others who lack an upper lip, a mouth, or even a head. From Egyptian sources Pliny was aware of African Pygmies, but he asserted that there were also people in Africa who were two or three times as tall as normal humans. Still others, his account relates, were deformed in intelligence, lacking speech or the knowledge of fire. Pliny's affirmation of the existence of monstrous Africans is particularly odd because in other places in his work he seeks to debunk fanciful interpretations, explaining, for example, the fact that one group of people were said to have extra eyes was a metaphorical way of saying they were skillful archers rather than a literal physical trait.[2]

Among the monsters Pliny's *Natural History* reported were the Blemmyes who are "said to have no heads, their mouths and eyes being seated in their breasts." This image is from Sebastian Münster's *Cosmographia* (1544). Source: Wikimedia Commons, public domain.

Why did Pliny present such strange tales? A harsh reading would be that he was a racist, who considered dark skin a deformity like the other monstrosities he describes. A gentler explanation would be that he was only reporting what others had written, something Herodotus also did, though he (unlike Pliny) had personally traveled up the Nile as far as Aswan. The two explanations are not mutually exclusive. We are on firmer ground in explaining the effects of what he wrote. For more than a dozen centuries, images of Pliny's deformed people decorated the interior regions of maps of Africa, continuing long after most outsiders had forgotten historically accurate details about Egypt, Meroë, and other parts of sub-Saharan Africa. Myths have amazing staying power.

Even though it can be difficult to explain the precise motives of individuals who have helped generate myths about Africa, it is possible to identify several factors that

2. Gaius Plinius Secundus, *The Natural History of Pliny*, trans. John Bostok and Henry T. Riley (London: H. G. Bohn, 1855–1857), bk. 6, chap. 35; Herodotus, *The Histories*, trans. Aubrey de Sélincourt (Baltimore: Penguin Books, 1954), bk. 2.

have generally been involved in such mythmaking. The first is ignorance. Pliny summarized what he could learn about Africa. Some of his evidence was factually accurate; some was wildly inaccurate. Accurate information about sub-Saharan Africa remained scarce for many centuries, in part because few outsiders penetrated those parts of Africa, in part because written accounts by sub-Saharan Africans were few, and in part because factual accounts did not circulate widely.

Eyewitness accounts of sub-Saharan Africa increased as Islamic traders penetrated south of the desert and down the east coast of Africa, but these did not usually circulate outside the Islamic world. Some accounts of West Africa came from Africans who crossed the Sahara, notably Muslims making the pilgrimage to Mecca. Some Africans also wrote letters and other accounts that survive in archives but were not widely known at the time. In the fifteenth century valuable information about sub-Saharan Africa begins to come from the new wave of Christian missionary expansion and the Portuguese explorations down the Atlantic coast of Africa. Some of this was published in Europe making use of the new technology of printing, but many accounts remained in archives until centuries later. Valuable Portuguese records were lost in 1755 when a massive earthquake, followed by fires and a tsunami, destroyed most of the capital city of Lisbon.

From the late 1700s onward Western explorers succeeded in reaching many parts of inland Africa, and their lengthy accounts were widely read in Europe and North America. Even so, ignorance about the large and diverse continent remained. During the twentieth century pioneering historians of Africa began to locate, collect, and critique information about Africa's past. Some of this writing was by African Americans associated with a growing Pan-African movement, and in time African-born historians began producing credible accounts of their history. An important milestone in the new scholarship was the launching of the *Journal of African History* in 1960 by Cambridge University Press. Diligent research, including interviewing African elders about their past, led to a flood of new studies and the growth of African history courses in schools and universities.

Ignorance has not been the only cause of mythmaking. Prejudice is another factor. Again, Pliny is a useful reference. On the whole he had a very open mind, for a mind circumscribed by ethnic or religious prejudices could never have undertaken an encyclopedic survey of the known world. As suggested above, Pliny seems to have harbored some prejudice with regard to sub-Saharan Africans, whether based on color or culture. Students of bias usually distinguish between simple prejudices and prejudicial ideologies. Simple prejudices against the unfamiliar are common but can be unlearned. Prejudicial ideologies, such as the hideous racism that developed in the 1700s and 1800s, are learned and, because they reinforce social or economic privilege, are very difficult to unlearn. If Pliny had had better evidence, he might have overcome his belief that the tropics fostered deformities.

In later centuries, Westerners' prejudices grew or waned depending on the circumstances. The Islamic conquest of Christian North Africa and most of Iberia stoked the fires of prejudice against North African Muslims, who were often described as "moors" or "blackamoors." On the other hand, Pope Leo X obtained an enslaved Muslim of North African origin, whom he freed, baptized with his own name, and set to work writing up what he knew from his travels in Africa. Despite its inaccuracies, Leo Africanus' *Description of Africa* (first published in 1550) made a major contribution to Western knowledge about the lands south of the Sahara. Western commercial contacts with Atlantic Africa beginning in the fifteenth century led to varied attitudes. The early Portuguese were particularly positive about Africans who might become Christians, feting ambassadors, educating youths, and even ordaining some African priests and consecrating an African bishop for the kingdom of Kongo. On the whole, European prejudice against Africans before the mid-eighteenth century was based on simple ignorance. Thus, prejudice tended to be strongest among Europeans who had never encountered an African or had done so only briefly. In contrast, Europeans who resided in African lands tended to harbor fewer prejudices, and the long-term residents regularly took African wives or mistresses and raised Afro-European children.

These examples of the spectrum of attitudes toward Africans contrast sharply in importance with the racist beliefs in African inferiority that became entrenched in the Americas as the Atlantic slave trade grew from the seventeenth century. Believing that Africans were inferior served to justify their enslavement. The abolitionist movement in Britain championed the human rights of black people, but ending slavery did not diminish racist ideas and practices, especially in the Americas. Finally, the European conquest and colonization of most of Africa at the end of the 1800s also had mixed results. Through personal familiarity with Africans, colonial officials often increased understanding and respect for their subjects. However, an ideology of African inferiority was integral to justifying colonial rule and subordination. Such prejudice and discrimination in turn encouraged Africans to claim equality and the right to govern themselves. In short, although ignorance declined, prejudice remained in many minds.

A third observable source of mythmaking about Africa has come from advocates of African equality. Some of these were African nationalist leaders, who mixed fact and myth in celebrating connections to ancient and medieval African states. At independence in 1960 the former French West African territory of Soudan renamed itself Mali after the medieval empire that had once occupied the same space. Nationalists in the former British colony of the Gold Coast in 1957 renamed their country Ghana, after an even older medieval empire whose territories had never included the new country's lands. These myths suggesting the rebirth of past glories were mild. More rigid and extreme were the myths that arose from movements for equality in the Americas identified with Africa.

Leaders of the Pan-African movement of the early twentieth century and the civil rights and the Black Power movements of mid-century saw connections between their struggles against prejudice and racial discrimination in the diaspora and the movements to liberate Africa from colonial rule and rehabilitate African history. The interesting and influential movement known as Afrocentrism in the 1980s and 1990s challenged the age-old European myth of African inferiority. That myth was already under strong attack by pioneering scholars of African history, but the Afrocentrists took their arguments to extremes. Rejecting accumulating factual evidence and scholarship about African history, they generated new myths that were often the mirror image of the Western prejudices being challenged. For example, the claim that Europeans discovered the American continents was countered by a claim that Africans had done so earlier. Such revisionist history was often accompanied by assertions that only "black" people could teach African ("Black") history, which suggested to many that the key issue was about control of the curriculum. Some Afrocentrists refused to subject any claim to factual analysis; others studied hard and became historians respected in the mainstream of African studies. This is not the place to extend the analysis of Afrocentrism or examine its continuing influence in some American educational circles. However, it is a good place to say a little more about what "myth" means.[3]

As the discussion has shown, some "myths" are simply falsehoods. There have never been people in Africa or elsewhere whose faces are in the middle of their chests. Other "myths" are part of efforts to make sense of complex problems. Pliny seems to have accepted the existence of a Greco-Roman pantheon of deities, which was part of an effort to understand connections between the natural and supernatural worlds. As an effort to make sense of things it might be said to have been half true, even if few today would give credence to the literal existence of these deities. Mythology ("the telling of stories" in Greek) is common to all human societies, so it is not surprising that modern people engage in mythmaking, too. To the extent that modern myths are efforts to get at a deeper truth they are admirable—at least partly so. Even historians have sometimes engaged in mythmaking, but modern historians are less sympathetic to even well-meaning representations of the past that are false or distorted. In criticizing the myths about the African past, this volume hopes to expose falsehoods and correct distortions. Since there are always limits to historical evidence and to the insight of historians, the effort to demythologize the past must be content with less than total success.

For the most part, the "myths" examined in the chapters that follow are connected to people no longer living. The reason for this is less because mistaken old ideas make easier targets (though they sometimes do) than because the intention of this book is primarily to set the record straight. Old myths often cast long shadows, but pointing an accusing finger at living students of African history has two unfortunate consequences. First, it will antagonize them and those who agree with them, most likely generating more smoke and heat than illumination. Even those who may have

---

3. Stephen Howe, *Afrocentrism: Mythical Pasts and Imagined Homes* (London: Verso, 1998); Mary Lefkowitz, *Not Out of Africa: How Afrocentrism Became an Excuse to Teach Myth as History* (New York: Basic Books, 1996).

wandered down a wrong corridor of interpretation are likely to be sincere in their quest for the truth. The second reason for limiting attacks on living people is more personal. In pointing out the mistakes of others past, the author of this book does not mean to claim that he is cleverer than they or always right himself. In the scholarly world, interpretations are often hotly debated in specialized journals best read by other scholars. Beginning students are better served by an introductory survey that interprets history from a long-term perspective. The better students will be able to recognize for themselves when a teacher, scholar, or writer has strayed from the evidence. Ideally, historical progress occurs slowly, as advanced students take exception to what an older generation of teachers has professed. If they are right, the newer interpretation should gain traction. As we'll see, however, bad old ideas can die slowly.

## Africa Is Not a Country

When I told a colleague that I was writing a book about the seven myths of African history, his reply was succinct: "Only seven?" His implication that there were many more is quite obviously correct. Several of the chapters that follow are concerned with a small bundle of related myths that can readily be examined together. One myth in particular is so fundamental and widespread that it needs to be examined here in the Introduction, namely the belief widespread in the United States, as well as elsewhere, that Africans share a common culture. The myth is expressed in a number of ways. For example, some people speak of Africa as a "country," suggesting it has less diversity than one would expect in a continent. Sometimes categories of ethnic discourse in the United States are extended overseas: just as the diverse peoples who speak Spanish are lumped together as "Hispanics" or "Latinos," the American category of "African American" or "black" is sometimes used to amalgamate the diverse societies of Africa. A particular example of this latter confusion occurred in the Afrocentric assertion that because ancient Egyptians were Africans, they had to be black Africans. A careful comparison of how Egyptians depicted themselves and how they depicted their African neighbors to the south shows that they were clearly aware of the physical differences that separated them.

As the second largest continent, Africa not surprisingly exhibits tremendous diversity in its geography, peoples, and histories. The Sahara is the world's largest desert, greater in its area than the continental United States. Africa also contains three of the fifteen longest rivers in the world, with the Nile ranking first globally. Humans originated in Africa, have lived there much longer than elsewhere, and, as a result, genetic diversity among the indigenous inhabitants of Africa is greater than it is among Europeans or Asians. The size of Africa, its human diversity, and the length of African history make summarizing difficult.

While this volume makes every effort to be inclusive, its themes inevitably focus more on what Africans have in common than on their diversity. One particular challenge is defining Africa. All the long-term inhabitants of the continent now call themselves Africans, but to the ancient Romans "Africa" was the lands northwest of the Sahara. Today "African" is frequently used to refer to the people dwelling south of the Sahara as distinguished from North Africans, whose identities and histories, though connected, have often been separate. The narrower sense of African as synonymous with black African shows up in speaking of African art, African hair, and African Americans. In the United States, people whose ancestors came from sub-Saharan Africa are commonly described as African Americans, whereas Americans of North African ancestry are more likely to be classified as Arab Americans. This volume addresses this division in two different ways. The earlier chapters include North Africa as part of the larger experience; in the later chapters North Africa is sometimes considered a place apart or not included.

Yet the most significant differences in Africa are cultural not physical. Today, as earlier, there are between 1,500 and 2,000 distinct languages spoken as mother tongues in Africa. To deal with this tremendous number of languages within their borders, most African countries have chosen to use a foreign language as their national language. That choice simplifies communication within a country as well as across the continent. But in the not-so-distant past, crossing political, linguistic, and other cultural barriers was much more difficult. Far from being a single country, Africa today contains more countries than either Europe or Asia and more countries than there are states in the United States.

The analysis leads to several general conclusions that will be explored in particular contexts in later chapters. First, the long, slow process of peopling the African continent inevitably led to cultural differentiation. Second, the fact that this diversification was expressed in new African languages and cultural identities did not mean that Africans could not recognize and utilize what they shared in common (something that occurred both in the diaspora and within modern political boundaries). Third, over the centuries Africans have joined world religions (notably Islam and Christianity), learned new international languages, and expanded their horizons through new systems of learning—all without necessarily abandoning fundamental values, beliefs, and knowledge. To understand Africans one must embrace their complexity.

## Chapter Overview

Chapter 1 takes on the myth that Africa has no history, or at least none worthy of study. It argues that not only do modern research methods demonstrate that Africans have the longest history of any branch of humankind, but that African history is also full of fascinating and unexpected discoveries. It catalogs the richly diverse kinds of evidence that can be used to bring African history to life, including the visual evidence of art and artifacts, historic buildings, and written texts and newer evidence brought to light by archaeology, linguistics, and genetics.

Chapter 2 examines a series of myths about Ethiopians. Jewish, Christian, and Muslim scriptures all assigned a special status to the "blameless" Ethiopians, even if they were rather expansive in the meaning they assigned to that name. Medieval Europeans believed in a powerful Christian prince called Prester John, whose realm they came to identify with the kingdom of Ethiopia. The Ethiopians themselves created an elaborate myth that their first king was the love child of King Solomon of Israel and the queen of Sheba.

Chapter 3 focuses on economic encounters between sub-Saharan Africans and outsiders from antiquity through the first three centuries of direct European contacts. It shows that sophisticated trading systems have a long history in sub-Saharan Africa, so it is not surprising that the dealings of earlier Egyptian, Hebrew, Arab, and Asian traders display remarkable similarities with those of the early Europeans. The contrary assertion that the arrival of European traders represented a sharp departure from the past is shown to lack a factual base.

Chapter 4 explores a number of myths about the European-run slave trade across the Atlantic. It challenges the common belief that Africans were "stolen" away rather than purchased. It takes issue with the common assertion that slavery did not exist in Africa and disputes both the older idea that African cultures perished in crossing the Atlantic and a newer notion that they survived intact. Finally, it contrasts the claim that Africa was irreparably damaged by the Atlantic slave trade with the factual record of the continent's rapid recovery, economically, demographically, and culturally.

The fifth chapter builds on foundations laid in Chapter 4 to demonstrate that African cultures, far from being fixed, were changing and evolving during the nineteenth and twentieth centuries. Larger identities grew from existing cultural roots, new state formations, and the influence of world religions and European colonial occupation. The chapter emphasizes that Africans were active participants in these changes, choosing or rejecting according to what they saw as their best interests.

Chapter 6 expands upon the theme of religious change by testing a nineteenth-century Afro-Caribbean educator's prediction that Islam would prove more suitable for Africans than his own Christian faith. For most of the 1800s he seemed correct, but, thereafter, greater numbers of Africans began to adopt Christianity. By the end of the twentieth century, Christians had become more numerous than Muslims in Africa. Both Islam and Christianity spread at the expense of traditional African religions, but African converts brought a lot of traditional beliefs and practices into the two world religions.

The seventh and final chapter looks at the modern myth that African independence from colonial rule would usher in a sort of golden age and its counterpart that independent Africa has failed to make reasonable progress. Winning independence was indeed a big step forward, but the magnitude of the tasks awaiting the new African governments was a greater challenge than anticipated. As the news from Africa shifted from the hopeful rhetoric of independence celebrations to the missteps and misfortunes of actual events, the prevailing news from Africa became overwhelmingly negative. While not denying the grim realities behind this bad news, the chapter identifies a number of important positive trends in twenty-first-century Africa. Literacy is rising, child mortality has nosedived, and life expectancy has shot upward. AIDS has ceased to be a death sentence; Ebola's spread has been halted; malaria deaths have fallen sharply; and polio may soon be eradicated. Africans have been taking more prominent roles on the world stage, in international organizations, as scholars, educators, and religious leaders, as well as musicians and other performing artists.

Taken together, the chapters provide a scintillating overview of the vast sweep of Africa's history. They show the similarities and differences among the continent's diverse ethnicities and cultures. Finally, the chapters point out the long history of Africans' connections with the peoples of other continents.

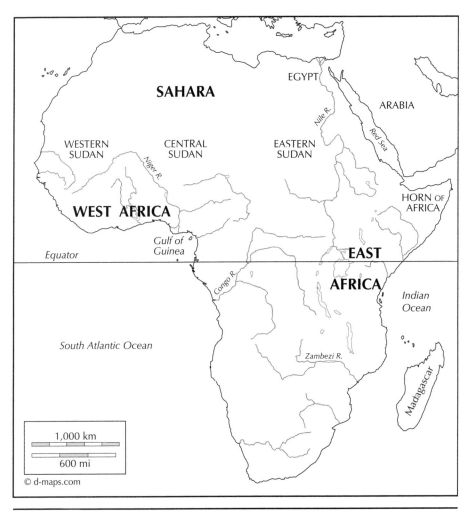

SAHARA

EGYPT

ARABIA

WESTERN
SUDAN

CENTRAL
SUDAN

EASTERN
SUDAN

Nile R.

Red Sea

Niger R.

WEST AFRICA

HORN OF
AFRICA

Gulf of
Guinea

Equator

EAST

Congo R.

AFRICA

Indian
Ocean

South Atlantic Ocean

Zambezi R.

Madagascar

1,000 km

600 mi

© d-maps.com

African Geography and Regions.

# 1. No History in Africa? Can the Oldest Humans Have the Shortest History?

What we properly understand by Africa is the Unhistorical, Undeveloped
Spirit, still involved in the conditions of mere nature, and which had to
be presented here only as on the threshold of the World's History.[1]
—*Georg Hegel, German philosopher, 1830s*

Perhaps, in the future, there will be some African history to teach. But at present
there is none, or very little: there is only the history of the Europeans in Africa.
The rest is largely darkness. . . . And darkness is not a subject for history.[2]
—*Hugh Trevor-Roper, professor of history, Oxford University, 1963*

In the 1830s, the hugely influential German philosopher Georg Hegel presented a
view of Africans that was both extraordinary in its negativity and lasting in its influence. "The Negro," he asserted, "exhibits the natural man in his completely wild and
untamed state," a being lacking morality, religion, a sense of individuality, or any
other higher human trait. For these reasons, he argued, Africa has no history worth
considering. Thirteen decades later, in 1963, Hegel's views were echoed in a celebrated public lecture by another distinguished European intellectual, Hugh Trevor-Roper, the Regius Professor of History at Oxford University. Africa below the Sahara,
Trevor-Roper declared, contains only "the unrewarding gyrations of barbarous tribes
in picturesque but irrelevant corners of the globe," and thus whatever history Africans
had was not worth teaching, aside from the history of Europeans in Africa.[3] Such
remarkably negative views have not entirely disappeared despite the successful efforts
of modern historians to replace willful ignorance and blatant prejudice with proven
evidence. Indeed, it is now possible to argue that Africa's history is not only distinguished but also considerably longer than that of any other continent and thus provides great insight into the remarkable story of human development.

Several assumptions besides ignorance and prejudice underlie the notion of an
unchanging, unprogressive Africa. One of these is the belief that true history is based
on written records, especially records that focus on the deeds of great men. This
belief holds that before there was writing there was only "prehistory," the domain of

---

1. Georg Hegel, *The Philosophy of History* (New York: Dover, 1956), 99.

2. Hugh Trevor-Roper, *The Rise of Christian Europe* (London: Thames and Hudson, 1965), 9.

3. Hegel, *Philosophy of History*, 93; Trevor-Roper, *Rise of Christian Europe*, 9.

archaeologists and folklorists. Another assumption is that meaningful history began in urban civilizations. The belief that history is impossible without written records is unsupported but still pervasive. While African history includes the deeds of many great men and women known from written records, recent African historians make use of many other kinds of evidence to reconstruct broader social and cultural themes. The rich history that scholars of Africa have crafted from different kinds of evidence and disciplines has led historians of other continents to imitate their approach.

Evidence for early African life in the different parts of the giant continent takes many forms. Africans deliberately left behind many kinds of evidence, including monumental stone buildings, art, oral traditions, and written records. Other evidence comes from accidental leavings, including physical remains, occupation sites, and even the plants and animals used by humans. Generations of archaeologists have skillfully located, excavated, and dated such evidence to reconstruct changes in Africans' lives and activities. Additional evidence about the movement of people in Africa comes from languages, which also provide important clues about the origins of beliefs, institutions, ways of life, and technologies, such as the invention of iron smelting. Although archaeologists were the first to discover evidence of human physical evolution in Africa, this once contentious subject has been irrefutably proven by the study of human genetic evidence (DNA) both within Africa and elsewhere in the world. Recent genetic evidence has also enabled historians to trace the movement and interaction of people within the African continent and how people from Africa spread across the face of the planet. These resources supply compelling evidence of African historical events dating to long before the appearance of writing in any part of the world.

The respectability of African history has made great progress, but disparaging statements like those by Hegel and Trevor-Roper about the history of Africa remain common. The present author's experiences suggest that large numbers of otherwise well-informed people still believe that African history is lacking—or at least not worth knowing. In gatherings of educated people, when I have disclosed that I was a professor of African history, I have regularly been greeted with blank stares or eyebrows raised in disbelief that someone could specialize in so meager a subject. Some folks, perhaps thinking they had misunderstood, ask me questions about African American history. The least guarded ask openly what there could possibly be to teach. At a major conference on Atlantic history, more than one of the eminent historians attending stated openly, "Oh, I don't know anything about Africa," as if one of the four Atlantic continents was not worth bothering to study. Such willful ignorance by academics claiming expertise in a region that ought to include Africa seems inexcusable, but it is not uncommon, despite the fact that two different eight-volume surveys of the African past were published in the 1980s.[4] For those with limited time to spare

---

4. J. D. Fage and Roland Oliver, eds., *The Cambridge History of Africa* (Cambridge: Cambridge University Press, 1975–1986); UNESCO, *General History of Africa* (Berkeley: University of California Press, 1981–1989).

shorter introductions to African history are common. Ignorance of the African past may have become inexcusable, but old habits of thought die hard.

Not only does Africa have a history, but also what is known and knowable about the African past has been expanding at a rapid rate. The history of Africa neither exhibits, as the German philosopher opined, "the natural man in his completely wild and untamed state," nor does it consist, as the Oxford professor asserted, of "the unrewarding gyrations of barbarous tribes in picturesque but irrelevant corners of the globe." During the first half of modern humans' existence the development of ethical standards, religious beliefs, esthetic and artistic sensibilities, music, dance, and literature took place exclusively in Africa. As Professor Roland Oliver, a pioneer in the teaching of African history in London, used to tell his students, the advantage of studying African history was that "you got to start at the beginning." An author in the first volume of the recent *Cambridge World History* begins with the simple factual statement, "Before about 48,000 BCE human history was African history."[5] Even today there is genetic evidence of African ancestry in the bodies of every human being. Willful ignorance cannot be refuted, but the demonstrable truth is that African history is as knowable as the history of humans anywhere else on earth.

It is true that the pace of change in sub-Saharan Africa was often slow and in some African societies glacially slow. Hagel and Trevor-Roper believed in the attractive proposition that progressive change was the crowning achievement of humans, and it alone was worthy of historical explanation. In the twenty-first century, we are beginning to realize that the speed of recent change has brought frightening risks as well as benefits. The extraordinary increase in human population from one billion in the early nineteenth century to seven billion in 2012 has put unsustainable demands on the planet, especially in light of rapidly increasing per capita energy use. Even optimists concede that the notion of bigger and better deserves only two cheers (not three). Maybe it would take a different historical experience, in which continuity and sustainability were more notable, to merit three cheers.

## Handprints: Deliberate Evidence

The range of evidence that historians use for reconstructing the African past can be divided into two categories. The first type is evidence Africans have intentionally left, which we can call *handprints*. Some of the oldest forms of intentional evidence are quite literally handprints, painted on the walls of caves along with other representations of people, animals, and symbols. The oldest known cave art in Africa comes from southern Africa, where paintings on rock dating to about 25,000 BCE clearly depict a rhinoceros, an antelope, and a zebra, animals that could have been hunted for their meat. More

---

5. Christopher Ehret, "Early Humans: Tools, Language, and Culture," in *The Cambridge World History*, vol. 1, *Introducing World History, to 10,000 BCE*, ed. David Christian (Cambridge: Cambridge University Press, 2015), 339.

mysterious in the same cave is a painting of a cat-like creature with human-looking rear legs, a reminder that evidence is not always self-explanatory. Studies of analogous images in the recent rock drawings of the Khoisan-speaking people of southern Africa, suggest that they represent mystical trances or dreams rather than realistic depictions. Interpreting these drawings and other evidence is not an exact science.[6]

Drawings of chariots incised into exposed rock faces in mountains in the central Sahara also are surprising as well as puzzling. The date of the drawings must fall during the two millennia after about 1700 BCE when such horse-drawn two-wheeled vehicles were in use in Egypt, but their significance is debated. Some take the chariot drawings as evidence of trans-Saharan trade, although they are too lightly built to carry goods. Another explanation is hinted at by the ancient Greek historian Herodotus, who writes that the Libyan people known as Garamantes were great chariot users and that some young men from the neighboring Nasamonians crossed the Sahara in a southwesterly direction until they reached a great river and a land inhabited by black people. If the great river was the Niger, it is possible that the rock drawings confirm this fifth-century BCE crossing of the Sahara or other subsequent crossings. However, this evidence is incomplete. Archaeologist Timothy Insoll argues that the absence of trade goods from Roman times in West Africa (except for one blue bead) negates the suggestion of a trade route across the Sahara in antiquity, though he readily concedes that the tomb of a tall women in the central Sahara has yielded a number of items of fifth-century (CE) Roman origin. Insoll also points out that the chariots in the drawings were built for speed and were incapable of carrying trade goods. Not until about the ninth century when camels came into use did the volume of trade grow to significant proportions.[7]

In addition to visual depictions, oral transmissions of history, literature, and beliefs are another form of handprints, though they might better be called voiceprints. Oral traditions in Africa include myths of origin, folk tales, lists of rulers and their accomplishments, and heroic epics. While varying in historical content and reliability, oral traditions can provide insights into how events were seen and interpreted. A well-known example is the *Epic of Sundiata*, the mid-thirteenth-century CE founder of the Mali Empire in the Western Sudan, who is described as a magician with supernatural powers, even though he was (also) a Muslim. Just as the Greek epics and the teachings of Confucius, the Buddha, Jesus, and Muhammad were transmitted orally before they

---

6. For southern African rock art, see Peter Garlake, *Early Art and Architecture of Africa*, Oxford History of Art (Oxford: Oxford University Press, 2002), 29–49, and Peter Mitchell, *The Archaeology of Southern Africa*, Cambridge World Archaeology (Cambridge: Cambridge University Press, 2002), 132–34, 192–226.

7. For illustrations of Saharan rock art, see Basil Davidson, *African Kingdoms* (New York: Time-Life Books, 1966), 43–57. For other evidence and interpretation, see Herodotus, *The Histories*, trans. Aubrey de Sélincourt (Baltimore: Penguin Books, 1965), 114, 301–4, and Timothy Insoll, *The Archaeology of Islam in Sub-Saharan Africa* (Cambridge: Cambridge University Press, 2003), 209–12.

Egyptian divine figures and hieroglyphs incised in stone at the Temple of Horus at Edfu, Egypt. Though built in the Ptolemaic period (273–57 BCE), the temple replicates older styles. The central figure wears the Double Crown of Upper and Lower Egypt. The male on the right wears the Red Crown of Lower Egypt and the woman on the left wears a headdress representing the solar disk between cow horns. Photo courtesy of N. R. Northrup.

were written down, so too were African historical traditions passed down orally before being reduced to print (in many cases within the last century).[8]

It is a small step (but an important one) from composing a text in the mind and reciting it to preserving it in writing. Once symbols were devised to represent sounds or words, the familiar handprint known as handwriting provided a way of preserving texts on papyrus and paper or carved into stone or other surfaces. It was a notable invention. The ancient Egyptians, the first in Africa to use the process, attributed the invention of writing to their god Thoth. In use before 3000 BCE, Egyptian writing had two early forms. Hieroglyphs were formal and artistic, using some five hundred symbols, many of which are easily recognized as different animals or human body parts, such as an eye or hand. Beautifully colored inscriptions using hieroglyphs

---

8. Jan Vansina, *Oral Tradition as History* (Madison: University of Wisconsin Press, 1985); Peter Schmidt, "Oral History, Oral Traditions, and Archaeology," in *The Oxford Handbook of African Archaeology*, ed. Peter Mitchell and Paul Lane (Oxford: Oxford University Press, 2013), 37–47; D. T. Niane, *Sundiata: An Epic of Old Mali*, trans. G. D. Pickett (London: Longman, 1985).

recounted the names and deeds of the pharaohs. Another sign of the supernatural aura of writing is that many early texts concern death and the afterlife. Egyptian scribes also used a more stylized form of cursive writing using ink on papyrus that could be written much more quickly than hieroglyphs. In both forms of writing the symbols stood for sounds. By the Egyptian Middle Kingdom (2050–1780 BCE) there are written literary works as well as the compilation in hieroglyphs of ritual incantations for the deceased known as *The Book of the Dead*.

Writing in ancient Africa was not confined to Egypt. From the second century BCE, writers in the Kingdom of Meroë (south of Egypt) used an alphabetic script that was influenced by Egyptian hieroglyphs. Although the script was deciphered in 1909, the language written in this Meroitic script is unknown. In the Horn of Africa, the state of Aksum, precursor to medieval Ethiopia, also developed a system of writing before the fourth century CE, which was partly borrowed from South Arabia and has remained in use (with modifications) up to this day. As Chapter 2 details, the most famous work written in it, the *Kebra Nagast* (Glory of Kings), probably dating to the thirteenth century, tells a story of supposed connections between medieval Ethiopian rulers and ancient Israel. It is written in the ancient language Ge'ez.[9]

Africans who produced written records during later centuries increasingly used languages and systems of writing that had originated outside the continent. The Egyptian city of Alexandria, named for its founder Alexander the Great, became home to the greatest library in the ancient Mediterranean world with tens or hundreds of thousands of papyrus scrolls, mostly written in Greek. After Egypt and the rest of North Africa became part of the Roman Empire, the region's writers grew famous for their contributions to literature, thought, and Christian theology, in both Greek and Latin. The incorporation of North Africa into the Islamic Empire of the Arabs in the seventh century and the movement of non-African and African Muslims below the Sahara and down the Indian Ocean coast of Africa resulted in a great many texts written in Arabic that are essential to African history. Some oral traditions in African languages were first written in Arabic script, for example, the *Kano Chronicle*, an account of the reigns of the rulers of an important Hausa city-state that goes back to the tenth century.

Writers of African origin became so numerous and will be cited so regularly in the following chapters that it would be tedious to attempt to list them here. Instead, let's mention two of Moroccan descent who authored wide-ranging and important accounts of sub-Saharan Africa between 1330 and 1550. The first was Ibn Battuta, born in the Moroccan city of Tangier in 1304, who recorded detailed descriptions of his travels in West and East Africa as well as in India and Arabia. His original Arabic texts, which have been translated into many other languages, provide significant

---

9. For texts see Constance Hilliard, ed., *Intellectual Traditions of Pre-Colonial Africa* (New York: McGraw-Hill, 1998); *Ancient Egyptian Book of the Dead*, trans. Raymond O. Faulkner (New York: Barnes & Noble, 2005); Richard Pankhurst, *The Ethiopians: A History* (Oxford: Blackwell, 1998), 24–25.

Known as the Rome Stele (or the Aksum Obelisk), this 160-foot tall granite structure has symbolic doors carved into its base and windows into the upper stories. It was removed from Ethiopia by the Italian military as war booty in 1937 and erected in Rome. After much negotiation, it was restored to Ethiopia in 2005. Source: Photo by Ondřej Žváček, 2009. Wikimedia Commons.

information about fourteenth-century life. The second, best known as Leo Africanus, was born in Muslim Spain about 1494 and originally named Hasan. He and his Berber parents soon returned to the city of Fez in their native Morocco, where he received a good education and about 1510 accompanied an uncle on a diplomatic mission across the Sahara as far as the city of Timbuktu. After visiting Cairo, Constantinople, and Mecca, Hasan was captured by a Spanish ship in 1518 and later presented to Pope Leo X. After instructing his youthful charge in Christianity, Pope Leo baptized him and conferred his own name on him. Thereafter known as Leo Africanus (Leo the African), he was put to work writing out what he knew of African history and geography. His substantial tome, published in Italian in 1550 and in English in 1600, became Christian Europe's most relied-upon source for Muslim lands on both sides of the Sahara.[10]

The most visible and enduring handprints in the landscape of Africa are stone buildings. In places where suitable rock is abundant, Africans have long erected monumental architecture, certainly for their own immediate purposes but also to remind future generations of their greatness. The most famous of these are the pyramids and temples of Egypt that go back to nearly 2600 BCE. Other notable examples are found in lands to the south of Egypt. The Kushitic kingdoms of Nubia, further up the Nile in what is now northern Sudan, erected pyramids of a different style, as well as temples, during the first millennium BCE. Still further south in Aksum (northern Ethiopia) there are rich examples of stone monuments, especially tall slender shafts known as stelae erected in the fourth century CE. Several are still standing, but the biggest one, the largest object ever carved from a single block of stone and weighing over five hundred tons, lies broken on the ground, perhaps having fallen while being hoisted into place. Other examples of skilled stone carving come from the early thirteenth century, when the Christian ruler of Ethiopia named Lalibela sponsored an extensive church building project. The churches are stylistically diverse, but each was hollowed out of "living" rock, that is, rock lying in its natural site.

10. N. Levtzion and J. F. P. Hopkins, eds., *Corpus of Early Arabic Sources for West African History* (Princeton, NJ: Markus Wiener, 2000); Said Hamdun and Noël King, *Ibn Battuta in Black Africa* (Princeton, NJ: Markus Wiener, 1994); Leo Africanus, *The History and Description of Africa*, 3 vols. (London: Hakluyt Society, 1896).

Of the many other stone buildings erected along the Indian Ocean coast of eastern Africa the most spectacular was the palace of the ruler of the city-state of Kilwa. Built of coral covered with lime plaster sometime around 1300, the extensive palace contained public and private quarters and courtyards, a pool, warehouses, and pavilions with barrel vaulted roofs and domes. Ibn Battuta, who visited Kilwa in the 1330s, judged it to be "among the most beautiful cities [of the world] and elegantly built" and said the mostly Muslim population of the city were devout and had extremely black skins. Kilwa's wealth came from its role as middleman in the trade in gold between the Zimbabwe kingdom and states around the Indian Ocean. The inland kingdom's capital city, known as Great Zimbabwe, had the largest complex of ancient stone structures in Africa south of the Nile River valley. The most monumental structures, built between the eleventh and the fifteenth centuries, are still substantially intact. They include the Great Enclosure, an oval structure the size of a football stadium, whose stone walls are over thirty-two feet high and sixteen feet thick. Inside the Great Enclosure is the Conical Tower (thirty feet high and eighteen feet in diameter). Both structures were built of layered granite stones without mortar.

Although all of these structures have been known to the outside world for many centuries, the belief in African inferiority was so strong that Europeans ascribed non-African origins to them. Ancient Egypt's magnificent structures were said to be sited on the African continent only incidentally, the product of a civilization that was Mediterranean, not African. Meroë's temples and pyramids were simply derivative of Egyptian influences. The monumental structures of Aksum and Ethiopia were dismissed as being of Arabian origin. The cities of the Swahili Coast were attributed to Arab and Persian origins, despite Ibn Battuta's eyewitness testimony that the inhabitants were not merely dark skinned but "extremely black." These tales of outside influences may have a grain of truth in them, but giving the outsiders all the credit and denying local Africans any credit is about as credible as saying the scientific breakthroughs of Copernicus, Galileo, and Isaac Newton were due to Asians because the numerals they used had first been devised in India. Great Zimbabwe posed a special challenge to such racist interpretations, not only because of its size and inland location but also because the structures and extensive artifacts showed no foreign influences. Nineteenth-century Europeans who saw Great Zimbabwe proclaimed its existence a "mystery" and speculated without any evidence that its builders were Phoenicians, Israelites, or other outsiders. The explanations shifted after archaeological excavations proved Great Zimbabwe was of local African origin. The site that had previously inspired wonder and whose carved stone birds had been looted as treasure then came to be disparaged, in terms Hegel and Trevor-Roper would have applauded, as "products of an infantile mind."[11]

---

11. The stone structures south of ancient Egypt are described and illustrated in Garlake, *Early Art*, 51–88, 117–120; his statement about Zimbabwe is at 23. The quotations from Ibn Battuta are from Hamdun and King, *Ibn Battuta*, 22.

Some of the monumental structures of eastern and northeastern Africa considered above were associated with the burials of important persons, whether as tombs, as in the case of pyramids, or monuments, or as in the case of the stelae of Aksum. As the ancient Egyptians had sadly learned, spectacular tombs had the unintended consequence of alerting thieves to the location of rich treasures interred with the departed rulers. As a result, survivors came to place memorials in a different place from the actual burial site so as to protect the graves and grave goods from looters. Nearly all the Egyptian treasures displayed in museums today come from tombs that escaped being robbed in antiquity, which is ironic because, while the monuments were meant to be enduring tributes to the lives of the departed, the grave goods were not intended to delight later generations, but were meant for the departed to enjoy in the afterlife.

In parts of Africa that lacked stone for building, the memorials erected to the memory of illustrious people are long gone because they were made of less enduring materials. Even so, chance discoveries of rich grave goods testify to similar burial practices. One of the oldest and most impressive of these is a site from the ninth century near the village of Igbo-Ukwu in southeastern Nigeria. The corpse was interred seated on a wooden throne dressed in rich garments that were decorated with more than 100,000 glass beads, along with copper armlets, anklets, and amulets beautifully fashioned by local artisans. Other grave goods included ivory tusks, a crown, a ceremonial staff, a fan, and a flywhisk. It is now beginning to be understood that the Igbo-Ukwu grave and accompanying site are part of a complex of rich burials widespread in West Africa, some of which have been destroyed by modern looters.[12]

## Footprints: Evidence by Chance

Another category of historical evidence can be called *footprints* because, like tracks across the sand, they have been left behind unconsciously or inadvertently. Wind and rain normally erase actual footprints soon after they are made, but on rare occasions ancient footprints across a wet surface have survived. Kenyan archaeologist Mary Leakey, for example, discovered a series of fossilized footprints of an upright-walking adult and a child in the East African country of Tanzania that may date to 3.7 million years ago.

Just as skilled trackers can follow the footprints of people or animals, so too can history detectives uncover the distant past from many kinds of footprints unconsciously carried forward or inadvertently left behind. In recent years historians of Africa have made exceptional use of two new sorts of evidence that living people carry with them. One astonishing link between the present and the distant past is carried in human genes, which, when decoded, can be used to trace lines of descent covering the entire span of human existence and even connections with our prehuman ancestors. Living languages can also be mined to reveal forgotten pieces of history and

---

12. Garlake, *Early Art*, 26–27, 97–115.

previously unknown relationships among societies. In addition, specialized archaeologists can construct remarkable histories from traces of human bodies and discarded fragments of household possessions.

Archaeology has made contributions to African history so immense that they can be called revolutionary. On the one hand, archaeologists' excavations and analyses have opened up the countless millennia before the last ten thousand years that historians had traditionally considered "history." Their work in this vast period of "prehistory" has documented changes and achievements in Africa before the monuments of Egypt were imagined, and has also documented the evolution of humans over millions of years.

On the other hand, archaeologists have greatly expanded what can be known about the doings of Africans during recent millennia and extended the focus from kings and conquerors to include the lives of ordinary men and women. These days archaeologists work across a very broad spectrum of fields, and many of the best are adept at interdisciplinary fields ranging from paleobotany to linguistics, geology, and history. For world historians the accumulation of archaeological evidence has made it possible to write an African history that includes the full range of human development in Africa. What was once called "prehistory" is now a major part of history.

Other archaeologists have reconstructed the lives of ancient Africans from bits of arrowheads or jewelry, broken pieces of pottery (potsherds), and the remains of fire pits and simple dwellings. Some have looked into graveyards and sifted through debris in old wells and trash dumps. It has become possible to learn more about what people were eating by sifting a site for fossilized seeds, pollen, and excrement. The mundane findings that are found add texture to our knowledge, and occasionally something quite special is found, as was the case at Igbo-Ukwu mentioned earlier. Archaeologists have also found ways to improve the precision with which sites can be dated. One can date very old remains by noting where they are found in geological layers. Dating remains such as charcoal from more recent centuries is possible using techniques that measure the decay of the radioactive carbon isotope known as carbon 14 ($C_{14}$).

The many kinds of evidence available for African history work best in concert. As one archaeologist has noted, "Archaeological evidence devoid of the supporting props of [written] historical sources . . . can appear dry and lifeless. . . . However, [although] the use of historical sources in isolation . . . might provide us with the basic chronological framework[,] . . . we must also turn to archaeology to begin to construct the diverse social, political, and economic" factors.[13] Linguistic studies have also proven very useful in framing the written, oral, and material evidence, as will be discussed below.

During the second half of the twentieth century archaeologists made some extraordinary discoveries of fossilized remains of early humans and of their pre-human ancestors, finds that supported the theory that humans evolved in Africa. As remarkable as

---

13. Insoll, *Archaeology of Islam*, 3.

these finds were, the evidence was too limited and spread over too long a span of time to convince skeptics that Africa was the birthplace of humankind. Nor was there any real hope that sufficient new archaeological evidence might be uncovered to tip the balance more decisively in favor of a single theory. And then, an astonishing breakthrough occurred that changed everything. The breakthrough came not from new archaeological finds, but from microbiologists studying the genetic code carried by modern humans. By comparing samples of genes (DNA) collected from large numbers of humans from around the world, geneticists were able to draw firm conclusions about human evolution.

The basic conclusion was that a quite small population of human hunter-gatherers emerged in Africa between 200,000 and 100,000 years ago. Then, between 200,000 and 70,000 years ago, these ancestral humans spread and diversified within Africa, and small groups of humans from northeastern Africa colonized Asia, Europe, and the rest of the planet. While this population dispersal led to a notable increase in the number of humans and in their biological diversity, human biological diversity in Africa remains greater than the differences between Africans as a whole and all the rest of humans outside of Africa. Although these findings will no doubt be refined by new research, the broad patterns are already well established: Africa is the mother continent of humanity.[14]

Another place where ancient footprints hide is in language. Languages tend to change very slowly, but over long periods of time changes within a language become extensive, and dialectical differences can become significant enough to form separate new languages. Like a cell that splits to form new cells, a mother language that divides no longer exists. In time the daughter languages may also divide. Even as this linguistic fragmentation occurs, the new languages inherit words and grammatical structures from their ancestor languages, which can reveal aspects of the language family's history. Vocabulary for things that remain important to the speakers of a language tend to change less, while new things are given new names, which may be words borrowed from other languages. The speakers of a language are seldom aware of all the historical baggage their language contains. For example, how many speakers of English know from what languages English has borrowed such words as capital, raccoon, pajama, and euphoria?[15] Specialists, however, can decipher the hidden historical evidence. Because linguistic evidence is passed along unconsciously, it is not subject to manipulation the way written evidence might be. Moreover, language evidence reflects the full range of human activity, not just the topics of interest to the political

---

14. Marta Mirazon Lahr, "Genetic and Fossil Evidence for Modern Human Origins," in Mitchell and Lane, *African Archaeology*, 326–40; Sarah A. Tishkoff, Floyd A. Reed, Françoise R. Friedlaender, et al., "The Genetic Structure and History of Africans and African Americans," *Science* 324 (2009): 1035–44.

15. Latin, Algonquin, Hindi, and Greek.

African Language Families. After a map by Mark Dingemanse, Wikimedia Commons.

or intellectual elite. Among historians, those studying Africa have made the greatest use of linguistic evidence.[16]

There are between 1,500 and 2,000 African languages today, so making sense of their diversity can be bewildering even to specialists. However, the map of language families in Africa is strikingly simple and reveals important historical realities. Most Africans speak languages belonging to one of two families. The dominant family in North Africa, the Sahara, and the Horn of Africa is called Afrasian (or Afro-Asiatic).

16. Christopher Ehret, "Writing African History from Linguistic Evidence," in *Writing African History*, ed. John Edward Philips (Rochester, NY: University of Rochester Press, 2005), 86–111.

As this name suggests, the family also includes languages, such as Arabic and Hebrew, spoken in parts of Asia adjacent to Africa. Within Africa this family includes the Berber languages of the Sahara and northwest Africa, the ancient languages of Egypt, and the ancient and modern languages of Somalia and Ethiopia, as well as the Hausa language of northern Nigeria and Niger, one of the most widely spoken languages in West Africa. As the result of the Arab conquest of North Africa in the seventh and eighth centuries Arabic has become widely spoken across that area as a first or second language. Additional issues about the Afrasian family are explored below in the context of the origins of the ancient Egyptians.

The second giant African family of languages is called Niger-Congo, a convenient and succinct name that describes its distribution across the vast area of West Africa through which the Niger River flows and the equally vast area of Central Africa drained by the Congo River and its branches. In fact, the Niger-Congo family stretches all the way from the Atlantic to the Indian Ocean, including the major languages of East and southeast Africa. Niger-Congo is one of the largest language families in the world, both in terms of the number of distinct languages it includes and the total number of people speaking these languages. Given its size, it is not surprising that the Niger-Congo family divides into two distinct sub-families with quite different histories: the languages of West Africa and the Bantu languages of Central and Eastern Africa. The West African languages are themselves highly diverse reflecting a very long history of development and differentiation. The Bantu languages, in contrast, are newer in origin, and, like the Romance languages of southern Europe, they share many common features. For example, the name "Bantu" comes from the term for person common to most of the languages of the sub-family. In the past two centuries, Swahili has become the most widely spoken Bantu language by spreading inland as a second language from its ancestral home on the Indian Ocean coast to as far as the eastern Congo.

In addition to these two giant language families, there are three smaller families. The inhabitants of the large island of Madagascar speak Malagasy, a language of the Austronesian family, whose other languages are found in Southeast Asia and the South Pacific. Linguistic and other evidence support the idea that the language was brought to Madagascar by Indonesian mariners, who settled there sometime before or just after the beginning of the Common Era, at a time when the island was uninhabited. The other two smaller families, Nilo-Saharan and Khoisan, are very ancient African language families, whose present speakers now survive only in arid and semi-arid areas that later intruders did not occupy because they were too dry for farming or raising cattle. Thus, the modern language map can reveal important patterns of historical change.

Languages and entire families can also go extinct, but language extinction is not the same as population extinction. For example, the many Pygmy societies that still inhabit the great equatorial rainforests of Africa have come to speak the Bantu languages of their neighbors. The ancestral Pygmy languages are gone, but Pygmy societies and cultures live on. Other societies have blended with the populations that intruded into their homelands. Speakers of languages known collectively as Khoi and San (or Khoisan) were once spread across much of the southern cone of Africa. In the face of the expanding Bantu-speaking populations, Khoi and San speakers either retreated or blended. The evidence is partly genetic, but the long blending of these populations shows up in the languages of the southeasternmost Bantu speakers. Over many generations speakers of Bantu languages like Xhosa and Zulu adopted click sounds from Khoisan speakers. Such click sounds have long been a normal part of Khoisan speech, but they are not found in any other Bantu-speaking areas.

As these remarks suggest, the modern map of language families reveals much about African history, but even more can be discovered by specialized linguistic studies. Through careful comparison of languages in a family, scholars can construct a family tree. If all the branches have similar words for something, such as cattle, then that vocabulary must derive from a mother language common to them all. If the technical vocabulary used in a specialized process such as iron working are different in the different languages then that activity must have appeared after the split from the ancestral language. Things can get more complicated because vocabulary can be borrowed as well as inherited, and because estimating when language splits occurred is imprecise. However, specialists have become adept in resolving such problems.[17] Therefore, linguistic evidence can provide suggestive evidence or indications of possibilities, but it generally does provide firm proof of historical events. Even so, linguistic evidence is an important tool because its findings encourage scholars in other disciplines to look for additional historical evidence.

## Combining Evidence: Three Case Studies

Each of these kinds of handprints and footprints provides important evidence for Africa's history. All historical evidence needs to be used critically, considering its inherent biases, omissions, and uncertainties. In addition to careful scrutiny of the evidence, combining different kinds of evidence can increase (or decrease) the likelihood of something being true. The examples that follow show how combining different kinds of evidence can illuminate the ancient African past. The first topic, the history of significant changes in how Africans obtained food, examines the hunting of wild animals and gathering of wild plants, the raising domesticated animals, and the transition to agriculture, that is, the deliberate cultivation of grains and other food plants. The second topic is the movement from wood and stone implements to tools fashioned out of metal. The final topic explores the long-standing controversies about ancient Egypt's place in history generally and in African history in particular.

---

17. Christopher Ehret, "Agricultural Origins: What Language Evidence Reveals," in *The Cambridge World History*, vol. 2, *A World with Agriculture, 12,000 BCE–500 CE*, ed. Graeme Barker and Candice Gaucher (Cambridge: Cambridge University Press, 2015), 56.

In Africa, as elsewhere, humans learned to feed themselves by exploiting the food available in particular environments. The first written evidence about African hunter-gatherer communities comes from the Portuguese explorer Vasco da Gama, who described the people he encountered living near the southern tip of Africa in November 1497. Those living near St. Helena Bay on the South Atlantic, he recorded, ate the meat of seals, whales, and gazelles along with "the roots of wild plants" and honey. They had domesticated dogs and hunted with wooden spears tipped with horn.

Rounding the Cape of Good Hope, the Portuguese encountered another people at Mossel Bay, pastoralists who had herds of domesticated cattle and sheep and so would not have depended so much on hunting and gathering for their food. They welcomed the Portuguese with flute music and sold them a fat ox, whose meat the visitors found tasty. As linguistic and genetic evidence attests, the hunter-gatherers near St. Helena Bay were following a way of life that had existed for many thousands of years over much of Africa. The pastoralists at Mossel Bay had added a newer and more secure source of meat, milk, and other animal products, but despite this significant change, they and the hunter-gatherers along the South Atlantic shared a long, common history.

It is not known how much these two communities were aware of their common past at the time of da Gama's visit. They certainly did not have a common name for themselves, but modern scholars have named them. At first the new names emphasized the obvious differences in how the two communities made their livings, the hunter-gatherers being called the San and the pastoralists called the Khoekhoe peoples. As linguistic evidence revealed their membership in a common language family, the two names were combined as Khoisan.[18] However much these peoples had no conscious memory of their shared history, their languages retained proof of it. As historian Christopher Ehret summarizes, "the earliest Khoisan languages included at least two verbs for hunting with a bow and arrows, along with nouns for two kinds of arrows and, most informatively, a noun for arrow poison [as well as terms that indicate] that honey collection was already an important subsistence activity for these people." The words had traveled a long way geographically over a very long span of time. These early words come from ancestral languages spoken some 22,000 years ago in East Africa, a location some 2,500 miles to the northeast. The San had changed the basic structures of the ancestral way of life little, aside from adapting to quite different environments. The greatest innovation was clearly the addition of seafood. Because Europeans named Mossel Bay for the sea mussels that abound there, it is not surprising that archaeologists have found early evidence of shellfish harvesting. The whale meat mentioned by da Gama probably came from whales that had beached themselves, since the San were not great mariners. Work was gendered: men hunted; women gathered wild plants. Khoisan speakers were also artists, as the rock art mentioned earlier attests.

---

18. Historians and linguists do not agree on the spellings of Khoe and Khoi.

Genetic evidence carries the history even further back in time, showing that the Khoisan speakers are one of the oldest strains of fully modern humans and suggesting that they made their way to the tip of South African sometime after 45,000 years ago. Pastoralism developed much more recently. It is likely that first stage involved the domestication of sheep, some fifteen centuries before da Gama's description. The transition from hunting and gathering required so many cultural changes that it must have taken place over an extended period of time. Perhaps, as in other cultures, younger people were assigned the routine tasks of tending the flocks, while adults continued to hunt and gather. Domesticated cattle existed in Africa several thousand years before they reached the southern tip of Africa, which occurred as late as 700 CE. So the cattle and sheep keepers whom da Gama encountered were a much more recent innovation than the hunter-gatherers he first encountered.[19]

The movement from hunting and gathering to pastoralism and agriculture was a momentous change in human history. Yet the fact that this transformation took place at about the same time around the world has been puzzling until recently. In the last few decades there have been great advances in specialists' ability to reconstruct the history of global climate changes. By drilling into sea floors and glaciers scientists have been able extract evidence of what climates were like in the distant past. It is now known that there have been long cycles of warmer and colder climates. The critical period for change in how humans obtained most of their food came after the tenth century BCE. For several millennia the world had been in the grip of the last Ice Age, when temperate rainfall froze and the accumulating ice cover led to decreased sea levels. Few places in Africa saw ice, but the vast quantities of frozen water elsewhere led to a climate that was generally drier as well as cooler. The rainforests along the equator shrank and were replaced with savannas. North and south of the Tropics, deserts expanded to their greatest extent. Then the cycle reversed: the ice melted, moisture returned, air temperatures rose, deserts shrank, and rainforests expanded. What had been exceptionally cold and dry a few centuries earlier became exceptionally warm and moist. Lake Chad, the largest lake in West Africa, grew to be almost as large as the island of Madagascar. This was when both pastoralism and farming spread.

However much the new wetter climate made agriculture easier, it did not *cause* pastoralism and farming to spread. So other, more particular, evidence must be considered. Until recently dating was uncertain, and it was widely assumed that Africans simply borrowed pastoralism and agriculture from Middle Eastern peoples. Some borrowing did indeed take place, but historians now believe that Africans were also innovators. They reason that most innovations in pastoralism, agriculture, and metals in Africa took place so early that borrowing is implausible.

---

19. Ehret, "Africa from 48,000 to 9500 BCE," in Christian, *Cambridge World History*, vol. 1, 372; Mitchell, *Archaeology of Southern Africa*, 227–48; Alvara Velho, *A Journal of the First Voyage of Vasco da Gama, 1497–1499*, ed. and trans. E. G. Ravenstein (London: Hakluyt Society, 1898), 7–10.

Pastoralism and agriculture developed separately in northern Africa, but it is widely agreed that both were essentially indigenous inventions. Archaeological and linguistic evidence suggests that wild cattle were first tamed in the far eastern Sahara during a wet period around 9000–8000 BCE. Archaeologists suggest the domestication of cattle occurred in western North Africa about 6000 BCE. Support for thinking these domestications were African innovations comes from two facts: archeological evidence shows they occurred as early as those in the Near East, and genetic evidence from the cattle shows that they had a separate linage. As the Sahara grew drier, the practice of cattle pastoralism gradually spread south. Later, cattle domesticated in India spread into Africa and bred with African cattle. Pastoralism has remained a sustaining way of life for many Africans.

At the time that African pastoralism was emerging, early African farmers were domesticating plant species. Although archaeology has unearthed convincing evidence of the domestication and improvement of a wide range of indigenous plants, including grains, coffee, and African varieties of peanuts and rice, the physical evidence for early agriculture in Africa is scattered and incomplete, yielding dates from the third and second millennia BCE. However, historian Christopher Ehret argues from linguistic and other evidence that there were two (or perhaps three) much earlier centers of agricultural innovation in northern Africa: one in the far eastern Sahara after 8500 BCE and a second just below the Sahara in West Africa by 9500 BCE. A third independent development of agriculture may have taken place in Ethiopia.[20]

While it may be tempting to regard the movement from hunting and gathering to farming and pastoralism as an advance, these changes were much more complex. Some African societies resisted abandoning a way of life based on hunting and gathering. Others became pastoralists but did not farm. Indeed, Africa has the largest concentration of pastoralists in the world. Those who did make transitions did so slowly and carefully, evaluating their costs and benefits. For example, the adoption of agriculture brought disadvantages as well as advantages. Cultivating crops or tending herds was a lot more work than hunting and gathering. Crops needed to be planted, fertilized, weeded, and watered. Domesticated herds needed feeding and watering. Both crops and domesticated animals had to be protected from wild predators. Moreover, both living in dense settlements so as to tend to crops and tending domesticated animals could be unhealthy because of diseases spread through exposure to human and animal waste. Studies have shown that early farmers were shorter in stature than hunter-gatherers and lived less long on average. Of course, there were advantages to the new ways of life, or else so many societies would not have adopted them.

---

20. Christopher Ehret, *The Civilizations of Africa: A History to 1800* (Charlottesville: University Press of Virginia, 2002), 59–100; Ehret, "Agricultural Origins," 59 ff.; Fiona Marshall and Elizabeth Hildebrand, "Cattle before Crops: The Beginning of Food Production in Africa," *Journal of World Prehistory* 16 (2002), 99–143; Paul J. Lane, "Early Agriculture in Sub-Saharan Africa to ca. 500 CE," in *Cambridge World History*, vol. 2, 473–97.

A different sort of change was taking place in technology. Early stone tools and weapons were durable and relatively easy to fashion for a variety of uses. Stone tools and weapons remained in use for millennia, but equivalent objects made of metal gradually displaced them. The fashioning of metals had begun for decorative purposes. Pure gold had long been sought for jewelry because of its naturally attractive gleam, and polished copper has a similar sheen. Refining copper and gold was also relatively easy because they may occur in relatively pure forms and do not require unusually hot temperatures to soften for shaping or to melt for casting. However, pure gold and copper were too soft to make durable tools. Alloys of copper, known as bronze or brass, were harder than pure copper and were used to make decorative objects for the rich and powerful, such as the man buried at Igbo-Ukwu mentioned earlier. Valuable trades in copper and gold became widespread in Africa, as the next chapter will relate.

Most iron deposits were mixed with impurities and required hotter temperatures to purify. Although mixtures of relatively pure iron and nickel occurred in meteorites,[21] such meteorites were so rare that their iron was used only to make weapons for powerful rulers, such as the pharaohs. Ordinary iron ore is abundant in Africa and elsewhere, but it took a long time for people to perfect the complex process of separating out pure iron from the slag. It was once believed that the technology of iron smelting was invented at a single center in Anatolia (now Turkey) about 1500 BCE and that the technology gradually spread from there to the rest of the world. A few years ago UNESCO supported an effort to prove that iron smelting had actually developed independently about the same time in what is now the country of Niger in West Africa. The location seemed possible because that area had been an important center of copper metallurgy several centuries earlier. As it has turned out, this effort became an exercise in mythmaking by supporters of African achievement. It is still possible to imagine that Africans could have invented iron smelting independently, but the evidence that the supporters cited for the dating of the Niger smelters did not stand up to critical examination. Not only were the charcoal samples used for radiocarbon dating contaminated, but it also turned out that individuals eager to make the case for the Niger site had selectively manipulated and exaggerated the evidence. For the present, the best consensus among scholars is that the archaeological evidence does not support a separate discovery of iron smelting in sub-Saharan Africa. Many also feel that the possibility of finding sufficient evidence is low, both because of the problems inherent in finding sites with datable evidence and because of too little effort is currently being made to locate and investigate sites in sub-Saharan Africa.

Is there another way to generate the proof? Christopher Ehret argues from linguistic and other evidence that there were multiple places in sub-Saharan Africa where

---

21. The largest iron meteorite in the world is the Hoba meteorite, discovered by accident in Namibia in the early twentieth century. Weighing some sixty tons, it is largely intact and lies where it was found, being too heavy to move.

people seem to have discovered how to smelt iron. The earliest African invention of iron smelting may date to before 1000 BCE in the Great Lakes region of East Africa and south of Lake Chad in West-Central Africa. From these places it could have spread to the rest of sub-Saharan Africa, except for the Horn of Africa, where the technology was borrowed from the Middle East. Thus, although independent African inventions of iron smelting are possible, the intriguing linguistic evidence does not seem sufficient, by itself, to convince the scholarly community.[22]

Although developments in food production and metallurgy spread slowly, they did produce some changes that in retrospect seem quite dramatic. One was a steady increase in population, due to improved nutrition. Another was transformation in the landscape as cultivation increased. The language map of Africa provides another striking perspective on the magnitude of the changes under way. Slowly but relentlessly a new group of languages known collectively as Bantu spread across most of Africa below the Equator. In the third millennium BCE, speakers of a language known as proto-Bantu began to expand out of southern Cameroon to the east and south. The proto-Bantu were Late Stone Age farmers, who initially cleared woodland for their crops using polished stone axes. By 1000 BCE, Bantu-speaking people had spread up the Congo River valley as well as along the southern edge of the great Central African rainforest. Over the course of next two millennia the frontier of advancing Bantu languages had reached the Indian Ocean and moved south of the Zambezi and Limpopo Rivers into eastern South Africa.

As they expanded generation by generation, these populations underwent many significant changes. One of the most obvious is that the ancestral proto-Bantu language gave birth to dozens and then hundreds of different languages, each language being associated with distinctive cultural features. Today there are some 350 distinct Bantu languages. A second change was the spread of iron smelting, enabling farmers to clear land more efficiently with iron tools, thus enabling their settlements to spread faster. The expansion of Bantu-speaking peoples altered the map, but the transformations occurred slowly over four thousand years. Once misleadingly called the Bantu migration or migrations, it was in reality a population drift, an oozing of people generation by generation through compatible environments. This expanding population interacted with other peoples, absorbing some of them and borrowing parts of their cultures. The driving force was population growth due the abundance of food and land. As one generation gave birth to a more numerous new generation, the surplus

---

22. Hamady Bascoum, ed., *Aux Origines du Fer en Afrique: Une Ancienneté Méconnu. Afrique de l'Ouest et Afrique Centrale* (Paris: Éditions UNESCO, 2002); David J. Killick, "Review Essay: What Do We Know about African Iron Working," *Journal of African Archaeology* 2.1 (2004): 97–112; Stanley B. Alpern, "Did They or Didn't They Invent It? Iron in Sub-Saharan Africa," *History in Africa* 52 (2005): 41–94; Ehret, *Civilizations*, 136–38, 159–62; Bertram B. B. Mapunda, "The Appearance and Development of Metallurgy South of the Sahara," in Mitchell and Lane, *African Archaeology*, 615–26.

population sought new lands nearby. As geographical distances multiplied, so too did cultural and linguistic differences. The map of the Romance language family in Europe corresponds to the borders of the Latin-speaking Western Roman Empire, but there was no Bantu empire to provide a cultural base. Thus, the spread of the Bantu languages involved greater cultural differentiation.

An example of this differentiation can be found in southeastern Africa where DNA evidence shows that Bantu-speaking people intermarried with Khoekhoe peoples, incorporating new genetic material into their own gene pools. Anthropological and linguistic evidence shows that the early Bantu also adopted some Khoekhoe customs. Khoekhoe influences appear to lie behind the fact that men of the southeastern Bantu devoted greater energy to cattle keeping than did other Bantu-speaking males, along with the greater role their women played in farming. As mentioned earlier, the several click sounds in some southeastern Bantu languages were one of the most obvious and persisting borrowings.[23]

The final case study concerns the evidence for ancient Egypt's African origins. One of the misinformed judgments about Africa offered by the German philosopher Hegel concerned ancient Egypt, whose historical importance even he found impossible to question. One cannot exclude Egypt, he stated, from consideration "in reference to the passage of the human mind from its Eastern to its Western phase, but it does not belong to the African Spirit." Although ancient Egypt merits a special place in human history, it did not emerge in isolation. Just as Western culture borrowed from the ancient Egyptians, Egyptians borrowed from African societies to the south. The African connection is clearly supported by linguistic, genetic, and other evidence. The ancient Egyptian language belongs to the Afrasian (or Afro-Asiatic) family and is the oldest written form of that language, going back to 3300 BCE. The prototypic Afrasian language emerged between 22,000 and 15,000 BCE in the Horn of Africa, probably in the Ethiopian highlands. Thereafter, Afrasian speakers moved northward through the hills along the western Red Sea coast into Egypt. Genetic evidence from modern Egyptians confirms the presence of a distinctive Y-chromosome deriving from that movement. Fully modern people already lived in Egypt at the time the Afrasian-speaking people arrived, but there is nowhere they could have come from except from earlier migrations originating in sub-Saharan Africa.[24]

The fact that the language spoken and written by ancient Egyptians belonged to the Afrasian family attests to the cultural importance of the newcomers. Further migrations spread the family of Afrasian languages into the Middle East. Along with other languages, ancient and modern Hebrew and Arabic belong to the Afrasian family. The Afrasian family also spread west across North Africa, giving rise to the Berber languages, and south of the Sahara into what is now northern Nigeria, giving rise to

23. Ehret, *Civilizations*, 241–43; Pierre de Maret, "Archaeologies of Bantu Expansion," in Mitchell and Lane, *African Archaeology*, 627–43.

24. Ehret, "Africa from 48,000," 379–87.

the important Hausa language. However, ancient Egypt was not just part of Africa; it also interacted with its neighbors, who sometimes invaded. The African kingdom of Nubia, for example, conquered ancient Egypt, and Nubians formed Egypt's twenty-fifth ruling dynasty in the eighth century BCE. Likewise, the Near Eastern states of Assyria and Persia also invaded and conquered the land of the Nile. Finally, Egypt was incorporated into the empires of Alexander the Great, Rome, and the Arab Muslims. For the most part the conquerors adopted much more from the Egyptians than the Egyptians did from them.

The linguistic evidence for Egyptians' African lineage is cultural not racial. In common with the Hebrews, Arabs, and some Berbers, the Egyptians did not regard themselves as sharing the same skin coloring as the "black" Africans further south. Nor does genetic evidence prove that Egyptians were biologically identical with the darker-skinned people of the Horn of Africa. After all, all humans have genes that can be traced back to Africa. As the Introduction warned, the Afrocentrists' claim that, because ancient Egyptians were Africans they must have been black, is a misleading oversimplification of the complexity of human biology and history.

## Conclusion

It will be clear that Africa has a history that is longer than any other continent and is equally full of interesting and important events and achievements. This chapter has concentrated on the earlier events in African history; later chapters will take up more recent topics. It will also be clear that the task of uncovering the secrets of the African past requires using many distinct and specialized disciplines. Rather than relying primarily on written sources, historians of Africa must be prepared to utilize a wide range of information that Africans have deliberately left behind (handprints) as well as evidence that they have inadvertently left behind or carried forward in their genes and speech (footprints). If Georg Hegel may be partly excused for his negative views of African history because he lived before modern historians had mapped the patterns of the African past, people in more recent times have no such excuse. The outline of African history is clear, and researchers have documented many particular details. Yet history is always a work in progress, so future scholarship will emend current ideas and interpretations.

# 2. How Special Can Ethiopia Be?

". . . [N]ine months and five days after she [the queen of Sheba, i.e., of Ethiopia] had separated from King Solomon . . . she brought forth a man child.[1]
—Kebra Nagast (Glory of Kings), *fourteenth century, linking the Ethiopian throne to ancient Israel*

[There was] not many years ago a certain John, a king and a priest, living in the Far East, beyond Armenia and Persia, who like all his people was a Christian.[2]
—*Hugh, Bishop of Jabala (Lebanon), 1145*

We know and we over-stand, Almighty God is a living man.[3]
—*Bob Marley, Jamaican singer, stating the Rastafari belief that Emperor Haile Selassie of Ethiopia was a deity*

The previous chapter argued that there is a great deal more evidence available for Africa's history than has been commonly assumed. This chapter narrows the focus to a single country—Ethiopia in northeast Africa—and looks critically at various widely held beliefs about its place in history that are myths in the sense that they oversimplify or distort the historical record. The many threads of the myth of Ethiopia as a special place arose at different times and in different places. While differing significantly from each other, these myths share the assumption that Ethiopia and Ethiopians are ultra-special, divinely elevated to a higher spiritual plain.

One must begin by saying that Ethiopians are indeed special. Their country has existed longer than any other south of Egypt and was the only African state to defeat a European takeover attempt in the nineteenth century and to escape a long period of colonial occupation, despite a later Italian conquest in 1936. Moreover, Ethiopia was the first independent African state to be a member of the League of Nations and one of four African founding members of the United Nations. Culturally, Ethiopians have the longest continuous traditions of literacy and Christianity in sub-Saharan Africa and also have distinguished art and architectural traditions. A final distinction is that Ethiopian cuisine has achieved the greatest international success of any from Africa.

---

1. E. W. Budge, *The Queen of Sheba and Her Only Son Menyelek (Kebra Nagast)* (London: Medici Society, 1922), 33.

2. Otto of Freising, *Historia de duabus civitatibus*, bk. 7, chap. 33, cited in C. F. Beckingham, "The Achievements of Prester John," in *Prester John: The Mongols and the Ten Lost Tribes*, ed. Charles F. Beckingham and Bernard Hamilton (Aldershot, UK: Variorum, 1996), 2.

3. W. B. Carnochan, *Golden Legends: Images of Abyssinia, Samuel Johnson to Bob Marley* (Stanford, CA: Stanford University Press, 2008), 134–35.

Other widely believed special qualities of Ethiopians are mythical, in the sense that they lie beyond what can be verified historically. Some myths are demonstrably false, while others appear to be exaggerated or are incapable of verification. After a brief examination of Ethiopia's special connections to Judaism, Christianity, and Islam, this chapter probes deeper into two medieval myths. The first is the Ethiopian legend that their country is the Second Zion and the successor of ancient Israel, a legend that intensified the sacredness its ruling dynasty. The second medieval myth arose among Western European Christians during the Crusades against Islam and concerned a Christian priest-king known as Prester John, who later came to be identified with the king of Ethiopia. The final section of the chapter looks at more recent myths from southern Africa and the African diaspora that gave Ethiopia special spiritual and political importance. Although these myths are quite distinct in their details, their common reference point joins them together like threads in a tapestry.

## Ethiopia's Many Names and Images

Over its long history, the diverse people now called Ethiopians have been known by various other names, and Ethiopia's political boundaries have also shifted greatly. Before 1900, the kingdom was most commonly called Abyssinia. After it expanded to its present extent in the late nineteenth century, political leaders began to promote the use of "Ethiopia" as the empire's official name, both to encourage a common identity internally and to clarify its identity internationally. To keep the narrative coherent, this chapter will follow the practice of using Ethiopia and Ethiopians throughout all periods, much as historians commonly use the term American in describing the Western Hemisphere in pre-colonial and colonial times. It cannot be said for sure when the initial Ethiopian state came into existence, but the first one with good historical evidence was known as Aksum (or Axum), the name of its capital. The state of Aksum was in existence during the first millennium CE.

The name "Ethiopian" is ancient, but it originally referred to a broad area of Africa south of Egypt. As the Introduction documented, ancient Greek and Roman writers from Herodotus to Pliny the Elder (and beyond) used Ethiopian as a generic name for all dark-skinned African people. Although Pliny suggested these "Ethiopians" were strange by virtue of their skins having been charred by the sun as well as being deformed in other ways, other ancient texts used the term in positive ways. The Greek poet Homer praised the "blameless Ethiopians," the noblest people in the world, whom the gods often visited. In the Hebrew Bible, Psalms 68:31 says, "Let envoys come from Egypt; let Ethiopia eagerly stretch forth her hands to God," and Amos 9:7 asks, "Are you not like the Ethiopians to me, O Israelites?" that is, beloved. An account in chapter 12 of the Book of Numbers says that when Moses was criticized by other Hebrews because he had married an Ethiopian woman, presumably a non-Jew, God came down in a column of cloud and silenced his critics. In the Acts of the

Apostles in the New Testament, there is a record of a meeting near Jerusalem between the Apostle Philip and an "Ethiopian," whom the apostle persuaded to become a Christian and baptized. In this case, because the "Ethiopian" is described as the chief treasurer of Queen Candice, we know that he was from the kingdom of Kush just south of Egypt. Although in all of these Biblical texts "Ethiopian" refers to black Africans generally, some readers have incorrectly interpreted these passages as referring just to the particular kingdom now known as Ethiopia.[4]

The Arabs called the people of Aksum and its successor kingdoms *Habshi* and their land *al-Habesh*, from which comes the name Abyssinia. The Prophet Muhammad and his early followers had a quite special relationship with Abyssinians. It is impossible to verify the historical accuracy of the statements about the Abyssinians in the Qur'an and the Hadith (the traditions about the Prophet's life), since there is no outside evidence to collaborate them. At the very least, the number of connections is remarkable. As an infant, Muhammad was nursed by an Abyssinian woman and was later raised by his maternal grandfather, who had many business connections with Aksum. In addition, a freed slave of Abyssinian origins was one of the earliest converts to Islam and served as the faith's first muezzin, the person who calls the faithful to prayer. The most substantial connection came about as the result of Arab persecution of some of Muhammad's followers, whom the Prophet advised to flee to Aksum, "a country where no one is wronged, a land of righteousness." Those refugees who were welcomed there included Muhammad's daughter, two of his future wives, his former wet nurse, and his future successor.

The king of Aksum treated the refugees with kindness and refused a large bribe offered by some Arabs to send them back to Mecca. When it was safe, the refugees returned to Arabia with such glowing accounts of their good treatment that, upon hearing that the Abyssinian king had died, the Prophet is said to have prayed for his soul and later ordered his followers to "leave the Abyssinians in peace." The many words in the Qur'an that derive from the Abyssinian language are evidence of close connections between Mecca and Aksum, as is the fact that Muslims did indeed leave the Abyssinians in peace for the better part of the next millennium.[5]

Despite the special relationship with Muslims, Aksum suffered a marked decline following the Islamic conquests in the seventh century. The evidence is incomplete, but one clear sign of the troubles is that the kingdom ceased to mint its own coins. Partly the decline stemmed from the wars' disruption of trade, partly from internal problems in Aksum, including, it has been argued, population pressures, drought, and famine. Declining strength led to local rebellions and an invasion from the west. Little is known of the particulars of Aksum's last days. In about 1137, when a new Ethiopian

---

4. Richard Pankhurst, *The Ethiopians: A History* (Oxford: Blackwell, 2001), 18, with citations and text from *The Complete Bible: An American Translation*, trans. J. M. Powis Smith and Edgar J. Goodspeed (Chicago: University of Chicago Press, 1939).

5. Pankhurst, *Ethiopians*, 45–46.

The Church of St. George, Lalibela, was painstakingly chipped away from bedrock to a depth of forty feet, carved into a cruciform shape, and then hollowed out. The people in the picture give an idea of the size of the church, which can be entered by means of a narrow subterranean trench. Photo courtesy of Alfred J. Andrea. All rights reserved.

dynasty called the Zagwé came to power, its founders claimed to be Aksum's successor. Little is known for sure about Zagwé history except that these rulers remained devoted to Aksum's Christian faith and continued the tradition of rock carving. Both traits are attested by the remarkable churches carved of out of solid rock under some of the later Zagwé kings. In 1270, following a period of decline, the Zagwé rulers were replaced by another dynasty. Like new dynasties everywhere, this royal family needed to establish its legitimacy, which its founders tried to do not only by claiming descent from Aksum's rulers but also from Solomon, the king of Israel in the tenth century BCE. Known as the Solomonic dynasty, it governed Ethiopia until 1974.

## Solomon and Sheba

The Ethiopian belief in a connection to the rulers of ancient Israel derives from the story of King Solomon and the queen of Sheba in chapter 10 of the first Book of Kings in the Bible (abbreviated I Kings 10), which states that "when the queen of Sheba heard of the fame of Solomon, . . . she came to test him with hard questions."

Impressed with his answers and the beauty of Jerusalem, she gave Solomon lavish gifts of gold, spices, and jewels. He reciprocated with splendid gifts, and she and her retinue went home. The Bible makes no mention of their lovemaking, unless one chooses to read that into the passage, "Solomon gave to the queen of Sheba all that it pleased her to ask for," which seems unwarranted. The Bible also does not say precisely where Sheba was located, but the passage about her is mixed in with accounts of the trade to Ophir, which appears to be located somewhere near the southern end of the Red Sea. Many scholars (but not all) identify Sheba with Saba, the southern region of Arabia.

The Ethiopian *Kebra Nagast* (Glory of Kings) presents a much more detailed and elaborate account of Solomon and Sheba. Where the Bible is general, the Ethiopian account is detailed. For example, while Kings says that the queen arrived in Jerusalem with "a very large retinue, with camels," the *Kebra Nagast* specifies that there were 797 camels along with mules and asses. The Bible is silent about the meals and entertainments that would have accompanied their conversations; the *Kebra Nagast* specifies the variety and quantities of food and wine served and the number of male and female singers who entertained. It relates, "every day [Solomon] arrayed [the queen] in eleven garments which bewitched the eyes." Like a modern writer of romantic fiction, the author of the *Kebra Nagast* describes the queen's inner emotions:

> she saw his wisdom and his just judgments, and his splendour, and his grace, and heard the eloquence of his speech. And she marveled in her heart, and was utterly astonished in her mind . . . how perfect he was in composure, and wise in understanding, and pleasant in graciousness, and commanding in stature . . . his voice, . . . his lips, . . . his wisdom.[6]

The mood and emotional context having been convincingly set, the author moves on to the central event in the expanded story. Solomon persuades the queen to sleep in his bedchamber, extracting from her a promise that she wouldn't take any of his possessions, while he promises in return not to make sexual advances during the night. But all this was a setup for seduction. Solomon had plied the queen with a feast of spicy food, so that when she awoke in the night with a raging thirst and drank from the water bottle at his bedside, he accused her of breaking her pledge, freeing him to break his. Solomon "worked his will with her and they slept together." Afterwards, there seem to have been no regrets on either side. The Bible itself concedes the king had a strong attraction to the opposite sex: "Now King Solomon was a lover of women; . . . he had seven hundred wives, princesses, and three hundred concubines" (I Kings 11), a passage the Ethiopian text repeats, noting that God permitted such excesses to Solomon back then, but Christian men may have only one wife.

The author of the *Kebra Nagast* adds other details. It reveals the unnamed queen in the Biblical account was named Makeda, and she was from Ethiopia, which in those days was always ruled by queens who were virgins. After returning home, Makeda

---

6. Budge, *Queen of Sheba*, 21.

gave birth to a son. When the son had grown into manhood, he learned his father's identity and persuaded his mother to let him go to Jerusalem to meet him. Solomon was delighted by the visit and presented rich gifts and ordered the eldest sons of the nobles of Israel to accompany him home. However, fearful of traveling unprotected in a strange land, the young men resolved to take with them the sacred Ark of the Covenant, a gold-covered box containing the tablets of the Ten Commandments. With the blessing of the Angel of God, they removed the Ark from the Temple in Jerusalem and took it with them to Ethiopia. Upon Makeda's death, her son became the first of the male kings of Ethiopia, taking the throne name Menelik.[7]

Evaluating the historical validity of this narrative is no easy task. The *Kebra Nagast* skillfully embellishes the Biblical texts, but logical problems are inherent in its account. For example, the account appears to blend details about the queen of Sheba from the Book of Kings with the mentions of "Ethiopian" Queen Candice in the Acts of the Apostles. In fact, Candice was not a personal name but the title of the queen mother of the kingdom of Kush, which was "Ethiopian" only in the broad sense used in antiquity, and she had no connection to the land now called Ethiopia. The Candices were not virgins but the mothers of kings, though they ruled when the male heir was underage. A more serious issue is the gap of over a thousand years between the time of Solomon and the earliest known existence of the kingdom of Aksum. There is an even greater temporal gap between the events regarding Solomon described in the *Kebra Nagast* and the oldest manuscript of that text, which dates to the early 1300s, some 2,250 years after the time of Solomon. This suggests that the account in the *Kebra Nagast* could not have been passed down orally over so long a period and that the story of Solomon and Sheba was most likely written shortly after the Solomonic dynasty seized the throne in 1270, so as to give it a legitimacy derived from prestigious origins in the ancient kingdom of Israel. Even so, parts of the story may have circulated orally before they were written down. A late twelfth-century Armenian account, for example, refers to the Ethiopians possessing the Ark of the Covenant. The bottom line is that the *Kebra Nagast*'s imaginative and emotive account of a line of descent from Solomon and Sheba to the kings of Aksum and the new Solomonic dynasty is highly improbable and unsupported by evidence. It is a myth.[8]

Another piece of the myth is that the Ark of the Covenant was brought to Ethiopia. If so, where is it? The Ethiopian tradition is that the Ark is in the city of Aksum in an outbuilding known as the Chapel of the Tablet in the precincts of the Church of Our Lady Mary of Zion. Zion is an ancient name for the kingdom of Israel that stresses its sacral quality. On the basis of the connection to Solomon and the Ark, Ethiopia becomes the Second Zion, heir to the special position of ancient Israel. In the *Kebra Nagast* the Ark is regularly referred to as Zion in that it is the repository of the special

---

7. Budge, *Queen of Sheba*, 26–37, 57–64.
8. Pankhurst, *Ethiopians*, 19, 54–55.

Church of Our Lady Mary of Zion, Aksum, in whose precincts the ancient Israelite Ark of the Covenant is said to lie. Photo courtesy of Alfred J. Andrea. All rights reserved.

spiritual compact between God and Israel. Normally the Ark is hidden from public view. In 2009 the patriarch of the Ethiopian Orthodox Tewahedo Church promised to exhibit the Ark but later withdrew that premise, while still affirming its existence.

The special connections of the Ethiopians to the three Abrahamic faiths are remarkable. Christian since the fourth century, ancient Ethiopia nevertheless gained special regard from early Muslims. Even before that, according to the *Kebra Nagast*, Queen Makeda of Sheba/Ethiopia converted to Judaism, thus suggesting that the earliest kings of Ethiopia must have been Jewish as well, on both their paternal and maternal sides. There is no reason to take this story literally, but it does point to a larger historical reality, namely that the region of the Horn of Africa had close cultural, commercial, and sometimes political ties to the Semitic world of Arabia and ancient Israel. The likely language of Aksum was Ge'ez, which is used as the liturgical language of the Ethiopian Orthodox Tewahedo Church. Along with Arabic and Hebrew, Ge'ez belongs to the Semitic branch of the Afrasian language family and contains many Hebrew loanwords and linguistic connections to southern Arabia. These cultural ties from ancient times were reinforced by commercial exchanges with gold, salt, and ivory traded from Africa to Arabia. Finally, at times between the eighth century BCE (or even earlier) and the first century CE, the south Arabian kingdom of Saba ruled lands on the African side of the Red Sea, where modern archaeologists have located more than a hundred Sabaean sites. Thus, while the queen of Sheba (Saba) may not have been an actual person (or if she was, may have lived later than the time of Solomon), the *Kebra Nagast*'s suggestion of links among Israel, Arabia, and Ethiopia are valid in general, if not in the particular details.[9]

In moving from legend to history, it is helpful to bear in mind that all history, but especially religious history, is layered. By this is meant that new additions lie atop older beliefs, which are sometimes displaced or altered. Sometimes remnants of old traditions lie in plain sight but may not be recognized by later generations. For example, the days of the week in English derive from three belief systems: the names behind the first two days, the Sun and the Moon, represent ancient deities widely worshiped around the world. The next four days are named after old Norse gods: Tiw, Wodan, Thor, and Frige (a female deity). Saturday is named for the Roman god Saturn. Even after English speakers became Christian, Sunday was not renamed the Lord's Day as happened in some other European languages. One would expect Ethiopian belief systems to be similarly layered, although one needs to keep in mind that there can be considerable feedback between older and newer layers. In simplified terms, the oldest layer would contain traditional African beliefs involving magic, witchcraft, and nature spirits, followed by a newer Semitic layer heavily skewed toward Jewish beliefs and practices, and overlain with a Christian layer. One might note that these layers are implicit in the *Kebra Nagast*, which says the queen of Sheba was a snake worshipper before Solomon convinced her to accept Jewish beliefs and customs, and that her descendants later became Christians and promoted that religion in their realms.

Although this simplified outline follows a chronological sequence, scholars know that the actual process of cultural change is more complex. Thus, it is clear that Ethiopian Christians have retained a large number of Jewish customs, but it is far from certain that these are all survivals from an earlier Semitic layer. Jewish customs could also have been introduced later along with the belief in an ancient connection to the Jewish Zion. For example, the fact that many Christian churches in Ethiopia resemble Solomon's Temple is more likely due to literate Christians following the detailed descriptions of the Temple in the Old Testament rather than to architectural norms that were passed down from generation to generation going all the way back to Solomon's time. Similarly, the fact that Ethiopian Christians observe Jewish dietary prohibitions, such as those against eating pork and the flesh of some other animals and fish, could date from three millennia ago or could have been introduced in Christian times as the result of knowledge of the Old Testament texts. The latter case is suggested by an Ethiopian saying about pork that is stricter than Jewish custom: "Pork taints not only him who eats it but him who hears about it." Likewise, Ethiopian observance of Jewish forms of ritual cleansing could date from Old Testament times or be a later

---

9. Pankhurst, *Ethiopians*, 9–10, 13–19, 20–26.

introduction. For simplicity, these possibilities have been posed as either-or choices, but, in fact, some blend of the two is also possible. Without evidence dating from before the writing of the *Kebra Nagast* in the early 1300s, it is impossible to choose among these possible interpretations.[10]

Furthermore, not all "Jewish" customs are necessarily derived from ancient Israel. The fact that Jews, Arabs, and Ethiopians all practice male circumcision and avoid eating pork suggests that these traditions are older than ancient Israel. A more complex issue is the origin of Ethiopian Jews known as the Falasha or Beta Israel. The airlift of over 80,000 Ethiopian Jews to Israel beginning in 1979 drew great attention to this Ethiopian minority and set off controversies about their origins. The official position taken in Israel was that they were the descendants of a "lost tribe" of ancient Israelites. Modern historians of Ethiopia have challenged this "myth." In the first place, while Jews were present in Aksum and older states, there is no evidence of a mass migration into the kingdom. Historians James Quirin of Fisk University, a historically black school in Nashville, Tennessee, and Steven Kaplan of Hebrew University in Jerusalem agree that the presence of the Beta Israel in Ethiopia cannot be traced earlier than the 1400s, so any earlier history is unknowable. In Quirin's words, "A sophisticated analysis . . . argues for the appropriation of Old Testament symbols by Christian Ethiopians after the Aksumite period rather than a more mechanical process by which elements were brought by migrants." Kaplan is more explicit: "From a cultural perspective there appears to be little question that the Beta Israel must be understood as the product of processes that took place in Ethiopia between the fourteenth and sixteenth century."[11] Both historians suggest that pressure from the Ethiopian Christian state led some communities with Hebraic and Judaic traditions to become more orthodox Christians while others hardened their attachment to Jewish identity and became a separate group, even though they suffered by being deprived of their land. The identities of both the Solomonic rulers and the Beta Israel were "invented," not out of thin air but by weaving existing cultural strands into a larger tapestry that gave them meaning. Bear in mind that there is no documentation of events before 1400. These identity myths are deeply important to their believers, but that does not prove their historical accuracy.

## Prester John

The myth of Prester John that became popular in medieval Europe might have been created out of thin air, but over time Ethiopia came to be seen as the home of that mythical

---

10. Edward Ullendorff, *Ethiopia and the Bible* (London: Oxford University Press, 1968), 73–145.

11. James Quirin, "Caste and Class in Historical North-west Ethiopia: The Beta Israel (Falasha) and Kemant, 1300–1900," *Journal of African History* 39 (1998): 198–99; James Quirin, *The Evolution of Ethiopian Jews: A History of the Beta Israel (Falasha) to 1920* (Philadelphia: University of Pennsylvania Press, 1992); Steven Kaplan, *The Beta Israel (Falasha) in Ethiopia: Earliest Times to the Twentieth Century* (New York: New York University Press, 1992), 157.

Christian priest-king. Although Ethiopia was a real place, Europeans tended to view it through mythical lenses. In the first recorded version of the myth in 1145 Prester John clearly did not dwell in Africa. That source named "a certain John, a king and a priest who dwells beyond Persia and Armenia in the uttermost East [and is said to be] a lineal descendant of the Magi . . . in the Gospel."[12] Prester John was said to be fabulously wealthy and a descendant of one of the Magi whom the New Testament states came to Bethlehem bearing gifts for the Christ Child.

The story of this mythical Christian ruler established itself in many European languages, including a work of fiction entitled *The Life of Prester John* that appeared in 1165. Despite obvious impossibilities, such as the survival of the same individual century after century, European travelers made fruitless attempts to locate the priest-king in Central Asia, China, or India. The Nestorian Christians found in Central Asia and China and the St. Thomas Christians in India did not rule powerful enough states to fit the myth. After a party of thirty Ethiopian monks visited the Italian city of Genoa in 1302, the search for Prester John turned to northeastern Africa. An Italian pilgrim to Jerusalem in 1335 reported the presence of Ethiopian monks at the Christian Church of the Holy Sepulcher (where they may still be found dwelling on the roof) and was the first writer to suggest that the Ethiopian monks were from the kingdom of Prester John. According to some accounts, the Kurdish Muslim military leader known as Saladin had made the Ethiopians guardians of Christian holy places in Jerusalem after driving out the Latin Christian crusaders in 1187. Saladin likely chose the Ethiopians ahead of other Christians because of their close ties to the Prophet Muhammad as well as because they had no part in the anti-Muslim crusades. Another Italian who had lived in Ethiopia for several years led a delegation of Ethiopian monks to Venice 1402, where they created a sensation, partly because they brought tame leopards with them and partly because they seemed to confirm that the existence of the kingdom of Prester John.[13]

The myth of Prester John was so entrenched that shifting his realm to Africa didn't seem to matter. Ethiopia was not located in the distant East, but in the elastic geography of the day it could still be considered a part of the Indies. Nor was it a problem that no Ethiopian emperors would be named John (Yohannes) until the mid-1600s. Nor did it matter that the kings of Ethiopia were not usually priests, but were they priest-kings? The best answer may be that all Christian monarchs in pre-modern times were considered sacral. Both in Europe and Ethiopia the coronation ceremony for monarchs involved anointing with holy oils in a manner very similar to the ceremony for consecrating a bishop. It was often believed that kings had the miraculous power to cure diseases. Kings were also immortal in the sense that, while their bodies

---

12. Matteo Salvadore, *The African Prester John and the Birth of Ethiopian European Relations, 1402–1555* (London and New York: Routledge, 2017), 4, quoting Otto of Friesing's *Chronica sive Historica de duabus civitatibus.*

13. Salvadore, *African Prester*, 2–3, 21–30.

were mortal, they passed their divine right to rule on to a legitimate heir, at least in theory.[14]

Although the realm of Prester John could be reconciled with Ethiopia, the size of its realm and the qualities of its ruler remained larger than life. The mid-1400s *Mappmundi* of Fra Mauro showed the kingdom of the Ethiopian Prester John extending from the Red Sea south across most of East and Southeast Africa. It also asserted that Prester John, the king of Abyssinia, controlled more than 120 kingdoms containing immense numbers of peoples speaking more than 60 languages. In the second half of the fifteenth century there were Portuguese reports that the kings of Benin in the Niger Delta of West Africa depended on a priest-king called Ogane for their consecration, whom some believed was Prester John. Other exaggerations reflected ancient beliefs about black Africans having superhuman qualities. The learned papal secretary Poggio Bracciolini (1380–1459) seriously reported that Ethiopians lived longer than other people, reaching an average span of 120 years, with some surviving for 150 or even 200 years. Another extraordinary belief was that the kings of Ethiopia possessed the power, or at least the physical ability, to stop of flow of the Nile waters to Egypt. Perhaps this mistaken idea was due to an understandably sketchy grasp of the geography of the Nile's headwaters (which do indeed lie partly in the Ethiopian highlands). It may also have stemmed from the supposition that Prester John possessed magical powers. In a letter to the king of France in 1448, the Grand Master of the Knights of St. John in Rhodes stated that "some Indian [Ethiopian] priests" had told him of Prester John's powers over the Nile's flow. It was not the first time this power was asserted, nor would it be the last.[15]

Besides the mythic beliefs, Europeans embraced locating the kingdom of Prester John in Africa for practical and strategic reasons. One was the need to halt the Muslim front advancing from the East. In 1453 the Ottoman Turks had captured Constantinople, the last outpost of Roman and Byzantine power and the seat of the patriarch of Eastern Orthodox Christians. Many on both sides of that front believed (quite correctly) that further advances would follow. Thus, impeding Muslim advances by having the Ethiopians turn Egypt into a desert would be a key part of the Christian strategy. To build a pan-Christian coalition it was necessary to heal the historic divisions among Christians. Even before the fall of Constantinople the patriarch of the West (the Roman pontiff or pope) had called church councils to promote Christian reunification. Some forty Ethiopian monks, including three ambassadors said to be from Prester John, had joined the delegates from Greek, Egyptian, and other Eastern churches attending a council in Florence in 1441. In the face of the impending advance of the Turkish Muslims, all sides were eager to talk about putting aside old

---

14. Ernst Kantorowicz, *The King's Two Bodies: A Study on Medieval Political Theology* (Princeton, NJ: Princeton University Press, 1957).

15. Salvadore, *African Prester John*, 1–6, 21–30, 63, 92–93, quotation 45; see also Beckingham, "Achievements of Prester John," 1–22.

theological differences. As the Byzantine Empire fell to the Turks, just as Christian Egypt had fallen to the Arabs centuries earlier, Christian Ethiopia's importance grew in the European imagination. In 1481 a monastery inside the walls of the Vatican was dedicated as an intellectual center for Ethiopian studies. Known as Saint Stephen of the Abyssinians, it housed Ethiopian monks who studied Latin Christianity and taught Europeans about Ethiopian Christianity. Either at the Council of Florence or shortly afterward, Ethiopians presented the papacy with a copy of the Book of Psalms in their language and script. In 1513 a printed edition of that Ge'ez text was published, the first such Ethiopian text to be mass-produced. By mid-century an Ethiopian and European team of scholars at Saint Stephen's had also published in Ge'ez a New Testament and a missal with the text of the Mass and other rituals. By that time the Ethiopian presence in Europe was also displayed in a bronze plaque on the central door of the new Saint Peter's Basilica, depicting the arrival of African delegates at the Council of Florence.[16]

These encounters with Ethiopia are well documented on the European side, but the Ethiopian leaders were just as interested in an alliance to meet the threat of Islamic advances. In addition to military support, the Ethiopians also saw their new Mediterranean connections as a source of skilled craftsmen, including printers. The Ottomans' advance along the Red Sea had slowed after they took control of Mecca and Egypt in 1517, though naval battles still occurred there. However, local Muslim warlords were prone to ignore the immunity Ethiopia had long been accorded by Muslims. In the early 1500s Ethiopian rulers sent new delegations to the Mediterranean with pleas for aid and alliances, despite the perils of passing through the intervening Muslim lands. A Portuguese embassy that made it to Ethiopia in 1520 produced a detailed description of the kingdom. Beginning a decade later, a furious Muslim assault on the kingdom destroyed monasteries and churches, slaughtered, enslaved, and plundered. The assault, led by the jihadist Ahmed ibn Ibrahim al-Ghazi, known as Gragn ("Lefty"), drove the imperial court into hiding. In part Gragn's attack had been provoked by Portugal's new and aggressive presence in the Indian Ocean. Motivated by the legend of Prester John and the new pan-Christian dialogue, the Portuguese came to rescue the Ethiopians. A large fleet dispatched from Goa, the Portuguese base in India, reached the Red Sea in 1541, and, after some misadventures, the small army made its way inland, successfully skirmishing with Gragn's forces, and joined up with the remnants of the Ethiopian army. In new battles Gragn gained the upper hand, but he was shot in 1543, and his followers fled. Ethiopia survived.[17]

The historical reality of Ethiopia was gaining focus in Europe, but mythic Prester John faded slowly. A Portuguese missionary, Francisco Álvares, who had traveled to

16. Salvadore, *African Prester*, 58–66, 71–72; David Northrup, *Africa's Discovery of Europe, 1450–1850*, 3rd ed. (New York: Oxford University Press, 2014), 2–5.

17. Giancarlo Casale, *The Ottoman Age of Exploration* (New York: Oxford University Press, 2010), 53–74; Salvadore, *African Prester*, 180–84.

Ethiopia in 1515–1520, combined the myth and the reality in the title of his report, "A True Relation of the Lands of Prester John of the Indies." Around 1570 a Venetian merchant appealed to the pope to launch a new crusade, invoking Ethiopia's alleged ability to alter the Nile's flow to Egypt. In the next century, when another Portuguese missionary wrote an account of his years in Ethiopia, it was translated into English with the fully historical title, *A New History of Ethiopia, Vulgarly, Though Erroneously, Called the Empire of Prester John.*[18] That myth had been put to rest, though new myths would in time emerge.

## Myths from the African Diaspora

Ethiopia came to global attention again in the second half of the nineteenth century, as the result of reform and modernization efforts by Ethiopian emperors and clashes with European invaders. Emperors Theodore II (r. 1855–1868) and Menelik II (r. 1889–1913) modernized Ethiopia's military forces and doubled the kingdom's size. Theodore committed suicide after a British invasion in 1867–1868, which had been launched to free an imprisoned British subject. The British withdrew from this well-publicized campaign, but that left the kingdom open to an Italian invasion that Menelik's forces crushed in 1896. News of Ethiopia's success was welcomed by black Christian communities on both sides of the Atlantic. In southern Africa the news resonated with new Christian converts who were struggling against an older system of white supremacy. In that racially charged environment some African ministers broke with the white-led missionary denominations and set up their own independent congregations. Combining the references to "Ethiopian" Christians in the New Testament with the triumphs of Emperor Menelik in modern Ethiopia, the independent church movement began calling itself the Order of Ethiopia, and "Ethiopianism" became the generic term for African-governed Christian churches.

The southern African connection to Ethiopia was soon linked to the struggles of African diaspora communities in the Americas. One of the African founders of the Order of Ethiopia, James Mata Dwane (1848–1916), went as a delegate to the United States to explore affiliation with an African American denomination, the African Methodist Episcopal Church (AME), which had earlier split off from white-run denominations. Accepting this new connection, AME leader Bishop Henry M. Turner went to South Africa in 1898 and ordained fifty-nine African clergymen and consecrated Dwane bishop of the new enterprise. Although Dwane's efforts to raise funds for Menelik's Ethiopia from African Americans were not successful,

---

18. Francisco Álvares, *The Prester John of the Indies: A True Relation of the Lands of Prester John*, trans. Lord Stanley of Alderly (London: Hakluyt Society, 1961); Matteo Salvadore, personal communication; Job Ludolf, *A New History of Ethiopia, Being a Full and Accurate Description of the Kingdom of Abyssinia, Vulgarly, Though Erroneously, Called the Empire of Prester John*, trans. John Phillips (London: Samuel Smith, 1684).

Ethiopia was becoming a beacon for Pan-African political and relgious independence movements.[19]

The first third of the twentieth century remained tumultuous for Ethiopia. After Emperor Menelik died in 1913 following a long illness, his successor (Iyasu V) faced encirclement by colonies of France, Britain, and Italy, who became allies in World War I, as well as internal opposition to his reformist policies. Emperor Iyasu was deposed in 1916 due to the unpopularity of his overtures to Germany and to anti-imperialists among his Somali neighbors and his grant of religious toleration to Muslims. His replacement was Menelik's daughter Zawditu, the first woman to rule in her own right, it was said, since the queen of Sheba. The Ethiopian prince Ras Tafari was named regent and heir to the throne, more for his education and administrative experience than for a strong claim to succession. Tafari courted foreign support and pushed reform as far as he dared in a traditional society. He succeeded in gaining membership for Ethiopia in the new League of Nations in 1923 and set out on a tour of European countries. For a time, membership in the League proved useful in deflecting imperialist intrusions and overturning an arms blockade that had been imposed on Ethiopia. At home, Tafari introduced the first printing press, opened a few modern schools, and imported some automobiles and airplanes, eventually establishing a small air force. After the death of the empress, Tafari was crowned emperor in 1930, taking the name Haile Selassie, and the titles Lion of Judah and King of Kings.[20]

Membership of the League of Nations and Selassie's coronation had made Ethiopia better known internationally. Additional "Ethiopian" movements developed in other parts of Africa. In the Americas, a "back to Africa" movement was growing, some of whose members regarded Haile Selassie as the divine king foretold in the Bible, who would be the Messiah of African Redemption. From Europe, however, Italy launched a new invasion of Ethiopia in 1935, which the League of Nations was too weak to stop because of the economic crisis of the Great Depression, the rise of aggressive nationalism, and fear of expanding Communism. When Italian planes bombed and gassed Ethiopians into submission in 1936, the outrage felt around the world was profound and rational. In the diaspora, responses were also emotional and mythic. Although black people in the Americas had no historic link to Ethiopia, they were moved by the references to Ethiopia in the Bible, its legendary origins, and the glorious trappings of the recent coronation. Ethiopia became a compelling symbol for what was happening everywhere to black people. A strong response from the African American leadership of the National Association for the Advancement of Colored People (NAACP) failed to persuade the Roosevelt administration to intervene on Ethiopia's side. Black

---

19. Richard Gray, "Christianity," in *The Cambridge History of Africa*, vol. 7, *1905–1940*, ed. A. R. Roberts (Cambridge: Cambridge University Press, 1986), 148; George M Fredrickson, *Black Liberation: A Comparative History of Black Ideologies in the United States and South Africa* (New York: Oxford University Press, 1995), 80–90.

20. Pankhurst, *Ethiopians*, 195–218.

Americans as a whole, however, "turned their attention to Ethiopia on a sustained level unmatched by that accorded to any pervious event in Africa," in the judgment of historian James Meriwether. Black people read news accounts of the Italo-Ethiopian War, attended lectures by the hundreds and thousands, and tens of thousands staged a protest march in Harlem. Editorials in black newspapers called for action, fund-raising events were launched, and black men thought seriously about volunteering, despite the threat of a fine and prison for serving in a foreign army. Two African American pilots did serve in the Ethiopian war. In the Caribbean black doctors worked with counterparts in the United States to collect medical supplies for Ethiopia.[21]

The impending return to global conflict in the late 1930s altered the prevailing European alliances. After Italy joined the enemy side, British forces moved to overthrow Italian rule in Africa and restored Haile Selassie to Ethiopia's throne in 1941. The restoration permitted renewed attention in the black diaspora to what historian Ibrahim Sundiata has called Ethiopia the *Totem* as distinguished from Ethiopia the *Place*. Totemic Ethiopia was "a heroic backdrop to a diasporic dream" of a promised land in Africa where all the injustice of the Atlantic slave trade, enslavement, and inequality would be undone. In the totemic dream of Ethiopia, mysticism and magic abounded. The place called Ethiopia also had a mystical side, as we have already seen, but the grim reality for most residents was poverty, oppression, and lack of opportunity in a land where feudal monarchy, feudal landowning, and chattel slavery were too deeply entrenched for even the sincerest reform leaders to undo. For the dreamers it was paradise on earth; for those in place it was no better and probably worse than the African diaspora.

The beacon of totemic Ethiopia had lured some even before the war. In the early 1930s some sixty-six members of a black Jewish sect from New York City settled on land near Lake Tana, but few prospered and many eventually returned to the United States. Other African American emigration movements that sprang up in Philadelphia, Chicago, St. Louis, and New York failed to send more than a handful of people to Ethiopia before the Italian invasion and World War II made such travel impossible. After the war, the largest group of migrants to Ethiopia came from Jamaica. Ironically they came out of the giant United Negro Improvement Association (UNIA), a black diaspora movement founded by Marcus Garvey (1887–1940), first in Jamaica and then in the United States. Though Garvey was associated with the slogan "back to Africa," he actually held Ethiopia in low esteem for its backwardness.

The movement to Ethiopia came from a mystical splinter group that shared little of the UNIA's activist hopes for black political clout and black-owned businesses. Believing that the Biblical prophecy of princes coming from Africa was fulfilled, followers of

---

21. James H. Meriwether, *Proudly We Can Be Africans: Black Americans and Africa, 1935–1961* (Chapel Hill: University of North Carolina Press, 2002), 27–56, quotation 43; Joseph E. Harris with Slimane Zeghidour, "Africa and Its Diaspora, since 1935," in *UNESCO General History of Africa*, vol. 8, *Africa since 1935*, ed. Ali A. Mazrui (Berkeley: University of California Press, 1993), 708–14.

the sect known as Rastafari held that Emperor Haile Selassie was divine and the Messiah of African Redemption. (Tafari was Selassie's birth name and *ras* a title he gained later.) These Rastafari also celebrated marijuana as a sacred drug and the *Kebra Nagast* as a lost sacred text. As Sundiata puts it, Rastafari leaders "sought refuge in a kind of recalcitrant quietism in which political action waited on the will of the divine." The United States government sent Garvey back to Jamaica when his movement became too troublesome; several early Rastafari leaders ended up in Jamaican jails. Though few went to Ethiopia the place, the mystical and mythical dream of Ethiopia lived on. When Haile Selassie visited Jamaica in 1966, he received a tumultuous reception. Tens of thousands of Jamaicans flocked to the airport to welcome the diminutive monarch. Large crowds also lined his parade route and met him at stations along the train route from Kingston to Montego Bay during his three-day visit. Selassie also met with Rastafarian leaders. When Haile Selassie died in 1975, shortly after being overthrown in a coup, the Rastafari refused to believe an immortal deity could be dead. In Sundiata's judgment, "Myth conquered reality."[22]

In the 1970s, the small Rastafari community in Ethiopia declined sharply after the ancient Ethiopian monarchy was overthrown and Selassie died in exile. Soon, however, the Rastafari movement was gaining new life through its most celebrated convert, Bob Marley, the Jamaican reggae singer whose name and music became world famous. Before his death of cancer in 1981, Marley's music spread his religion far and wide. "We know and we over-stand," he sang of Haile Selassie, "Almighty God is a living man." However, Marley was disappointed enough by his 1978 visit to a Rastafari settlement in Ethiopia, then at a low point, to encourage followers to consider repatriating themselves mentally rather than physically. "Repatriate" is the term Rastafari use for going back to mother Africa so as to rid themselves of the cultural legacy of Babylon (the West). Just before his death, Marley was baptized into the Ethiopian Orthodox Tewahedo Church, perhaps completing the circle of his spiritual journey.[23]

In the wake of the reggae surge and the overthrow of Ethiopia's Marxist regime in 1990–1991, the Rastafari resumed their efforts at repatriation, with Ethiopia again being acclaimed as the promised land and the New Jerusalem or Second Zion, but some went to other African countries. The size of the Rastafari community in Ethiopia in recent years might be something like a thousand, half in the capital, Addis Ababa, and half in a settlement of Shashemene (Shashmane) some 160 miles south of the capital. The numbers are hard to pin down and many members are on temporary visas. A recent scholarly study by historian Erin McLeod identifies a highly significant contrast between how Rastafari immigrants and Ethiopians regard each other. For the West Indian Rastafari, home is black Africa ("Ethiopia" in the ancient usage), and within the African continent the nation of Ethiopia is where they think

---

22. Ibrahim Sundiata, *Brothers and Strangers: Black Zion, Black Slavery, 1914–1940* (Durham, NC: Duke University Press, 2013), 289–303, quotations 277, 301, 303.

23. Carnochan, *Golden Legends*, 134–35.

they belong (though in fact none of their ancestors actually came from there). For most Ethiopians, the Rastafari immigrants are *ferenjoch* (Franks, i.e., Westerners), people who cannot in practice became citizens or own land in Ethiopia. The images of each other that two sides have constructed are incompatible. As scholar Edward Chamberlin puts it with honesty and sympathy, "What Rastafarians have done is to make up a story—and I say this in high tribute—that will bring them back home while they wait for reality to catch up with their imaginations." Myth can be a bridge from aspiration to reality.[24]

## Conclusion

Several sources contributed to the construction of the myths that swirl around Ethiopia. The links that Ethiopians felt with their Judaic and Christian pasts led to the embellishment of the Old Testament story of Solomon and Sheba to enhance how the past is perceived. Medieval Europeans pinned onto Ethiopia the legend of a Christian priest-king descended from one of the Magi, thereby gaining hope of a pan-Christian unity that could stop the advance of the Muslim frontier into Europe. Similarly, people in the African diaspora pinned unrealistic hopes on modern Ethiopia as a place of refuge and on the last Ethiopian emperor as a black god incarnate. Calling these constructions "myths" does not disparage the aspirations behind them nor the depth of the hopes that feed them. Mythmaking is a natural human impulse, but setting the historical record straight is also a worthy task.

24. Erin C. McLeod, *Visions of Zion: Ethiopians and Rastafari* (New York: New York University Press, 2014), 1–10, quotation from Chamberlain 7–8; Jahlani Niaah, "The Rastafari Presence in Ethiopia," in *Rastafari in the New Millennium: A Rastafari Reader*, ed. Michael Barrett (Syracuse, NY: Syracuse University Press, 2014), 66–89.

# 3. Encounters with Non-Africans: Good, Bad, or Complicated?

> . . . [F]or four and a half centuries . . . Africa helped to develop Western Europe in the same proportion as Western Europe helped to underdevelop Africa. To discuss trade between Africans and Europeans in the four centuries before colonial rule is virtually to discuss slave trade.[1]
>
> —*Walter Rodney, Guyanese historian and political activist*

Nearly half a century has passed since Walter Rodney (1942–1980) published *How Europe Underdeveloped Africa*. Most other books published in the early 1970s have gone out of print or, if still in circulation, have been extensively revised and updated. Rodney's volume is the exception. It was originally published in 1972 by two small presses: Bogle-L'Ouverture Publications in London, a small Guyanese press founded in 1968 to showcase black authors and topics, and Tanzania Publishing House in Dar es Salaam, the capital of the Republic of Tanzania in East Africa. Two years later an American edition appeared from Howard University Press, an arm of that historically black institution specializing in books about African Americans and Africa. After Rodney's death in 1980, that press brought out a new edition of *How Europe Underdeveloped Africa*. Bogle-L'Ouverture Publications is now defunct; Tanzania Publishing House survives as one of 149 members of the African Book Cooperative; and Howard University Press ceased operations in 1981. Rodney's book lives on, however, not only surviving the author and the early publishers, but also selling briskly from Black Classic Press in Baltimore, which acquired the Howard University Press catalog.

Rodney was born in Georgetown, the capital of what was then British Guiana (now Guyana). He was bright, athletic, articulate, and politically engaged. As a young man, his abilities won him scholarships to an outstanding secondary school in Georgetown, to the University College of the West Indies in Jamaica, and to the School of Oriental and African Studies (SOAS) of the University of London. Brilliance and diligence enabled him to earn a Ph.D. from SOAS at the age of twenty-four and to publish three well-received books in rapid succession: a volume on his activities in Jamaica, a revision of his doctoral dissertation,[2] and *How Europe Underdeveloped Africa*.

---

1. Walter Rodney, *How Europe Underdeveloped Africa* (Baltimore: Black Classic Press, 2011), 75, 95.

2. Walter Rodney, *Groundings with My Brothers* (London: Bogle-L'Ouverture Publications, 1969), and *A History of the Upper Guinea Coast, 1545–1800* (Oxford: Clarendon Press 1970).

However, opponents of Rodney's political activism derailed what might have been a stellar academic career and provoked his assassination. Like many other black activists of the 1960s and 1970s, Rodney was deeply attracted to Marxism. Following Marx, Rodney identified capitalism as the root cause of plantation slavery, of the oppression of workers, and of black exploitation. Unaware of the changes the passage of time would bring, Rodney praised the communist governments of the Soviet Union, the People's Republic of China, and North Korea as leading the way to a better future.

That heady era of Black Power and black liberation movements was also a time of struggles against colonial rule and white supremacy in Africa and the Caribbean. It was as well the height of the American-led Cold War against the spread of communism, which vigorously challenged political movements that seemed too radical or too much aligned with communism. After Rodney accepted a position teaching African history at his alma mater in Jamaica in 1968, the Jamaican government charged that his fiery political speeches had provoked the so-called Rodney Riots and withdrew his welcome while he was out of the country. In 1974, the Guyanese government rescinded Rodney's appointment as professor and the chair of the history department at the University of Guyana before he could take it up. Even so, Rodney continued to be an academic-activist in Guyana, writing an acclaimed book on the Guyanese working class and helping to found a radical Working Peoples Alliance Party that challenged those in power. Political enemies were behind the car bombing there that killed him in 1980.[3]

Walter Rodney is remembered fondly for his academic accomplishments as well as for his activism. Even those who disagree with his politics respect his sincerity and talents. It must be said, however, that skillful mythmaking was among Rodney's many talents. A few academic books are so well done that they become classics, but most are replaced in a few years by newer research. Thus, it is suspicious when a book remains in print for so long. To be sure, the most recent publisher of *How Europe Underdeveloped Africa* calls it a "black classic," but, strictly speaking, that seems more a political judgment than an academic one. Indeed, even though Rodney was a brilliant academic, this particular book is not really an academic book. Written for a popular audience, it contains no footnotes and only general recommendations for further reading. Examples marshaled in support of arguments in critical places are not very convincing, and the thesis is more explicitly ideological than empirical, that is, more based on Marxist theory than on historical evidence and analysis. Moreover, the research on which the book rests has become outdated. It can be said that the reason for the success of this little book is twofold, it is well written, engaging, and provocative, and it a presents a myth whose appeal has grown over the decades. However, popularity is not proof.

This chapter challenges the thesis put forward in the three chapters in Rodney's book that deal with the pre-colonial period. His second chapter examines African

---

3. Rodney, *How Europe*, 11; Vincent Harding, Robert Hill, and William Strickland, "Introduction" to Rodney, *How Europe*, xi–xxi.

development during the period before the coming of the Europeans around 1500. At one level the chapter is a nice (though now quite dated) introduction to African societies, explaining ways of life, social systems, technologies, and political structures. But it is also a retelling of the Marxist stages of history: how primitive accumulation was replaced by feudalism, which was replaced by capitalism in the West, and which needs to be replaced everywhere by socialism. Marx knew little about Africa, and Rodney struggles to improve on what he wrote, detecting evidence of "feudalism" in ancient Egypt and medieval Ethiopia, but no hint of "capitalism" anywhere on the continent. Though admitting slavery existed in Africa, Rodney categorically denies this was comparable to the capitalist plantation slavery of the Americas, declaring, in Marxist terminology, "slavery as a mode of production was not present in any African society." Rodney gives some attention to the trans-Saharan trade (though not to the large number of slaves in it), but, given the book's concern with "development," it seems to give too little attention to the economic importance of this long-distance trade. Rodney's chapter also seems to understate the level of development in Africa, so it is a bit odd that the chapter concludes with the statement, "the first Europeans to reach West and East Africa by sea . . . indicated that in most respects African development was comparable to that which they knew."[4]

Rodney's next two chapters deal with the arrival of these Europeans. Chapter 3 contains some sweeping generalizations that are central to the thesis of the book's title but are rather simplistic in their analysis. The chapter opens with a classic Marxist oversimplification of economic relations: "it is necessary to reemphasize that development and underdevelopment are not only comparative terms, but that . . . Western Europe and Africa had a relationship which ensured the transfer of wealth from Africa to Europe." He goes on to state, "The contention here is that [from about 1500 to 1950] Africa helped to develop Western Europe in the same proportion as Western Europe helped to underdevelop Africa."

The first half of the statement is not contentious: Western Europe did gain from trade with Africa, although its gains were due even more to Europe's participation in larger Atlantic and global trading systems. The second half of Rodney's thesis is much more ideological. The contention that Europe's development caused Africa's underdevelopment seems predicated on the notion that if one side gains, the other must lose. The reasoning seems analogous to the Marxist thesis that, because labor alone is responsible for the increased value of a manufactured product, owners' profits are stolen from the workers, whereas most modern economists argue that investment, machinery, and management are inputs like labor and so deserve a share of the profits. Modern societies still argue about where the line should be drawn between a fair wage and a fair profit, but to assert that Europe won and Africa lost seems at odds with the historical facts. Another sweeping oversimplification occurs at the beginning of

---

4. Rodney, *How Europe*, 69.

chapter 4, where Rodney asserts that from 1500 to 1900 "trade between Africans and Europeans [was] virtually . . . slave trade."[5] Indeed, it has become common in world history texts to reduce African history from the late 1400s to the late 1800s to the history of an unequal trade involving the export of slaves into the Atlantic. Chances are very likely such chapters will be entitled something like "The Era of the Slave Trade." This is true of most one-volume high school or college textbooks or multi-volume collections.[6] Whether this is due to the influence of Rodney's book or for other reasons is hard to say, but this myth and others need correcting. This chapter presents evidence that slaves were traded, but the slave trade did not dominate the exchanges between Europe and Africa during the first two centuries of contacts. It further argues that European trade in that period closely resembled the trading by Arabs and others along the Indian Ocean coasts and across the Sahara. Chapter 4 will evaluate the consequences for Africa of the peak two centuries of the Atlantic slave trade.

## Eastern Africa to 1500

The earliest evidence about how sub-Saharan Africans traded with outsiders comes from the part of the continent adjoining the Indian Ocean. Because this evidence is largely external and fragmentary, let's begin by considering what a fully documented record would look like. The sources emphasize the goods outsiders obtained from a particular African locale, but there is every reason to expect that Africans were also very active in creating a market in goods that would be attractive to customers from afar. For example, the Book of Kings in the Hebrew Bible contains an account of King Solomon sending a fleet of ships in the tenth century BCE south on the Red Sea to a place called Ophir. The account says that "they took from there gold in the amount of 420 talents [over 28,000 pounds] and brought it to Solomon," but the mechanisms of trade are not described. That the gold was simply seized seems impossible, because the account says that such fleets went to Ophir every three years and brought back "gold, silver, ivory, apes, and peacocks," and in another place it mentions a trade in "sandalwood and precious stones." People would not be waiting around for someone to come to rob them every three years, nor would they be collecting quantities of so many different goods if they were not expecting to receive goods of equivalent value in return. As has long been observed, a functioning market requires willing buyers and willing sellers. The list of goods also suggests that merchants in Ophir must have had a broad network of suppliers.

---

5. Rodney, *How Europe*, 75, 95.

6. For example, John Thornton, "The Slave Trade and the African Diaspora," chap. 6 in *The Cambridge World History*, vol. 6, part B, ed. Jerry H. Bentley, Sanjay Subrahmanyam, and Merry E. Wiesner-Hanks (Cambridge: Cambridge University Press, 2015).

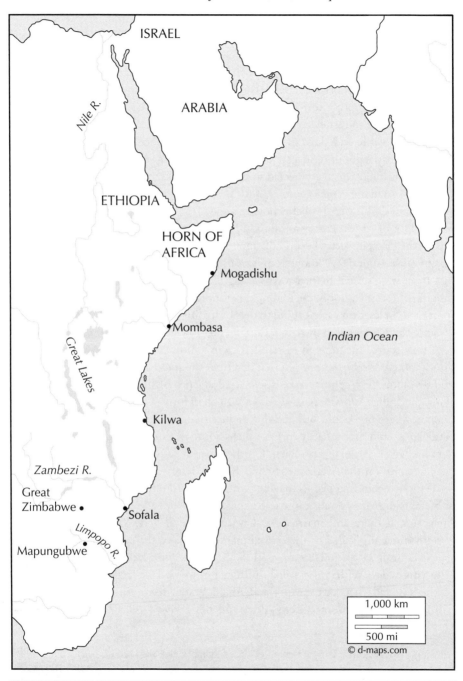

Eastern Africa.

The trade in that locale was already centuries old by the time of King Solomon. Inscriptions going back to the Fifth Dynasty of the Old Kingdom of Egypt (2500–2350 BCE) tell of expeditions south on the Red Sea to a place called "Punt" to obtain aromatic spices (frankincense and myrrh) and electrum (a naturally occurring alloy of silver and gold), substances that were very important in Egypt's relations with the Near East. An Egyptian text from the fifteenth century BCE tells of eleven expeditions to Punt for spices, electrum, ebony, slaves, and cattle. Other inscriptions tell of purchases of cattle and skins of panthers or cheetahs. Here, too, the details of what Punt's merchants got in return are omitted, but logic suggests and later history shows that they must have been connected to trading networks reaching far inland to obtain supplies of so many varied goods.[7]

Punt and Ophir were probably not the same place, but they were both in the region of the Horn of Africa. Punt was south of Egypt along the coast of the Red Sea; Ophir was on the Horn of Africa beyond the mouth of the Red Sea. It is not unusual for markets to move around. We know from later times, when the volume of trade was larger, that there were several market towns along the coast of the Horn and other parts of eastern Africa. In addition, the trading expeditions of ancient Egypt were government-sponsored. In later times, as private traders or trading alliances came to dominate long-distance trade, individual merchants and market towns competed for their business.

A final source for trade in eastern Africa in antiquity is a merchants' guide called the *Periplus of the Erythraean Sea* that describes the trade of the Indian Ocean in the middle of the first century CE. There were a series of independent market towns along the Indian Ocean coast of Africa. On the Horn of Africa was a town named Opone, where one could buy locally produced cinnamon, aromatics, "slaves of the better sort," and high-quality tortoise shell. South of Opone lay the region of Africa then known as "Azania," an ancient Greek name for eastern Africa. The market town farthest south on the Azanian coast was Rhapta, whose name comes from the boats made there by binding planks together with stout cord rather than with wooden pegs or metal nails. Many Arabs came to Rhapta to buy ivory and tortoise shell, and some Arabs settled there and married local women. The *Periplus* says that traders from western India also sailed to the coastal market towns of the eastern Africa, bringing clarified butter, sesame oil, cotton cloth, waist bands, and a kind of sweet syrup. Some historians believe traders also sailed to Rhapta from the East Indies.[8]

The sea trade between Rhapta and Arabia ended some time between 350 and 650 CE, and trade from eastern Africa did not revive until around 1000. In the

---

7. 1 Kings 9:26–28, 10:11; Barry J. Kemp, "Old Kingdom, Middle Kingdom and Second Intermediate Period in Egypt," in *The Cambridge History of Africa*, vol. 1, *From the Earliest Times to c. 500 BC*, ed. J. Desmond Clark (Cambridge: Cambridge University Press, 1982), 723–24; Bill Manley, *The Penguin Historical Atlas of Ancient Egypt* (London: Penguin Books, 1996), 74.

8. William H. Schoff, trans., *The Periplus of the Erythraean Sea: Travel and Trade in the Indian Ocean by a Merchant of the First Century* (New York: Longmans, Green, 1912), secs. 13–16.

Ruins of the Great Mosque at Kilwa, 1100–1300. Source: Photograph by Claude McNab, public domain, Wikimedia Commons.

1300s Ibn Battuta, a Moroccan Muslim who had just completed his pilgrimage to Mecca, has left a fairly detailed, eye-witness description of what was happening along the East African coast. He sailed in a ship similar to the one described in the *Periplus*, a vessel (in Arabic known as a *dhow*) whose hull planks were sewn together with stout coconut-fiber cords. Along the Horn of Africa he called briefly at two "Barbara" (Somali) ports: Zeila in the north, "a big city and has a great market," and Mogadishu, a fifteen-day sail south, which he described as "endless in its size." Ibn Battuta records being welcomed by that city's ruler (the sheik), a dark-skinned Somali who spoke Arabic. On Friday the sheik led all the townsmen in prayers at the great mosque. Both Zeila and Mogadishu were noted for their camel products, and Mogadishu was also known for its high-quality cloth.

From Mogadishu Ibn Battuta sailed along what he called *Sawahil*, that is, the Swahili coasts, to the city of Mombasa and to Kilwa, which he called "a great coastal city" and "amongst the most beautiful cities and most elegantly built," fitting praise for a place famous for its gold and ivory exports. Ibn Battuta also praised the people of Kilwa as virtuous and righteous Muslims. Merchants at Kilwa told him of the city of Sofala half a month's journey farther along at the southern end of the Swahili Coast, but he did not visit it, probably because making such a journey so late in the season would have risked missing the chance to catch the monsoon winds back north.[9]

It is clear from these descriptions that there were periods, with some interruptions, over nearly three thousand years during which East Africa was involved in important commercial transactions with lands around the Indian Ocean, the Red Sea, and the eastern Mediterranean Sea. The descriptions written by outsiders focus on the ports where the overland and sea trades met and tell us more about what trade goods left Africa than about what Africans imported. Nevertheless, it is possible to infer a great deal about the trading networks that fed goods into the coastal ports and redistributed the trade goods received in return. The coastal merchants had links to many different African suppliers. Fishermen captured large sea tortoises, whose meat would have been consumed locally, but whose high-quality shells, mentioned in the *Periplus*, were bought by foreign traders who would market them to places where tortoise shell was in

9. Said Hamdun and Noël King, *Ibn Battuta in Black Africa*, rev. ed. (Princeton, NJ: Markus Wiener, 1994), 13–25; Ross E. Dunn, *The Adventures of Ibn Battuta, a Muslim Traveler of the 14th Century*, rev. ed. (Berkeley: University of California Press, 2005), 106–28.

**45**

demand for making jewelry and inlays on wooden boxes. The involvement of hunters is evident in the lists of live animals (apes, peacocks, panthers, and cheetahs) as well as animal products, of which elephant tusks would have been the most valuable. The participation of African pastoralists in the supply chain is evident from the accounts of the cattle sent to ancient Egypt and the mention in the *Periplus* of camel products. The accounts do not directly mention African farmers' roles, but farmers must have sold provisions to the coastal towns and to the visiting mariners for their return voyages.

Besides the involvement of the African suppliers already listed, there were special networks that supplied precious metals, especially gold, and other minerals for the internal and overseas trades. It is difficult to reconstruct exactly where the gold traded to ancient Egypt and Israel originated, since gold washed downstream by streams could have been panned in many places. In medieval and modern times, most of the gold mines were in southeastern Africa. However, some of the clearest evidence of East African mining for export concerns a different mineral. Archaeological evidence shows that in the tenth century rock crystal (transparent quartz) was a new and profitable export from the northern Swahili Coast. The deposits worked by Africans were located in what is now Kenya some one hundred miles inland from the ocean. Much of the crystal went to Venice, Italy, where carved quartz objects were in high demand.[10]

In later medieval times, the rise of powerful inland states is associated with the increase in gold exports from Kilwa, Sofala, and other coastal states. The earliest site where evidence of the gold trade has been found is Mapungubwe, the earliest known large town in the region, which flourished in the twelfth and early thirteenth century. It was located south of the Limpopo River, which today forms the boundary between the countries of South Africa and Zimbabwe. Mapungubwe was strategically sited to market ivory from the Limpopo Valley, copper from the south, and gold from the north. It is unclear when these inland exchanges became connected to the coast, some 375 miles away, but it was probably early in the process. That Mapungubwe's foreign trading connections were substantial is evident from archaeological finds of rare Chinese pottery, cowries and other Indian Ocean seashells, and thousands of glass beads that might have originated in India and Southeast Asia. In addition, archaeologists have found evidence of cloth manufacturing at Mapungubwe, using cotton from plants originally brought from India. A similar connection might lie behind the cotton used for making the cloth mentioned by Ibn Battuta at Mogadishu. Although East Africans were clearly supplying some of their own clothing needs, that did not mean that market for imported Indian textiles had shrunk, since their superior colors and low coast would have kept them in demand.

By the time Ibn Battuta visited the Swahili Coast in 1331, Mapungubwe was in decline and a new larger state farther north on the Zimbabwean plateau was becoming a key player in the trade to the coast. The capital of the new empire, known as Great

10. Christopher Ehret, *The Civilizations of Africa: A History to 1800* (Charlottesville: University of Virginia Press, 2002), 249.

Zimbabwe, benefited from a location closer both to the gold fields and to the coastal port of Kilwa, which Ibn Battuta had admired so much. As Chapter 1 indicated, the site of Great Zimbabwe exhibits the largest complex of monumental stone structures in Africa south of the Nile River valley. It was also the largest city in southern Africa with some eighteen thousand inhabitants, about as many people as lived in London in the twelfth century. Great Zimbabwe's size, splendid structures, and wealth are indications of a powerful monarchy and a prosperous economy. The traditional source of wealth among the Shona people who lived there was cattle, but it is clear that by the thirteenth century that metalworking and trade were important as well. The trade in copper and tin was mostly internal, but gold and ivory were major components of the rising Indian Ocean trade. Historian Ralph Austen has estimated that between 1100 and 1450 southeast African gold exports averaged 1.5 tons *a year*, which is a volume as great or greater than the more famous gold trade across the Sahara during that period. An external sign of the export trade's rising importance is the fact that within two decades of Ibn Battuta's visit a new dynasty from South Arabia seized power in Kilwa and then took control of the more southerly port of Sofala, which also had good links to Mapungubwe.[11]

This review of the commercial life of eastern Africa reveals a number of points. Overseas trade was ancient and valuable enough to attract merchants from considerable distances. Much of the trade across the Indian Ocean moved in stages from one port to another through many middlemen. Thus, although enough Chinese pottery reached the Swahili Coast that its different styles are used by modern archaeologists to date excavated sites, no Chinese ships are known to have sailed to the Swahili Coast until the fifteenth century, and those exceptional voyages would not be repeated until quite recent times. For our purposes, the commercial networks within eastern Africa during the centuries before 1500 are the most interesting. These networks distributed goods produced by a broad spectrum of African specialists within the region and sent to the coast for export, as well as marketing imported goods inland. As the volume of trade grew after about 1000 CE, some African political elites also became deeply involved, using the wealth from trade to build up their power and erect architecturally impressive structures. Along the Swahili Coast a hybrid society of local Africans and Middle Eastern settlers evolved to negotiate transactions between inland Africans and overseas visitors. In the coastal ports Africans predominated numerically and the ruling political and commercial elites in these city-states were at least as much African as foreign.

Although most people in eastern Africa in these centuries were far from the mainstream of such commercial networks, the growth of trade, mining, and manufacturing would have disproportionately large historical effects. In contrast to Walter Rodney's argument that "external demand" was mostly responsible for the growth of gold

---

11. Peter Mitchell, *The Archaeology of Southern Africa* (Cambridge: Cambridge University Press, 2002), 300–305, 312–31; Ehret, *Civilizations of Africa*, 248–56; Dunn, *Adventures of Ibn Battuta*, 126–28; Ralph Austen, *Africa in Economic History: Internal Development and External Dependency* (London: James Currey, 1987), 59, 276.

mining, most archaeological evidence supports the opposite interpretation: internal activities initiated the growth of trade and political systems to which foreign traders connected. The trade of eastern Africa before 1500 was certainly dynamic, and mining, smelting metals, and making cloth had many more multiplier effects than Rodney's language suggests. In addition, the distribution of imported goods (whether from Europe or Asia) to eager inland customers and the export of their production would have a developmental impact that only a Marxist would try to deny. Just as internal factors were responsible for the rise of Great Zimbabwe and the trading systems that enriched it, internal factors also brought about the abandonment of Great Zimbabwe in the fifteenth century and the decline in the gold trade. Historians do not agree on precisely what caused Great Zimbabwe's decline. Many suspect that the growing human and cattle populations in and around Great Zimbabwe strained the environment to a breaking point. It may also be that the most accessible deposits of gold on the Zimbabwean plateau had been worked out. In any event, a new kingdom of the Mwenemutapa took over territories along the Zambezi River well before 1500.[12]

## West Africa to 1500

Eastern Africa was well placed to connect with the vibrant trade of the Middle East and the Indian Ocean, but the Sahara had long been a formidable barrier to trade between North Africans and the people of West Africa south of the desert. Occasional ocean voyages may have by-passed the desert in antiquity, but no recurring trade resulted.[13] There were also occasional contacts across the desert in antiquity, but not until the eighth century CE did caravans using domesticated camels cross the Sahara on a regular basis. The frequent mention of gold in later North African accounts suggest that this valuable commodity motivated North Africans to make the slow, arduous, and costly trans-Saharan crossing. Before such regular crossings came into existence, West Africans had developed internal trading networks, market towns, and large states. The economic stimulation of regular trans-Saharan trade in the savannas of the Western and Central Sudan after about 750 CE was accompanied by increased exchanges among West Africans, both in the savannas and with Africans in the forested regions to the south.

There is ample evidence that West Africans had developed their own trade routes and markets well before connections were made across the Sahara. As in eastern Africa, these networks involved exchanges of goods produced by many specialists, including fishermen, rice-growing farmers, herders, blacksmiths, weavers, and potters. These specialists took their products to local markets where merchants bought them and carried them to more distant markets. The largest West African regional markets were in or near market towns and cities. For example, radiocarbon dating indicates that the

---

12. Rodney, *How Europe*, 66; Austen, *African Economic*, 74.

13. Sanford Holst, *Phoenician Secrets: Exploring the Ancient Mediterranean* (Los Angeles: Santorini Books, 2011), 261–65.

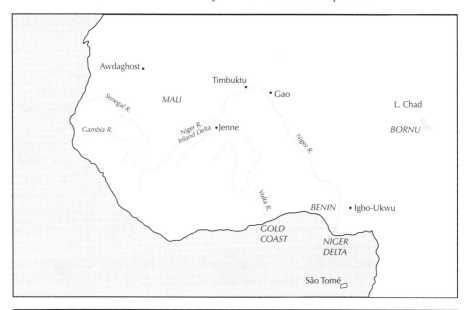

West Africa

trading city of Jenne on the Niger River was founded in the third century BCE, too early and too far south of the desert for its creation to have been stimulated by trade with North Africa. In the early centuries CE, a trade in gold from lands southwest of Jenne joined with the older trade in copper and iron arriving at Jenne by boat or by donkey from the east and south. By about 300 CE another new market city, Gao, had come into existence 375 miles northeast of Jenne on the Niger Bend.

The political amalgamation of these trading centers into states and empires began earlier in West Africa than in southeastern Africa. The oldest empire was Wagadu, which outsiders generally called "Ghana," after the title of its ruler. When Wagadu was founded is not known, but it was important enough in the 750s for Arab invaders from the north to attempt (unsuccessfully) to conquer it. A few decades later another Muslim described Wagadu as "the land of gold," which clearly represents the image it had in North Africa. At its greatest extent Wagadu occupied the lands between the inland Niger River delta and the upper Senegal River, but it did not include the lands to the southwest from which the gold came, nor did it include the trading cities of Jenne and Gao. In 1065, the Arab geographer al-Bakri, relying on a tenth-century text, described Wagadu's capital as consisting of two separate settlements, one for the ruler and his subjects and the other for the extensive population of foreign traders. Archaeologists have excavated a site called Kumbi Saleh, a walled town covering a square mile, which may be the foreign merchants' town, along with a cemetery outside the wall that was twice as large. The principal city in Wagadu was Awdaghost founded about 700 CE, whose excavated site displayed abundant evidence of foreign trade. Al-Bakri's account

**49**

provides evidence that Wagadu was at the center of three important regional trading systems: from the Sahara came salt and copper, which were taxed both when entering and leaving the state for lands further south, though he seems to know little of the trading networks there. The third system was the gold trade from lands to the southwest of Wagadu. This trade could have been critical in making Wagadu "the land of gold," since we are told that all gold nuggets found in Wagadu itself belonged to the *ghana* (king), and only gold dust from streams could be freely traded.[14]

By the 1100s Wagadu was in decline, and the new empire of Mali was expanding in the Western Sudan, eventually becoming larger than Wagadu had been. When Mali weakened, it was succeeded by Songhai, the largest empire of the Western Sudan, which flourished between 1375 and 1591. In the Central Sudan, the empire of Kanem-Bornu gained a dominant position in the trans-Saharan trade during the eleventh century. Not every state was an empire: between Kanem-Bornu and the empires of the Western Sudan were a number of autonomous city-states of the Hausa people, which were also important regional commercial and manufacturing centers with ties to the trans-Saharan trade. The rest of this section will look at a number of common themes rather than examining each state separately.

Just as in the city-states of the Swahili Coast, ensuring the security and safety of visiting merchants was an important factor for continuing long-distance trade. The camel caravans traveled with armed escorts through the Sahara, but they could be vulnerable once they reached the Sudanic region unless accorded protection by local rulers. Ibn Battuta, who traveled in Mali in the 1350s, emphasized that foreign visitors there were welcomed hospitably and their host's protection ensured they had no reason to fear thieves or other violence. In addition, he noted that the goods of foreigners who had the misfortune to die in Mali were even entrusted to another person until they could be returned to the rightful claimant. Security and trust were also enhanced by the fact that visitors from North Africa and their hosts and counterparts in the Western and Central Sudan shared a common religion. Well before Ibn Battuta's time, the rulers and merchants of these sub-Saharan states had all adopted the Islamic faith. That faith also encouraged Muslims who could afford it to travel across the Sahara on pilgrimages to Mecca. The first ruler of Kanem-Bornu had made the pilgrimage in the 1200s. The size of pilgrimage entourage led by the Mali ruler Mansa Musa in 1324–1325 had created a sensation in Egypt and elsewhere, especially for the amount of gold the ruler distributed.[15]

---

14. Graham Connah, *African Civilizations: Precolonial Cities and States in Tropical Africa: An Archaeological Perspective* (Cambridge: Cambridge University Press, 1987), 97–120; for a translation of al-Bakri's account, see N. Levtzion and J. F. P. Hopkins, eds., *Corpus of Early Arabic Sources for West African History* (Princeton, NJ: Markus Wiener, 2000), 79–85. Cf. Roderick J. McIntosh, *The Peoples of the Middle Niger* (Oxford: Blackwell Publishers, 1998).

15. Hamdun and King, *Ibn Battuta*, 50–57; Timothy Insoll, *The Archaeology of Islam in Sub-Saharan Africa* (Cambridge: Cambridge University Press, 2003), 273–78.

In addition to information from outside visitors like Ibn Battuta, there are also useful internal records. Chronicles of the rulers of both Kanem-Bornu and the Hausa city-state of Kano, which were first transmitted orally and then written in Arabic script, reveal important information about trans-Saharan connections. The Kano Chronicle traces rulers from the tenth century, and the Kanem-Bornu king-list begins several centuries earlier. Besides information about political dynasties, these chronicles mention the diffusion of new military technology and enslavement. The Kano Chronicle tells of a ruler named Kanajeji (r. 1390–1410), who introduced from Egypt quilted armor, iron helmets, and coats of mail for both horses and riders. With this advantage he was able to lay siege to a neighboring people until they gave him a total of 4,400 slaves, half of whom were their own children. A Bornu chronicle of King Idris Aloma (r. 1570–1602) describes his returning from the pilgrimage to Mecca and bringing with him Turkish and slave musketeers, the first known importation of firearms via the Sahara. With these additional military resources, King Idris waged several campaigns, enlarging his kingdom and taking slaves, but prohibiting the long-standing custom of enslaving fellow Muslims.[16]

These records of the link between military resources from across the Sahara and the capture of slaves are clues to an important trans-Saharan connection besides the celebrated trade in gold. Al-Bakri mentioned that Wagadu had a large army of 200,000 men, including a cavalry unit, using small horses. The diminutive size of the breed of horses that existed in West Africa limited their military effectiveness, so it grew common to import larger Arabian horses from North Africa. Two centuries later, the chronicler al-Umari (1301–1349) noted that Mali's army had ten thousand horse-mounted cavalry and that the rulers of Mali had to spend considerable sums of money purchasing Arab horses to maintain their numbers. Two centuries after that, an account by Leo Africanus added a final piece of evidence that clarified how imports of horses were linked to the export of slaves. The kingdom of Kanem-Bornu, he wrote, had a cavalry of three thousand. The horses were brought from North Africa, and each horse was exchanged for fifteen or twenty slaves. If a horse survived for a year on average, then the slave trade from Kanem-Bornu would have been on the order of 4,500 to 6,000 annually. Historical archeologist Timothy Insoll argued that in the Sudanic regions of West Africa the "employment of cavalry was almost cyclical in purpose": men on horses captured slaves in raids and wars; a portion of the slaves were then sold to acquire more horses.[17]

The nexus of empires, horses, and slaves is a vital key to understanding Sudanic West Africa. Wagadu, Mali, Songhai, and Kanem-Bornu had military might for two reasons. One was to protect themselves from attacks from the north. The old

---

16. For royal chronicles see Robert O. Collins, ed., *African History in Documents: Western Africa* (Princeton, NJ: Markus Wiener, 1997), 42–56.

17. For al-Bakri and Al-Umani see Levtzion and Hopkins, *Corpus*, 81, 266; for Leo Africanus see Collins, *African History in Documents*, 31; Insoll, *Archaeology of Islam*, 299.

kingdom of Kanem had moved its capital south of Lake Chad to protect itself from desert Berbers (the Tuareg). Wagadu had been severely weakened by an invasion from North Africa; Songhai had collapsed in the wake of a Moroccan invasion armed with firearms. Although these outside attacks were rare events, it was common for West African rulers to use of military power to expand their realms. They also needed a strong military to maintain control over the annexed territories. These conquest states, usually peaceful internally (as Ibn Battuta noted in the case of Mali), were inclined to disintegrate into their component parts when the center became weak.

Slavery was a common institution in Sudanic West Africa, just as it was in eastern Africa and North Africa. Muslim Arabs were not alone in trading in slaves, but they were successful in organizing slave trades from East and West Africa on a large scale. Slaves were essential in North Africa and the Middle East to staff households, workshops, and armies. Slaves were similarly important in sub-Saharan Africa. Ibn Battuta noted that when the sultan of Mali held audiences in his throne room, he was attended by some three hundred slaves, many armed. His predecessor Mansa Musa took hundreds of slaves with him on his pilgrimage to Mecca. While visiting Mali, Ibn Battuta purchased several slaves and received others as presents. Under Islamic law it was forbidden to enslave another Muslim, but it was laudatory to convert one's slaves to Islam. The law limited the number of wives a man might have to four, but he might have an unlimited number of concubines, all of whom were slaves. Ibn Battuta related that the head interpreter in Mali brought his four wives and about a hundred concubines to the sultan's court sessions. All were richly dressed, and they provided song and music. Ibn Battuta tells candidly of purchasing two educated (Arabic-speaking) slave women in the Saharan town Takedda, where there was a copper mine. In response to their former owners' pleas, he reluctantly sold both back. The Western Sudan was not only an exporter of slaves. In a very detailed description of the *ghana*'s throne room, al-Umari mentioned that about thirty slaves (he uses the Arabic word "mamluk," a term for slave soldiers) stood behind the ruler, identifying them as "Turks and others who are bought for him in Egypt." Other slaves also held important positions. For example, the commander of Songhai's armies was a slave named Askia Muhammad Ture, who staged a coup in 1493 and made himself the ruler.[18]

The expansion of trading connections southward from the savannas into the forests is not attested in written sources until the arrival of Portuguese observers by sea in the fifteenth century. Nevertheless, archaeological evidence reveals connections that are surprisingly rich and surprisingly early. The most celebrated site was excavated in 1959 in the southeastern Nigerian village of Igbo-Ukwu, about twenty miles east of the lower Niger River and ninety miles north of the Atlantic. The site contained a collection of bronze ceremonial objects and the grave of a man in elaborate regalia and flanked by elephant tusks and additional bronze symbols of high office. The exceptional quality

---

18. Hamdun and King, *Ibn Battuta*, 47–48, 68–69; Levtzion and Hopkins, *Corpus*, 265.

of the workmanship on the copper and bronze objects astonished historians, but it was the early dating obtained from radiocarbon analysis of charcoal to the ninth and tenth centuries that set off the greatest controversy. The bronze objects unearthed showed no sign of European or North African influence, suggesting they were crafted locally. Both the materials worked locally and other objects crafted elsewhere indicated distant trading connections. The copper used for the locally made castings came from a distance of two hundred miles or more to the north. Some of the tens of thousands of glass and stone beads were of local and regional manufacture, but others appear to have come from India and from Venice. The goods unearthed at Igbo-Ukwu suggest that long-distance trade routes ran north from there to the Sudan, most likely along the Niger River, where by the early 1600s a string of markets operated.

If regular trade passed between the upper Niger and the lower Niger before 1500, it is also likely that similar commercial routes reached the Atlantic elsewhere in West Africa. This was certainly true for the Senegal and Gambia River valleys, which were closely tied to the merchant empires of the Western Sudan. There is also suggestive evidence that a trading connection reached the ocean along the lower Volta River. The presence of Arabic speakers there seems to be the reason why the name the Portuguese gave their outpost, *la mina* (the mine), later changed to *el mina* (Arabic for "the port").[19]

## Contacts with Europeans to 1700

Was the arrival of the first European merchants along the Atlantic and Indian Ocean coasts of sub-Saharan Africa in the 1400s, as Rodney asserted, a sharp break with the patterns that had been going on for many centuries with outside traders? In fact, a comparison of the trading relations of Europeans and of earlier outsiders seems to show more similarities than differences. In contrast, Rodney's claim that from the beginning European contacts consisted very largely of slave trading is also untrue for the first two centuries of European contacts. The goods coastal Africans sold Europeans during those centuries included many items, of which gold and ivory were predominant, along with some slaves. Just like the Arabs and others, Europeans had to deal with powerful African partners, who often held the upper hand. In addition, Africans gradually acquired languages and some cultural practices from the Europeans, just as they had from the Arabs.

Africans were no more passive in their contacts with Europeans than they had been in earlier outside encounters. As in eastern Africa and the Western Sudan, coastal West Africa's well-established merchant communities quickly recognized

---

19. David Northrup, *Trade without Rulers: Pre-Colonial Economic Development in South-Eastern Nigeria* (Oxford: Clarendon Press, 1978), 17–29; Peter Garlake, *Early Art and Architecture of Africa* (Oxford: Oxford University Press, 2002), 117–20; David Northrup, "The Gulf of Guinea and the Atlantic World," in *The Atlantic World and Virginia, 1550–1624*, ed. Peter Mancall (Chapel Hill: University of North Carolina Press, 1996), 171–73.

The Oba of Benin and a Portuguese visitor, ca. 1500 CE. Source: From a photograph by Mike Peel taken in the Horniman Museum and Gardens, London. Wikimedia Commons, CC-BY-SA-4.0.

the potential economic benefits of partnering with seaborne Europeans, especially since the lower shipping costs enabled Europeans to offer better prices for the commodities Africans were already selling to the north. Thus, the early Portuguese found willing trading partners along the lower Senegal and Gambia Rivers, where Africans were already long connected to the Sudanic and trans-Saharan trade networks. For Senegambian merchants, Europeans provided an alternative outlet to the merchants from across the Sahara.

Farther south, along the Gulf of Guinea, early Europeans sold copper for much lower prices than that brought overland from Sahara mines, and they were willing to pay more than traders from the north for locally produced gold. Very early on, in 1482, a ruler on what came to be known as the Gold Coast agreed to allow the Portuguese to erect a trading fort, stating the hope that it could be advantageous to both sides but warning that, should the Portuguese step out of bounds, he could easily terminate the trade. Down the coast, near the lower Niger River, the ruler of the powerful kingdom of Benin sent an ambassador to Portugal in 1486 to check out whom he was dealing with. The ambassador returned with rich presents for the king of Benin and evidently with a favorable report, since commercial relations were opened. Palace officials closely regulated Benin's markets, which Europeans had to pay fees to "open." In 1553, the king of Benin personally welcomed the officers of an English ship that had come to purchase pepper, spoke with them in Portuguese, and even offered them credit, if they lacked sufficient trade goods to complete their purchases.

Once Portuguese ships reached the Indian Ocean in 1498, they were back in a well-established trading area. Relations on the Swahili Coast were complicated by Portuguese antipathy to Muslims, who were also highly suspicious of the Christians' intentions. Early in the 1500s, the Portuguese attacked Muslim-ruled city-states on the Swahili Coast that had refused to cooperate with them. An exception was the city-state of Malindi, which entered into an alliance with the Portuguese and allowed them to build a trading fort in hopes of gaining an advantage over its rival Mombasa. As was described in the previous chapter, the Portuguese also forged an alliance with the kingdom of Ethiopia based on their common Christian faith. Further south the Portuguese established an outpost at Mozambique (an island, not the colony of the same name that came much later) and small outposts on the Zambezi River to gain access to the gold trade. However, the gold trade was already in decline due to African political rivalries and depleted gold fields. The eclipse of the Portuguese empire in the 1600s by other Europeans with greater interest in Asian trade meant that the eastern African trade became less important than the new coastal trade in West Africa.

Unlike those in West Africa and eastern Africa, people along the Atlantic south of the Equator had not been able to participate in long-distance trade before the arrival of Europeans along their shores. This may help explain why their commercial relations with the new visitors developed along different lines. The rulers of the kingdom of Kongo along the lower Congo River welcomed the Portuguese and even adopted Christianity. Their common faith led the Portuguese to accept pleas to intervene on Kongo's side in inter-African conflicts and led African rulers in this region to seek firearms from the Portuguese, with some success. In turn, military intervention in Kongo led to a greater presence of Portuguese agents in coastal enclaves and much deeper inland than was the case in West Africa. The region of West-Central Africa (also known as Angola) in which the kingdom of Kongo was located was also the only region where slaves became the major basis of the export trade during these early centuries. In the seventeenth century, the Dutch displaced the Portuguese in Angola.

After the Dutch were driven out in 1648, inland African rulers had to renegotiate alliances with the Portuguese in order to preserve their independence. Later the Portuguese were able to subjugate some African states and punished their African rulers for their "disloyalty."[20]

The Dutch became the foremost European nation in global trade in the seventeenth century, challenging the Portuguese in Asia and South America as well. The Dutch East India Company established a way station in 1652 at the southern tip of Africa, where they might take on fresh water and food on the long sea voyages between Europe and Asia. Over time, that small outpost grew into the port of Cape Town. To provide a labor force in and around Cape Town the Dutch imported slaves from islands around the Indian Ocean. Relations with local Africans were often cordial, and in 1664 a high company official married a local Khoekhoe woman, known as Eva, who was a trusted translator. Only after a small pox epidemic devastated local Khoekhoe peoples in the early 1700s were white settlers able to advance inland along with their slaves.

In the period before 1650 gold was the principal export from West Africa to Europe, averaging 0.7 tons a year between 1471 and 1600 and 0.9 tons a year in the first half of the 1600s. Most of the gold came from African mining operations farther inland and passed through the outposts on the aptly named Gold Coast. This gold, and another half ton or more a year the Portuguese bought from southeastern Africans in this period, made Africa Europe's most important source of gold. Gold was not the only commodity Atlantic Africans sold to Western Europe. Benin exported ivory and a West African black pepper that was well received in Europe until it was displaced by Indian pepper. Benin also sold the Portuguese locally made stone beads (*coris*) and cotton textiles, as well as some slaves, all of which were destined for resale on the Gold Coast. Senegambia and the Gold Coast were also important sources of ivory along with other animal and forest products. Sugar became a major export from West Africa in the sixteenth century. The sugar was grown by Africans, but they were slaves that the Portuguese had purchased from mainland Africa and resettled on the formerly uninhabited island of São Tomé near the Equator, where enslaved Africans numbered 64,000 by 1600. After that date African slaves in Brazil would become the major producers of sugar.[21]

Although slaves were important in the trade from Angola and into São Tomé, the evidence does not support Rodney's claim that the slave trade was virtually all there was in Africa's trade with Europeans during the first two centuries of contacts. As Chapter 4 recounts, at the time Rodney wrote, estimates of the volume of the Atlantic slave trade were too uncertain to calculate the relative value of the trade in

---

20. John K. Thornton, *Warfare in Atlantic Africa, 1500–1800* (London: UCL Press, 1999), 99–125.

21. David Northrup, "Africans, Early European Contacts, and the Emergent Diaspora," in *The Oxford Handbook of the Atlantic World, 1450–1850*, ed. Nicholas Canny and Philip Morgan (Oxford: Oxford University Press, 2011), 43–45.

slaves and commodities, but research into numbers and values has greatly improved since then. Bear in mind that what is being calculated is the selling price of slaves and goods, not the incalculable value of human lives. For most of Atlantic Africa the slave trade was of comparatively modest proportions before the late seventeenth century. Before 1525 the trade in slaves in the Atlantic was primarily from one part of Africa to another: about 300 a year to the Gold Coast, 740 a year to the sugar plantations of island of São Tomé, and about 800 a year to the Cape Verde Islands. In that period, another 500 to 750 slaves a year were shipped to Portugal, many of whom went on to Spain and a few were taken to Spanish America. After the first slave ship sailed directly from Africa to the Americas in 1525, the numbers reaching the Americas slowly rose and the numbers shipped to European and African destinations declined, except for São Tomé. The average annual volume of slaves from Africa to the Americas in 1525–1549 was just under 2,500 a year, much the same as the slave trades to African islands and Iberia had been during the previous quarter century. During the second half of the 1500s, the transatlantic slave trade from Africa rose to an average of about 4,270 a year (still fewer than the estimated 5,420 taken annually across the Sahara in that period). However, in the first half of the seventeenth century the number crossing the Atlantic (13,350 a year) pulled ahead of the trans-Saharan slave trade (then about 8,950 a year). Thereafter, the transatlantic slave trade rose to new heights peaking at an average of over 80,000 a year in the last quarter of the 1700s. More than 90 percent of the Atlantic slave trade occurred between 1650 and 1850. But what is equally important to grasp is that between 1551 and 1650 more than three-quarters of the enslaved people came from the single region of Angola. The slave trade dominated that region of Africa before 1650 (as well as after that date) but not the rest of Atlantic Africa. Historian David Eltis has calculated that it was only from about 1700 that the value of slave exports from West Africa surpassed the value of other West African exports.[22]

If the export of slaves from most of Africa was far from dominant before 1700, what were Africans receiving in return? Rodney underestimated the market sophistication of African buyers in alleging that they eagerly accepted "old sheets, cast-off uniforms, technologically outdated firearms, and lots or odds and ends . . . , often of poor quality." Some such items were traded, but Africans were much more discriminating in their choice of imports. During these first two centuries of contacts the commodity Africans sought most was cloth, a demand which the Portuguese were hard-pressed to keep up with. Initially, the Portuguese bought cotton cloth from Benin to exchange for gold on the Gold Coast and also purchased woolen cloth from Morocco for resale elsewhere in sub-Saharan Africa. Portugal produced little cloth suitable for export, so other European traders collected textiles from across the face of

---

22. Northrup, "Africans, Early European Contacts," 45–48; Austen, "Trans-Saharan Slave Trade," table 2.8; David Eltis, *The Rise of Slavery in the Americas* (Cambridge: Cambridge University Press, 2000), 150–51.

Europe to meet African demand. Rodney also argued that European traders brought to Africa only goods they made in Europe, but, even in these early centuries, Africans demanded imports from Asia and the Americas as well. Although Africans purchased some linen and woolen cloth from Europe, their preference was for lightweight, washable cotton cloth, which was mostly produced in India, Southeast Asia, and China. The Dutch and English were soon supplying Atlantic Africans with large quantities of Asian textiles. Metals were the second most sought-after commodity. Large quantities of copper, copper alloys, and iron flowed into African markets, much in the form of bars that African smiths then turned into useful objects. Africans also sought hardware, such as knives, axes, hoes, and spears, as well as firearms. Though the Portuguese refused to sell guns to Africans who were not Christians and didn't sell many to those who were Christians, Dutch and English traders were more willing to keep their African customers happy. Before 1700 most of these arms were for military use, providing a cheaper alternative to the importation across the Sahara mentioned earlier. Thereafter, cheaper weapons for individual use became more common.[23]

Whether these imports "underdeveloped" Africa is an issue best saved for the next chapter, which considers later centuries when the volume of such imports was larger. Before concluding, it is worth considering the non-material exchanges that took place between Africans and Europeans during the period before 1700. Sub-Saharan Africans borrowed culturally from the Europeans who came to trade with them, much as they did from the Arabs. The early Portuguese had found some rulers receptive to Christian teachings. A few coastal rulers chose to become Roman Catholics, notably at Benin and Kongo. Because of conflicts with traditional ideas of divine kingship, the rulers of Benin to discontinue their Catholic links, but the rulers of Kongo actively promoted the new faith. As was seen earlier, the Portuguese also made contact with Christian Ethiopia and helped rescue it from a Muslim neighbor. Protestant Europeans were largely uninterested in spreading Christianity in Africa at this time.

Overall, religion was less important in these early contacts with Europeans than were other cultural exchanges that enhanced commercial exchanges. Africans proved adept at learning the languages of their European visitors, just as they had been in learning Arabic. Schools taught in European languages became a feature of coastal African communities with important trading connections. The earliest such schools were in Kongo and used Portuguese as the medium of instruction. Africans saw the benefit of learning European languages not just for oral communication but also because these languages (like Arabic) could be used for reading and writing. Just as Africans in the Sudan had used Arabic script to write their own languages, so too the Roman alphabet was used for published translations of Christian texts in the Kongo language in the sixteenth century. The Royal African Company, an English trading company that needed literate clerks, founded the first English-language school along

---

23. Rodney, *How Europe*, 77–78; David Northrup, *Africa's Discovery of Europe, 1450–1850*, 3rd ed. (New York: Oxford University Press, 2014), 83–114.

the Gold Coast in 1694. More educational efforts appeared in the second half of the eighteenth century. One of the first pupils at the new school was an African named Philip Quaque who, after additional training in England, became the schoolmaster and served as the chaplain for both British and African Christians. Schools were small and apt to founder because European settlements were so small and potential teachers were busy with other duties. Nevertheless, both Africans and Europeans recognized the importance of literacy. When there was no functioning school, Africans hired tutors to educate their children and those who could afford it sent their sons (and occasionally daughters) to study in Europe so that they could deal competently and comfortably with European trading partners. An African named Antera Duke made regular entries in English in his diary for several years in the 1780s about events in the trading port of Old Calabar. The French, Dutch, and Danes also made modest efforts to educate Africans in their languages and cultures, but the greatest promoters of such cultural broadening were African parents.[24]

## Conclusions

Rodney's claim that European trade with sub-Saharan Africa was significantly different from the trade with other outsiders does not appear to accord with the facts. Europeans sought products in Africa that were quite similar to what ancient and medieval traders had purchased: gold, ivory and other exotic animal products, along with mineral and vegetable products and slaves. Before the late 1800s Europeans generally lacked the power and motivation to penetrate into Africa beyond coastal outposts and had to draw upon global trading networks to supply the goods Africans demanded in return. Long before the appearance of the first Europeans at their shores Africans already had extensive trading networks, powerful political systems, and efficient systems of production, which enabled them to deal with Europeans from positions of strength not weakness. Rodney's more particular claim that the trade with Europe was little more than slave trading has been demonstrated to be false before 1700, except in Angola. Given how similar European trading arrangements were to those of other outside traders before 1700, it seems improbable that their economic effects could have been appreciably different. The particular consequences of the peak decades of the Atlantic slave trade and the period of European colonial rule will be examined in later chapters.

---

24. Northrup, *Africa's Discovery*, 25–77; Stephen D. Behrendt, John Latham, and David Northrup, *The Diary of Antera Duke, an Eighteenth-Century African Slave Trader* (New York: Oxford University Press, 2010).

# 4. THE ATLANTIC SLAVE TRADE: STOLEN BODIES, STOLEN IDENTITIES?

... [O]n the whole, the process by which captives were obtained on African soil was not trade at all. It was through warfare, trickery, banditry, and kidnaping. . . . The majority of the imports [Africans received in the slave trade] were of the worst quality even as consumer goods—cheap gin, cheap gunpowder, pots and kettles full of holes, beads and other assorted rubbish.[1]

—*Walter Rodney, Guyanese historian and political activist, 1972*

[Although the] principal secondary authorities and the principal textbooks are . . . in remarkable agreement on the general magnitude of the [Atlantic slave] trade . . . [the] authority [behind the agreed figure of at least 15 million is] an [obscure] American publicist of the 1860s.[2]

—*Philip D. Curtin, pioneer in African history in the United States, 1969*

This myth of the Negro past [includes this belief:] Since the Negroes were brought from all parts of the African continent, spoke diverse languages, represented greatly differing bodies of custom, and . . . were distributed in the New World so as to lose tribal identity, no least common denominator of understanding could have possibly been worked out by them.[3]

—*Melville J. Herskovits, anthropologist and founder of African Studies in the United States, 1941*

There are probably more myths about the transatlantic slave trade than any other subject involving Africa—and for good reasons. Because the legacies of the slave trade, despite the passage of time, remain so evident in the Americas, they are ongoing and often heated parts of contemporary political and social debates. Such contemporary concerns can cause new distortions, but entrenched, older myths distort the history of the Atlantic slave trade even more. One source of misunderstanding came out of the long, passionate campaign by British abolitionists in the eighteenth and nineteenth centuries. Although the abolitionists were careful that the information about the slave trade they uncovered was accurate (lest their arguments be proven false),

---

1. Walter Rodney, *How Europe Underdeveloped Africa* (Baltimore: Black Classic Press, 2011), 95, 102.

2. Philip D. Curtin, *The Atlantic Slave Trade: A Census* (Madison: University of Wisconsin Press, 1969), 3, 6.

3. Melville J. Herskovits, *The Myth of the Negro Past*, 2nd ed. (Boston: Beacon Press, 1990), 1.

they naturally publicized the most shocking conditions in the trade so as to convince lawmakers that drastic actions were needed. Recent textbooks and popular histories still tend to highlight the extreme examples the abolitionists documented rather than the complex realities discovered by modern scholars. In addition, the abolitionists' success in forcing Great Britain to abandon the slave trade in 1808 has made it nearly impossible for most people today to imagine that there was ever a time when upright people could have thought buying and selling slaves was not a moral evil. Unbalanced evidence and the lack of historical imagination can lead to misunderstandings about the actual operations of the slave trade.

For understandable reasons, activists in the twentieth-century movement for black civil rights in the United States often revived the moral perspectives of the abolitionists, viewing the struggle for legal, social, and economic equality as a continuation of the older struggle against slavery and the slave trade. In many ways such views were correct, but a narrow, moralistic treatment of the slave trade also simplified and distorted its historical complexities, leading, for example, to the commonly repeated charge that Africans were "stolen" away from their homes. In addition, the many positive aspects of African Americans' subsequent embrace of their African roots, by adopting African hairstyles, clothing, and names, sometimes led to exaggerated beliefs that these modern borrowings reflected unbroken chains of cultural transmission from the mother continent.

The 1960s and 1970s were also a time when historians around the Atlantic were engaging in a rigorous re-examination of African history, seeking to amend interpretations of Africa formulated in Europe and the New World with factually grounded accounts and authentic voices from Africa. Although many students welcomed the evidence that people in Africa were not rude barbarians but had a remarkable history, those steeped in the prevailing narrative of the slave trade found troubling the fact that African traders could have dealt with European traders as equals. Some, as will be seen below, even denounced efforts to re-calculate the size of the Atlantic slave trade and where slaves were landed in the Americas. The resulting controversies (and acrimony) sometimes became mixed with radical ideologies rising out of African movements for independence and out of African American desires to embrace their African roots. The movement known as Afrocentrism was another response to the re-discovery of African history, a movement that sought with some success to impose a rigid and unscholarly orthodoxy on the teaching of African history in American schools. Given the long neglect of many historical questions about Africa, the slave trade, and the African diaspora, such debates were healthy, even if they sometimes generated more heat than light.[4]

---

4. Mary Lefkowitz, *Not Out of Africa: How Afrocentrism Became an Excuse to Teach Myth as History* (New York: Basic Books, 1996); Stephen Howe, *Afrocentrism: Mythical Pasts and Imagined Homes* (London: Verso, 1998); Ibrahim Sundiata, *Brothers and Strangers: Black Zion, Black Slavery, 1914–1940* (Durham, NC: Duke University Press, 2003).

From the perspective of the twenty-first century, it may be hard to believe that in the 1960s the most popular histories of the Atlantic slave trade in use in the United States were written by journalists—admittedly talented journalists. These books were useful teaching tools in their day, but unrevised versions of them remained in classroom use even as new research undermined some of their central arguments. One was *Black Cargoes*, written by two American literary journalists, Daniel P. Mannix and Malcolm Cowley. Their well-written text emphasized the horrors of the slave trade exposed by British abolitionists and generally left American readers with the mistaken impression that the slave trade went largely to the United States rather than to Brazil and the West Indies. Despite its shortcomings, unrevised editions of *Black Cargoes* were still being reissued forty years later. Basil Davidson, a British journalist who would become one of the most influential pioneers of African history, wrote the second study, originally entitled *Black Mother*. Besides being less sensational, *Black Mother* differed from *Black Cargoes* in emphasizing African involvement in the trade and on the trade's effects in Africa. Davidson's framing of the Atlantic slave trade as a story of Africa's engagement with the Atlantic world on unequal terms was a welcome improvement on Mannix and Cowley's much narrower depiction of the trade as a sort of preface to the story of slavery and exploitation in the United States.[5]

Despite stimulating interest in their subject, both books have been overtaken by more recent scholarship. Writing at a time when the volume of the Atlantic slave trade was so uncertain that estimates started at an already inflated fifteen million and often went much higher, the authors were unable to resist the abolitionist impulse to exaggerate the Atlantic slave trade's impacts on both sides of the Atlantic. The long history of the slave trade from Africa is now knowable with greater certitude—an important step toward understanding why Africans were brought in chains and what that trade meant (and means) for Africans and people of African descent in the Americas. Yet, even today few popular accounts manage to tell the whole story and fewer do so dispassionately.

This chapter focuses on three interconnected myths about the slave trade, which were highlighted by the quotations at the beginning of the chapter. The first is that, as Walter Rodney charged, it was not trade at all but theft. The second myth, as Philip Curtin demonstrated, involves inflated guesses about the volume of the Atlantic slave trade, which are then used to support an argument that the trade caused irreparable demographic, social, and economic damage in Africa. The third myth, concerning the survival of African culture in the Americas, appears in two diametrically opposed versions. The older one, challenged by Melville J. Herskovits and now largely extinct,

---

5. Daniel P. Mannix and Malcolm Cowley, *Black Cargoes: A History of the Atlantic Slave Trade, 1518–1865* (New York: Viking Press, 1962); Basil Davidson, *Black Mother: The Years of the African Slave Trade* (Boston: Little Brown, 1961), the American edition was subsequently retitled *The African Slave Trade*.

holds that African cultures perished in the course of the Middle Passage from Africa to the Americas. But the ghost of the older myth haunts the newer version, which places an exaggerated emphasis on African "survivals" in the Americas, especially in the United States. As we have seen already, an assertion of the opposite of a mythical argument is likely to be as unfounded as was the original. Solid ground usually lies somewhere in the middle.

As has already been suggested, these myths exist for good reasons, but correcting the historical facts is still vitally important, not just to set the record straight but also to overthrow another even more insidious myth that underpins them. This myth holds that Africans were easily exploited, and that their societies were weak and brittle. This myth of weakness is so attractive because it can be used to place all blame for the slave trade on Europeans. However, by oversimplifying the complexity of these events in this way, this myth also underestimates Africans' strength, intelligence, and adaptability.

## The Mechanisms and Morality of Slave Trading

Language reveals and conceals. Those who speak of Africans being "stolen" may have several meanings in mind. Some believe that Europeans quite literally kidnapped coastal Africans and spirited them away, rather than that the slave trade was an exchange of people for goods. Other people find it impossible to believe that Africans could have sold "their own people," a wording that reflects a misunderstanding of the complexity of historical identity in the giant continent. While admitting that slaves were obtained in Africa primarily through trade, Rodney, nevertheless describes the trade as "warfare, trickery, banditry, and kidnaping," blending three mechanisms by which Africans secured the slaves they traded to Europeans with the charge that European slave traders used "trickery" to get their African partners to accept cheap and valueless goods. Let's examine each of these issues in turn.

Were the Africans transported across the Atlantic to the Americas literally "stolen"? Certainly some kidnappings did occur, especially in the early years. The earliest Portuguese explorers sailing down the Atlantic coast regularly kidnapped a few Africans who were taken back to Portugal, taught Portuguese, and used as interpreters on subsequent voyages. After a few years of service many, if not most, were freed and returned to their homelands. In 1567–1568, the famous English adventurer John Hawkins made an expedition to West Africa where his attempt to seize coastal Africans by force succeeded in capturing only a few and those at a great cost. Many of Hawkins' men were injured or killed by poisoned arrows. Hawkins led the survivors further down the coast, where they entered into an alliance with one African ruler to wage war against a neighboring African community. Attacking by land and sea, Hawkins' force, despite casualties, managed to capture 250 men, women, and children. His African ally captured 600 people but failed to keep his promise to let Hawkins take his pick of them. The lesson was learned: African resistance made even a surprise attack too costly to be profitable.[6] Thereafter, European slave traders followed the practice already used for trading in gold and other commodities, buying what they wanted from African rulers and traders in exchange for goods. If a European dared to supplement his cargo of slaves by kidnapping a few coastal Africans, local rulers and traders would boycott trading with him and all his fellow countrymen until those stolen away were returned or a heavy fine paid.

The evidence is clear that all but a few of those crossing the Atlantic had been bought and paid for before they boarded slave ships, but the word "stolen" is often still used by those who cannot believe that Africans could have sold people as they sold gold or ivory. Students frequently object that Africans couldn't possibly have sold their own people. It is true that, under normal circumstances at least, people try hard to protect those close to them. At times, ideas of commonality can be expanded to include quite large groups, so that people may go off to war to defend their nation or religious tradition. Yet these examples imply that humans also draw a line between those inside their group and those outside it, between "us" and "them." Judaism, Christianity, and Islam all taught that people should not enslave members of their own faith, but that it was permissible to enslave those outside their faith. In early modern times, North African Muslims enslaved Christians they captured in conflicts in the Mediterranean, just as European Christians enslaved indigenous people in the Americas to provide a labor force for colonies.

For our purposes, the key question is where sub-Saharan Africans drew the line between themselves and others. As was suggested in the Introduction, the first part of the answer is that there was no common "African" identity. People whom outsiders grouped together as "Africans" thought of themselves in quite different terms in the past, distinguishing variously on the basis of kinship, alliances, and religious beliefs. Much as Europeans shrank from enslaving co-religionists but did not see any problem with trading in African bodies, people in Africa generally refrained from selling people with whom they felt a common bond, but were willing to sell people whom they regarded as foreigners or enemies.

It is important to understand that, just as people in earlier times did not see identities the way people do today, the modern idea of universal human rights is quite a new idea. By modern standards, slavery is abhorrent. It is illegal to buy and sell people as though they were cattle, but such views were rare in the era of the slave trade. If we are to understand how the slave trade could have continued for centuries, then we must accept that, for sellers as well as buyers, slaves were commodities even though they were also humans. The slave systems that were established in the Americas are often called "chattel" slavery. The word "chattel" and the word "cattle" both ultimately derive from the same Latin word, *caput*, meaning "head." Like land, money, and other possessions, slaves were "capital," a third word English derives from *caput*.

---

6. John Hawkins, "Third Voyage," in *Voyages of Hawkins, Frobisher and Drake*, ed. Edward John Payne (Oxford: Clarendon Press, 1907), 69–71.

Referring to all those in the slave trade as "captives" is another interesting usage that has become popular in recent years. This usage may derive from the declaration by historian Walter Rodney, "Strictly speaking, the African only became a slave when he reached a society where he worked as a slave. Before that he was first a free man and then a captive."[7] To a degree the statement is true. Many of the enslaved had been captured in wars among Africans or kidnapped by unscrupulous African neighbors. It is also true that on the slave vessels crossing the Atlantic at least the grown men among the slaves were held captive in chains and shackles. However, it is not easy to distinguish clearly between captives and slaves. Nearly all those writing about plantation life in the Americas refer to the black workforce as "slaves," though, not being free, they were also captives. In a recent study, historian Stephanie Smallwood, for example, sometimes calls the enslaved people on the Middle Passage "slaves," but generally prefers "captives." Echoing Rodney, she constructs a two-step process of "turning African captives into Atlantic commodities" and "Atlantic commodities into American slaves."[8]

People are free to use language as they wish, and scholars need to be able to use the language that best conveys their meaning. Still, it is worth asking how Africans entering the Atlantic slave trade described their condition. We can never know what most of those transported thought, but those individuals who left a record of their thoughts suggest a surprising answer. Samuel Crowther, originally named Ajayi, penned one of the most complete narratives in 1837. Sixteen years earlier, Ajayi and several close relatives had been taken prisoner in his homeland by invading Muslims. Writing in English, he first he describes himself as a "captive," but, after being sold several times to other Africans, he writes that he had become "a veteran in slavery" by the time he reached the port of Lagos, where he was again sold, this time to the first Europeans he had ever seen. Ajayi had the good fortunate to be on a ship that was intercepted by a British patrol ship in June 1822. He was liberated and resettled in the small West African colony of Sierra Leone, where he soon learned to read and write English, became a Christian, and eventually chose to be ordained as an Anglican priest. As the next chapter will recount, he later was consecrated as a bishop and became a missionary to his home country. One of Ajayi's countrymen, known as Joseph Wright in Sierra Leone, wrote a similar description of his capture in those wars and of the several times African traders bought and sold him on his way to the ocean. He consistently refers to himself as a "slave" from the point of capture until he was rescued and liberated by the British. Sierra Leone is also the source a large body of other narratives collected by a nineteenth-century German missionary, S. W. Koelle, from resettled liberated Africans whom he used as the informants for his study of African languages. The missionary recorded what 143 informants told him about how they became part of the Atlantic slave trade. Nearly two-thirds reported that other Africans had seized them

---

7. Rodney, *How Europe*, 95.

8. Stephanie Smallwood, *A Middle Passage from Africa to American Diaspora* (Cambridge, MA: Harvard University Press, 2007), the phrases quoted are from her chapter titles.

in wars or kidnapped them; 14 percent were sold by relatives or superiors, often for debts; 11 percent has been sold into captivity after being convicted of crimes, such as adultery or for a serious religious infraction. Koelle's informants appear to confirm that (like Ajayi and Wright) they recognized their passage from free to slave had occurred before they ever left the African continent. Some of them told of being held as slaves for years before being sold overseas.[9]

These accounts suggest that most who entered the transatlantic slave trade had been captured or kidnapped but also that these unfortunate souls regarded themselves as slaves before they entered a slave ship or saw a plantation. The point is not that historians must call them "slaves" and not "captives," but rather that, if the term "slave" is reserved exclusively or primarily for those under European control, that usage risks obscuring something very important in the minds of those entering and leaving the slave trade. For too long African history has been written in ways that prioritized European or American perspectives, while omitting or minimizing how Africans saw things. Redressing the balance is one of the highest priorities of recent historians of Africa. Besides respecting the perspectives of Africans who became enslaved, one must also pay close attention to the perspectives of those who actively participated in the buying and selling of slaves. It is doubtful that the African merchants who engaged in the slave trade would have described what happened as "stealing" or called those they traded "captives," or accepted the implications that what took place in Africa was not *real* trade and that the institution of slavery in Africa was not *real* slavery.

European slave traders' thinking is spelled out in many firsthand accounts. The African side of the story is harder to tell because the sources are fewer and rarely firsthand. Nevertheless, African traders generally make it clear that they understood what slavery was and believed they were partners in trading in slaves. A particularly strong statement came from King Osei Bonsu of the powerful Asante Kingdom, who told a British representative at his court in 1820 why he objected to Britain's efforts to suppress the Atlantic slave trade. He first asked rhetorically how Britain could have moved from active participation in the slave trade to opposing it as evil, adding:

> Is not your law an old law the same as the Crammo [Muslim] law? Do you not both serve the same God, only you have different fashions and customs? Crammos are strong people in fetische [religion], and they say the law is good, because the great God made the book; so they buy slaves, and teach them good things, which they knew not before. This makes every body love the Crammos. . . . If the great king [of England] would

9. Crowther's and Wright's accounts are in Philip D. Curtin, ed., *Africa Remembered: Narratives by West Africans from the Era of the Slave Trade* (Madison: University of Wisconsin Press, 1967); S. W. Koelle, *Polyglotta Africana* (London: Church Missionary House, 1854), 1–24; P. E. H. Hair, "The Enslavement of Koelle's Informants," *Journal of African History* 6 (1965): 193–203.

like to restore this trade, it would be good for the white men and good for me too, because Ashantee is a country for war, and the people are strong.[10]

The king even offered to pay a large amount of gold in return for Britain's resuming participation in the slave trade. Rather than multiplying similar statements from other African rulers and merchants, let's turn to Chief Antera Duke, a powerful African merchant in the port of Old Calabar, who kept a personal diary in English for several years in the 1780s. This document is unique because it neither argues for the slave trade nor against it. Antera Duke simply recorded the mundane details of his commercial dealings with his inland African trading partners and with the European captains who came to trade, including details of his efforts to settle disputes among all these parties, so that the trade might continue uninterrupted. Slaves featured prominently in the trade of Old Calabar in those years, and, like the enslavement narratives, Antera Duke used the word "catch" to describe the seizure of war captives and "slave" to designate someone held in captivity in Old Calabar or sold into the Atlantic trade. His diary includes references to European vessels that took away over 14,500 slaves during the years 1785–1788, and it is known from other sources that another 3,400 slaves left Old Calabar in these years. He also refers to his own and other domestic slaves, who would appear to have been treated fairly well, were it not for the fact that some were used as human sacrifices at the funerals of important men. African slavery might differ from the plantation slavery of the Americas, but it was not, therefore, benign.[11]

As the previous chapter recounted, the European traders who came to Africa were not all-powerful. They had guns and cannon but normally did not make large conquests in the centuries of the slave trade. The Europeans had the capital to undertake long voyages to and from African coasts, but they could not make such ventures profitable unless they found African partners who were willing to exchange their goods for those the Europeans brought to their coasts. Economists have long insisted that willing buyers and willing sellers are necessary for markets to function. Africans could not be coerced into giving up their gold and ivory in exchange for cheap or worthless trinkets unless they were both powerless and simpleminded—neither of which was the case. As the previous chapter has shown, centuries before the first Europeans showed up on their shores, Africans understood how markets work and how to drive a hard bargain. The gold, ivory, and other exports came from inland territories in African hands. Any European who attempted to pass off shoddy goods soon found that markets were closed in his face or even found himself taken prisoner.[12]

---

10. Joseph Dupuis, *Journal of a Resident in Ashantee* (London: Henry Colburn,1824), 163.

11. Stephen Behrendt, A. J. H. Latham, and David Northrup, *The Diary of Antera Duke: An Eighteenth-Century Slave Trader* (New York: Oxford University Press, 2010), 77 and passim.

12. David Northrup, *Africa's Discovery of Europe, 1450–1850*, 3rd ed. (New York: Oxford University Press, 2014), 83–97.

This brings us to an additional insight into how African merchants thought about the slave trade. For obvious reasons, most studies focus on the unfortunate people leaving Africa. But one may gain important insights by looking at the other half of this trade, the goods those remaining in Africa received in exchange. Slave trading was part of the much larger Atlantic exchange of goods that, as the previous chapter has shown, began with Africans selling gold, ivory, and other items because they wanted what was offered to them in return. Africans were not predisposed or compelled to sell slaves into the Atlantic, but neither did they oppose the institution of slavery and the trade in slaves. The idea that Africans participated for profit gains strength when one looks at what happened after the Atlantic slave trade came to an end in the nineteenth century: Africans developed new "legitimate" exports so that could continue to import the goods they wanted from the Atlantic.

Thus far it has been argued that those Africans who participated willingly in the slave trade were not constrained from doing so by any moral belief that slavery was wrong nor by a belief that all black people shared a common identity. It has further been proposed that Africans' reason for doing so was rational and universal, the profit motive. These ideas lead us to explore two historical questions: What exactly did Africans receive in return and how did people at the coast obtain people to be sold into slavery? The short answer to the first question is that Africans got pretty much what they wanted in exchange for the goods and people they sold away. The next section of this chapter provides more detail. Establishing exactly where in Africa the slaves who were sold at the coast came from is more complicated, but during the peak years of the slave trade most came from inland communities rather than from the immediate vicinity of the coastal ports. As demand for slaves grew in the Americas and the price Atlantic slave traders were willing to pay also increased, African traders extended their contacts inland. In some places, they developed new routes; in other cases they enlarged existing trading networks. Although it is difficult to be precise about the numbers and origins of those sold abroad, as seen above, a place to start is Koelle's interviews in Sierra Leone with individuals from West, West-Central, and southeast Africa who had been liberated from slave ships. The informants tell where they started their journey into slavery and in some cases the routes they took to the coast.[13]

The sources of slaves changed over time in Africa, but in the first part of the nineteenth century many of Koelle's informants taken in war came from the hinterland of the Gulf of Guinea where two prolonged conflicts raged. One conflict was associated with the formation and expansion of the giant Islamic caliphate headquartered in Sokoto in what is now northern Nigeria. These wars united under common rule an ancient group of city-states among the Hausa and also spread to adjoining areas. The

---

13. Koelle, *Polyglotta Africana*, 1–24; Philip D. Curtin and Jan Vansina, "Sources of the Nineteenth-Century Atlantic Slave Trade," *Journal of African History* 5 (1964): 185–208; P. E. H. Hair, "The Enslavement of Koelle's Informants," *Journal of African History* 6 (1965): 193–203.

ruling group, the Fulani, generally made peace with the Hausa who submitted, while engaging in large-scale enslaving of other people. Most of those captured became slaves within the caliphate, some were exported across the Sahara, and others were sold into the Atlantic slave trade. Because the caliphate lay at a considerable distance from the coast, the captives headed to the Atlantic tell of passing from hand to hand over lengthy periods of time.

The second war, in what is now southwestern Nigeria, was a civil war among the kingdoms of the Yoruba people in the 1820s and 1830s. Early in the conflict one Yoruba faction invited forces associated with the Sokoto Caliphate to join their side, which had led to a great escalation of fighting that overthrew all of the Yoruba kingdoms. During the decades that these conflicts lasted, huge numbers of Yoruba captured in raids and battles were sold into the Atlantic slave trade, most ending up in Cuba or Brazil, the two principal main states still importing African slaves in the Americas. (The British and Americans had abandoned importing new slaves from Africa in 1808.) As we will see later in this chapter, the infusion of so many Yoruba had immediate and enduring effects on those societies. The British resettled many Africans rescued from slave ships in Sierra Leone, where Yoruba, Hausa, Igbo, and other languages rose to prominence.

Drawing a clear distinction between prisoners of war and victims of kidnapping is not always easy because these wars were often conducted by small bands of volunteers who were prone to capture easy civilian targets to resell or hold for ransom. In southeastern Nigeria the distinction is easier because the Igbo and neighboring peoples lived in autonomous communities not kingdoms, so their conflicts were on a small scale. Of the five accounts of Igbo enslavement collected in Sierra Leone, three individuals were kidnapped and the other two sold by their families or communities, one as punishment for adultery, the other as a young child for reasons unknown. Of the three victims of kidnapping, one was an adult who was taken captive and sold away "by a treacherous friend." In his famous autobiography, Olaudah Equiano wrote that he and his sister were kidnapped as children in the previous century and sold into the Atlantic slave trade. Although doubts have been raised about Equiano actually having been born in Africa, his account very likely is based on the experiences of other Igbo.

A few words need to be said about the networks of trails and markets that blanketed most of West Africa because they served the dual functions of moving captive people in stages to buyers and of moving goods from the Atlantic to customers across the densely populated interior region. One of the Igbo victims of kidnapping interviewed in Sierra Leone told of being sold to the Igala people on the Niger River, from where he would have been moved downstream in stages through the network of riverine markets, a fate that befell many others. Another Igbo said he was kidnapped as a boy and sold to the Aro people, who were famous inland traders in the region operating an extensive overland network of goods and slaves. When this individual was in his mid-twenties, the Aro sold him to European traders at the African port of Bonny. Referring to earlier times, the paramount chief of the Aro stated, "In some cases, when women left their children at home while they went to the farms, kidnappers would take them and sell them to the Aro."[14]

The records of the slave trade into the Atlantic make it clear that Europeans did not steal slaves but bought them for prices negotiated with their African trading partners. It also seems that those who were sold away already considered themselves slaves. Speaking of people "stolen" away or who were only "captives" until they reached the Americas may obscure these realities. Once one accepts that there was no pan-African identity at this time and that Africans had no absolute moral objections to enslavement, the reason for their engaging in the trade become obvious: they desired the trade goods they received in return. Only people clinging to outmoded beliefs in African inferiority find it difficult to accept the evidence that African trading communities operated over large areas of inland Africa, making use of rivers and overland routes to visit well-established markets to exchange local and imported goods for slaves and other exports.

## Economic Effects in Africa

In addition to stressing the sufferings of those enslaved, British abolitionists also argued that the trade had destructive effects within Africa. Reversing the prevailing notion that Africans' backwardness justified their enslavement, the abolitionists argued that it was the slave trade that was responsible for their dehumanization. The abolitionists believed, as historian Philip Curtin put it, "If the trade were to blame for African barbarism, its abolition would be the first step in bringing about the cure."[15] Some modern historians have taken up the abolitionists' argument, perhaps none so provocatively as Walter Rodney. While conceding, "Many things remain uncertain about the slave trade and its consequences," he asserts that a "general picture of destructiveness is clear" destructiveness that was "the logical consequence of the manner of recruitment of captives in Africa." The destructiveness was many-faceted: population loss, promotion of warfare and kidnapping, and economic harm. Rodney even dismisses the value of the imported goods by insisting that they caused "technological arrest" by driving African craftspeople out of business and by asserting, somewhat contradictorily, that "the majority of the imports were of the worst quality even as consumer goods—cheap gin, cheap gunpowder, pots and kettles full of holes, beads, and other assorted rubbish."[16]

---

14. Olaudah Equiano, "The Early Travels of Olaudah Equiano," ed. G. I. Jones, in *Africa Remembered: Narratives by West Africans from the Era of the Slave Trade*, ed. Philip D. Curtin (Madison: University of Wisconsin Press, 1967), 76; David Northrup, interview with Kanu Oji, Arochukwu, December 12, 1972.

15. Philip D. Curtin, *The Image of Africa: British Ideas and Action, 1780–1850* (Madison: University of Wisconsin Press, 1964), 68.

16. Rodney, *How Europe*, 95–96, 101–2.

For Rodney's thesis about the effects of the slave trade on Africa to be true, either Africans must have been forced to participate in the trade, which the author concedes they were not, or they must not have seen the harm that their participation was causing to their societies over several centuries. The latter explanation appears to demean African intelligence, although, as the previous chapter described, much of the popularity of Rodney's book has been among people of African descent. The appeal of Rodney's book is neither its scholarship nor its intellectual depth, but the way its message resonates with some audiences. The appeal has a certain logic to it: since the slave trade was terribly destructive to those enslaved, it is only proper that it was terribly destructive to the people remaining in Africa, and, as Rodney asserts, Europeans were to blame. Unfortunately, appealing interpretations do not need to be true.

If the central thesis about the slave trade in Rodney's *How Europe Underdeveloped Africa* is ideologically extreme and factually weak, a more balanced interpretation does not lie at the opposite extreme. Rodney's assertion that he wrote the book because white historians were asserting that the Atlantic slave trade was good for Africa is a deliberate distortion of what was happening at the time he wrote. It is true that the pioneers of African history (both white and black) were revising accounts of the slave trade, but what they were doing was moving away from the abolitionists' belief that both the enslaved and their African enslavers were victims—victims who needed redeeming. As was suggested earlier in this chapter, the new African history argues that African traders were acting from positions of strength and in pursuit of their own self-interests. Since the 1970s, historians of Africa have continued to uncover evidence that the slave trade was a partnership between two sides, not the relationship envisioned by Rodney in which the Europeans always had the upper hand.

As in history generally, it necessary to test the particular arguments about the effects of the slave trade in Africa against the historical evidence. One of the negative effects on Africa that abolitionists and Rodney believed was taking place was a rising level of violence that extended far beyond those sold into the slave trade. Knowing that war was an important means of enslavement, they charged the slave trade was the main cause of African warfare. King Osei Bonsu was adamant that this was untrue, at least in his powerful kingdom of Asante:

> I cannot make war to catch slaves . . . , like a thief. My ancestors never did so. But if I fight a king, and kill him when he is insolent, then surely I must have his gold, and his slaves, and the people are mine too.[17]

Historian Philip Curtin has tested whether West African rulers in the region of the Senegal and Gambia Rivers went to war for reasons of state, as the Asante king maintained, or for economic gain from selling the slaves that might be captured. He reasoned that if the economic thesis were true, wars would have been more frequent when the price of slaves was high than when the price was low. However, he found

---

17. Dupuis, *Journal*, 163.

that the correlation was weak at best. In Senegambia, as in Asante, economic motives appeared to have been a relatively unimportant cause of warfare.[18]

Besides the charge that economic motives led to slave capturing, some historians have argued that the importation of guns led to increased warfare in Africa. The plausibility of this guns-for-slaves hypothesis decreases as one looks at the evidence. Except for the West African kingdom of Dahomey, African military forces did not make significant use of firearms in these centuries, preferring instead to rely on traditional weapons and/or cavalry units. Another problem with the theory is that the demand for guns was often just as strong in regions that did not experience major wars as in those that did. Southeastern Nigeria was one place where the export slave trade was large, demand for firearms was strong, but states and wars were small. The demand for guns there seems to have been from individuals seeking to protect their homes and families.[19]

The economic argument that Rodney makes assumes that Africans were poor traders, selling people in exchange for shoddy goods and trifles. In effect, as we saw in Chapter 3, he argues that slaves were stolen, since the goods received in return did not represent adequate compensation for their loss. While this interpretation distorts the facts, it does direct attention to the importance of the goods Africans received in return for slaves, gold, or ivory. Accounts of the hard bargaining that took place along the coasts of Africa make it clear that Africans had strong preferences in trade goods and that their preferences forced important changes in what they received. As the previous chapter mentioned, African tastes in textiles shifted away from European-made linens and woolens to brightly colored textiles from India and other parts of Asia. Similarly, African demand for firearms became so great that it broke down European reluctance to sell them such weapons. The distribution of trade goods varied by coast and European nation as well as over time. (See the charts on the next page from the late 1700s, one British, the other French.) Having good access to textiles from India as well as sources of iron, the British provided larger proportions of these items. The French compensated with Brazilian tobacco and cowry shells from the Indian Ocean (much in demand as a currency in parts of West Africa), along with greater amounts of French-made brandy.

The goods Africans imported were largely of their own choosing, but they were not of equal value. Luxury goods such as top hats, frock coats with gold epaulets, and carved canes were intended for African elites. Most imported goods were intended for more ordinary customers who were hungry for cloth, refined metals (especially iron and copper), tobacco, and weapons. An expanding economy is evidently behind a third category of imports, including cowry shells and metal bars, which were widely used as currencies. African consumer preferences were so strong

18. Philip D. Curtin, *Economic Change in Precolonial Africa: Senegambia in the Era of the Slave Trade* (Madison: University of Wisconsin Press, 1975), 156–68.
19. For a survey of views see Northrup, *Africa's Discovery*, 97–106.

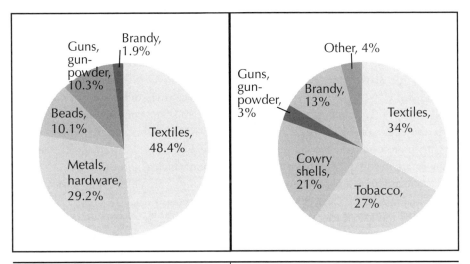

| Distribution of goods paid by Capt. John Potter to Chief Antera Duke at Old Calabar 1769–1770. Source: Stephen Behrendt, A. J. H. Latham, David Northrup, *The Diary of Antera Duke: An Eighteenth-Century Slave Trader* (New York: Oxford University Press, 2010), Table. 2.3. | Average distribution of goods paid in the Bight of Benin by captains of the *Marquis of Bouillé*, 1787, 1789. Source: David Northrup, "New Evidence of the French Slave Trade in the Bight of Benin," *Slavery and Abolition* 24.3 (December 2003): 64. |

and important that Europeans circulated detailed guides to the particular goods in demand on different coasts.

A variation of Rodney's argument that imports were of low quality argues instead that they were of such fine quality and so cheap that they undermined African industries such as cloth making and iron smelting. The theory rests on weak assumptions: first, that the volume of the imports was large enough to have had so major an impact in the vast area where they were eventually marketed; second, that African production was already fully meeting the demand for things like cloth, iron, and beads. In fact, it has been calculated that the imports were a small percentage of the total goods available in Africa and that the market for consumer goods was elastic, that is, Africans (like people elsewhere in those centuries) bought imported goods *in addition to* local manufactures. Some inefficient local smelters may have lost out to imported iron, but the additional work for African blacksmiths who turned imported metal bars into finished iron tools and weapons and copper or brass jewelry would have more than offset the negative impact on smelters.[20]

Older arguments about the destructiveness of the slave trade in Africa also needed to be scaled down after Curtin demonstrated in 1969 that the widely accepted figure of fifteen million or more Africans being transported lacked credibility and showed

---

20. Northrup, *Africa's Discovery*, 106–10.

that the actual figure was closer to ten million. While the new total was tentative and presented with many caveats, it produced two major responses. One was a great howl of protest from some quarters, charging that those arguing that the evidence suggested a smaller volume for the slave trade were actually trying to minimize the moral injustice of enslavement. A few even objected to the heartlessness of counting people as though they were pieces of wood, as though quantitative studies were not common in all areas of life. Other critics pointed out errors and omissions in Curtin's census.[21]

If the angry objections were an unwelcome (but not unexpected) consequence of Curtin's recount, the second response was one he had hoped for: new research in archives and newspapers for records of voyages upon which a more reliable count of the slave trade might be built. It was a huge task requiring a careful combing of the records of the major national carriers and of the ports slave ships reached. Led by historians David Eltis and David Richardson, the first published database included details of over 27,000 distinct voyages, a number that has now grown to almost 36,000 voyages. The new "Transatlantic Slave Trade Database" is freely available to anyone with Internet access for searching, analysis, and updating. On the basis of what is now knowable, the size of the Atlantic slave trade was somewhat higher than what Curtin initially estimated but still substantially lower than what most of his critics had suggested. Making allowances for missing data it is now estimated with a high degree of confidence that 10.7 million enslaved Africans were landed alive in the Americas after crossing the Atlantic. The number who left Africa was as high as 12.5 million.[22]

The debates about the volume of the Atlantic slave trade are over, but the detailed evidence these immense research efforts provide is far more revolutionary than the overall total. It is now possible to know, decade by decade (even year by year), which African ports slaves sailed from, where they were landed overseas, the role of different nations in the trade, the age and sex of those transported, and how mortality in transit varied over time. Although the database does not document directly what happened in Africa before ships were loaded or what occurred in the Americas after they discharged their cargoes of slaves, knowing the size and distribution by age and sex of the slave trade from ports and regions in Africa does refine the process of estimating these demographic, social, and cultural effects.

One application of the database has been to model the probable demographic effects of the slave trade in Africa, an effort led by historian Patrick Manning. Because in any society some people die and some are born in the course of a year, one important calculation is the rate of natural increase, which is generally assumed to have been

21. Curtin, *Atlantic Slave Trade*. For a review of the early reactions see Paul E. Lovejoy, "The Volume of the Atlantic Slave Trade: A Synthesis," *Journal of African History* 23 (1982): 473–501.
22. David Eltis and David Richardson, "A New Assessment of the Transatlantic Slave Trade," in *Extending the Frontiers: Essays on the New Transatlantic Slave Trade Database*, ed. David Eltis and David Richardson (New Haven, CT: Yale University Press, 2008), 1–60. The website is Voyages; The Transatlantic Slave Trade Database, [1514–1866], http://www.slavevoyages.org.

74

low in Africa during these centuries due to high childhood mortality, disease, famine, and warfare. The impact of the departures, therefore, could have been substantial at the peak of the trade in the decades before 1810, were it not for several factors. First, those enslaved were young, on average in their late teens or a bit older, meaning that the lost population could be replenished in a couple of decades. Second, the potential losses to Africa were lessened by the fact that twice as many males as females departed in the transatlantic trade (in contrast to a higher proportion of females in the trans-Saharan trade), since birthrates closely follow the number of fertile females. The third mitigating factor is that the Atlantic trade introduced new food crops to Africa from the Americas, notably maize, manioc (cassava), sweet potatoes, and other crops, which improved nutritional resources. The introduction of drought-resistant manioc to famine-prone West-Central Africa seems to have been particularly important in curtailing losses in famine years. Even so, it is probable that the populations of Africa most affected by the slave trade declined during its peak decades. Not surprisingly different historians produced somewhat different estimates of the demographic effects depending on how much weight they attached to each of the variables. Though the range of differences among scholars has narrowed considerably due to new evidence, the limits of what is knowable make it unlikely that a further consensus can be reached.[23]

Describing Africa's recovery from the effects of the slave trade is somewhat easier. In 1808, the British withdrew from the transatlantic slave trade and thereafter devoted considerable resources to enforcing the ban on its citizens and persuading other nations to withdraw from slave trading as well. As a result, the trade declined sharply in second quarter of the 1800s and came to an end in 1866. Because the British had had the largest share of the transatlantic slave trade during the century before 1808, the British government's abolitionist efforts curtailed the profits that its citizens had once made in Africa, but only for a time. British and African merchants did not abandon interest in trading and went on to build an even larger "legitimate" trade. Africans sold the British and other Europeans vegetable, animal, and mineral products in exchange for imported goods, exchanges that were quite similar those before the peak decades of the slave trade. The earliest and most dramatic changeover came in what is now southeastern Nigeria, where Africans dramatically increased their export of palm oil, whose commercial value by mid-century had become greater than the value of the outlawed slave trade had been. Great Britain imported so much palm oil because the growth of industrialization there had increased the market for vegetable oils to lubricate machinery as well as to make candles and soap.

The ability of ordinary Africans in southeastern Nigeria (and elsewhere) to increase production of palm oil so rapidly is evidence that the devastating social damage

---

23. Patrick Manning, "Contours of Slavery and Social Change in Africa," *American Historical Review* 88.4 (1983): 835–57, and *Slavery and African Life: Occidental, Oriental and African Slave Trades* (New York: Cambridge University Press, 1990); Joseph C. Miller, *The Way of Death* (Madison: University of Wisconsin Press, 1988), 3–169.

abolitionists had imagined the slave trade to have caused was an exaggeration. The new trade not only made use of the same African routes, markets, trading professionals, and coastal ports that had underpinned the commerce of the slave trade, but it also testifies to the importance of imported goods in motivating African producers to devote themselves to this new export. Eyewitness reports from European explorers, especially those sailing up the Niger River in the middle 1800s, provide additional evidence contradicting the social destruction the abolitionists had imagined in Africa. Instead of finding societies broken by the slave trade, they observed bustling towns and markets, stable institutions, and people eager to expand trading connections. Finally, there is evidence of demographic recovery. The losses of the enslaved were very real, but what became obvious as the nineteenth century advanced was that West African populations were recovering quickly from whatever demographic losses they had suffered.[24]

Research continues on the history of the slave trade from Africa and historians will continue to debate the details and meaning of this era, but the consensus has moved away from the views of abolitionists and Marxists. Instead of those who remained in Africa being seen as victimized almost as severely as those who were shipped away, it is now clear that Africans continued in control of their territories, of their inland trading networks, and of their participation in the Atlantic exchanges. As historian John Thornton has put it, "[W]e must accept that African participation in the slave trade was voluntary and under the control of African decision makers."[25] The myth that Europeans were all-powerful and African traders were easily duped is unsupportable. Though the trade in slaves across the Atlantic continues to shock modern sensibilities, the African demand for imported goods during the height of the Atlantic slave trade (as well as earlier and later) was a major reason why the trade took place. If Africa suffered from violence and population loss, it also gained in economic strength. Those who assume African societies were fragile need to re-examine the robustness shown in that era. The robustness of those who departed across the Atlantic is the subject of the third part of this chapter.

## Survivals and Transformation in the Americas

In 1941, anthropologist Melville J. Herskovits, a pioneer in the study of Africa and the African diaspora, published a book entitled *The Myth of the Negro Past*. The heart of the myth that Herskovits attacked was that African Americans had no past. More explicitly, he disputed the belief that early African Americans could not have worked out any "common denominator of understanding," because they "were brought from

---

24. David Northrup, *Trade without Rulers: Pre-Colonial Economic Development in South-Eastern Nigeria* (Oxford: Clarendon Press, 1978), 80–84, 114–223; Curtin, *Image of Africa*, 253–58; Robin Law, ed., *From Slave Trade to "Legitimate" Commerce: The Commercial Transition in Nineteenth-Century West Africa* (Cambridge: Cambridge University Press, 1995).

25. John Thornton, *Africa and Africans in the Making of the Atlantic World, 1400–1800*, 2nd ed. (New York: Cambridge University Press, 1998), 125.

| W. E. B. Du Bois, 1918. Bain Collection, Library of Congress. | Booker T. Washington, 1905. Library of Congress, Prints and Photographs Division. |

all parts of the African continent, spoke diverse languages, represented greatly differing bodies of custom, and, as a matter of policy, were distributed in the New World so as to lose tribal identity." Rather, Herskovits argued, African Americans in the United States had continued to exhibit numerous African traits and customs in their social, religious, linguistic, and artistic lives, just as had descendants of Africans in the West Indies, Brazil, and elsewhere in the Americas.[26]

Herskovits' work was widely praised and has become a classic that inspired much additional work. An early review of the book by the eminent African American educator W. E. B. Du Bois (1868–1963) declared it "epoch-making," and insisted its conclusions "must be regarded seriously in all future writing on the subject."[27] Du Bois was raised in Massachusetts and became the first African American to earn a Ph.D. from Harvard University, so he had moved far from his African cultural roots in his personal and professional lives, but he was keenly interested in connections to Africa. Du Bois' image of Africa was sometimes romantic, but he lived long enough to be buried as an honorary citizen in the newly independent West African country of Ghana. In part, Du Bois was nostalgic for the Africanness that long ago had been taken from him. Four decades before the publication of Herskovits' book, in an essay in *The Souls of Black Folks*, Du Bois had described how slave ships had taken black

---

26. Melville J. Herskovits, *The Myth of the Negro Past*, rev. ed. (Boston: Beacon Press, 1990), 1–2. "Negro" was then the term both blacks and whites used to designate people of African ancestry.

27. W. E. B. Du Bois, review of *The Myth of the Negro Past*, *The Annals of the American Academy* 222 (1942): 226–27; Sydney W. Mintz, introduction to the 1990 edition of Herskovits, *Myth*, xviii.

people from their African homes and how the plantation had erased "the old ties of blood relationship and kinship." All that survived of Africa on the plantation at that point, he believed, was religion in the form of "the healer of the sick, the interpreter of the Unknown, the comforter of the sorrowing, the supernatural avenger of wrong, and the one who rudely but picturesquely expressed the longing, disappointment, and resentment of a stolen and oppressed people." Later, he suggested, the spiritual priest became the black preacher and the founder of "the first Afro-American institution, the Negro church."[28] Du Bois stressed that this early church was more heathen than Christian, but that over time missionary efforts and motives of expediency led the black church to become increasingly Christian. Yet he also stressed that black churches never lost their African spirituality. In later years Du Bois became active in civil rights struggles in the United States and in the larger pan-African movement, experiences that prepared him to be receptive to the richer vision of an African heritage that Herskovits detailed.

Just as reverence for Africa and pursuit of mainstream American achievement mixed in Du Bois' own life, so too had this dual identity competed in earlier times. As will be shown in more detail below, plantation slaves in the American South mixed African traditions with a pride in speaking English well. After emancipation, the practical advantage of assimilating American culture persisted and even increased. The great educator Booker T. Washington (1856–1915), born in slavery, believed the salvation of black people lay in gaining the linguistic, social, and professional skills that would convince their white compatriots that they were their equals. In 1901 he published an autobiography entitled *Up from Slavery*, in which there is no reference to Africa except perhaps in this passage: "When persons ask me in these days how, in the midst of what sometimes seem hopelessly discouraging conditions, I can have such faith in the future of my race in this country, I remind them of the wilderness through which and out of which, a good Providence has already led us." Dr. Washington's immediate meaning of "wilderness" was slavery, but it may be that he was also referring to their escape from pre-Christian Africa, for just a few lines earlier he had written, "Negroes in this country, who themselves or whose forefathers went through the school of slavery, are constantly returning to Africa as missionaries to enlighten those who remained in the fatherland."[29] Dr. Washington believed that Africans (as well as African Americans) were in need of Christian enlightenment, but he did not despise Africa. For a time he had considered helping African Americans to go to Africa to escape discrimination and proudly sponsored African students at the school he founded in Tuskegee, Alabama.

Washington and Du Bois had different views of Africa's importance and sparred over what strategy African Americans should pursue in their efforts to gain equality,

---

28. W. E. B. Du Bois, *The Souls of the Black Folks*, ed. David W. Blight and Robert Gooding-Williams (Boston: Bedford Books, 1997), 152.

29. Booker T. Washington, *Up from Slavery: An Autobiography*, Project Gutenberg Ebook #2376, 39–40.

but they also had much in common. Both men spent most of their professional lives in black institutions of higher learning in the South, Washington as president of Tuskegee Institute from 1881 to 1915, Du Bois as professor of economics and history at Atlanta University from 1897 to 1910 and from 1934 to 1944. While Du Bois described his mission as educating the "talented tenth," Washington's Tuskegee Normal and Industrial Institute aimed at producing a less elite cohort of people with practical skills: teachers, technicians, and farmers.

The tensions between reverence for African ways and achievement in American society that were evident in the approaches of Du Bois and Washington were echoed in the movements for equal civil rights in the second half of the twentieth century. The cultural embrace by some African Americans of Afro hairstyles, African-style cloth and clothing, African names, and African religions did not change the fact that most Americans, black and white, were deeply estranged from the real Africa. The subsequent establishment of Black Studies or Africana Studies programs in the late 1960s and 1970s, however, helped foster serious scholarship, even if it sometimes also led to mythmaking.

The central myth that Herskovits fought against has largely disappeared from contemporary scholarship and discourse. Although it would be hard to find a respected scholar who denies the importance of African cultural heritage in the Americas, a heated debate has developed over the way to frame these phenomena. One school of interpretation sees the movement of identifiable and self-conscious African nationalities to the Americas. There are several problems with this interpretation. Because the interpretation appears to be modeled (consciously or not) on the movement of European nationalities across the Atlantic, it is worth taking a brief look that experience. Two points are relevant. The first is that many influential scholars have emphasized that nationalities in Europe were "invented," mostly in the nineteenth century, the age of nationalism. Their use of "invention" is deliberately provocative, intended to focus attention on the fact that identity formation is a dynamic process: identities do not pass unchanged from generation to generation. The second point is that many European immigrants to the Americas arrived with a weak or unformed sense of any larger nationality. German speakers came from numerous distinct states and principalities, mostly well before the formation of a united German state in 1871. Most immigrants from Italy arrived in North America when Italian unification was still underway and well before the Tuscan dialect became the national language. The Irish migration largely occurred when the Irish counties were part of Great Britain. It certainly can be argued that these (and other) groups had the potential for national identities, but the actual identities individual immigrants brought with them were far more local than national. Thus, it has been argued that German Americans, Italian Americans, and Irish Americans invented themselves in a two-step process: first identifying as Americans and then accepting an ethnic sub-category reflecting a European national origin that had often formed after their departure.

Similar themes have arisen in discussions of identity formation both in Africa and in the diaspora. First, as Chapter 5 argues, modern African ethnic or national identities mostly formed late, sometimes due to internal forces of state formation in the nineteenth century or as a response to external forces of colonialism in the twentieth century. Second, ethnicity for African individuals was, in historian Adrian Hastings' words, "in most places a very flexible identity" that they could adapt to changing circumstances.[30] Third, the process of identity formation in the Americas was a complex process of self-invention, enlarging African cultural roots, borrowing beliefs and customs from others (both African and European), and building institutions that helped them survive. Survival required change, but preserving what Herskovits called a "common denominator" of cultural traditions enhanced one's chances of surviving.

Anthropologists Sydney Mintz and Richard Price have argued since 1976 that enslaved Africans' most important achievement in the Americas was building new societies and identities. Readily admitting that elements of African beliefs, cultural traditions, and language survived in plantation societies, they stress that such "survivals" were less significant historically than the construction of new institutions and identities based on shipboard friendships and plantation alliances that blended and borrowed from diverse African traditions. In addition, they stress, interactions between those newly arrived in the Americas and those born and raised in the Americas had a comparable importance for both blacks and whites: "African-American social and cultural forms were forged in the fires of enslavement, but these forms could not, and cannot be defined by confining them to those peoples and or societies whose physical origins were African any more than Euro-American social and cultural forms are limited to those whose physical forms were European." Mintz and Price also quote with approval Herskovits' observation that "whether Negroes borrowed from whites or whites from Negroes, . . . it must always be remembered that the borrowing was never achieved without resultant change in whatever was borrowed."[31]

The broad thrust of Mintz and Price's analysis, though differently nuanced, echoes those of Herskovits and Du Bois cited earlier. When a new edition of *The Myth of the Negro Past* was called for in 1990, Mintz wrote a new introduction praising the work. Those espousing a greater emphasis on finding African "survivals" in the Americas also praised the pioneering efforts of Herskovits. Despite this common tradition, somehow small differences in interpretation became exaggerated. A group calling itself "Africanists" began campaigning against Mintz and Price's interpretation, often using emotive language and falsely charging the two with holding the mythic position Herskovits had challenged decades earlier, namely, that the African cultures had not survived the slave trade. It is hard to say what was at the root of the vitriol, for the

---

30. Leroy Vail, ed., *The Creation of Tribalism in Southern Africa* (Berkeley: University of California Press, 1989); Adrian Hastings, *Construction of Nationhood: Ethnicity, Religion and Nationalism* (Cambridge: Cambridge University Press, 1997), 149.

31. Sidney W. Mintz and Richard Price, *The Birth of African-American Culture: An Anthropological Perspective* (Boston: Beacon Press, 1992), 82–83.

difference often seemed to be a pointless dispute over whether the glass was half full or half empty. One side emphasized the importance of creating vital new societies in the Americas; the other emphasized African survivals. Both sides believed in cultural continuity and both acknowledged change. Sometimes the two sides are difficult to distinguish. For example, though not citing Mintz and Price, historian Paul Lovejoy has suggested that what occurred among Africans in the Americas was a cultural "resurrection," not a transfer of actual cultures from Africa, but a rebirth of neo-African cultures in the Americas.[32]

Working with the evidence in the transatlantic slave trade database, a new generation of scholars is shining fresh light on these old disputes. It is now clear that the origins and the destinations of the slave trade were highly varied. Brazil was the destination of the majority of slaves brought directly from Africa in the 1600s, 1700s, and 1800s. The lands that became the United States received a tenth that number from Africa, yet in the mid-nineteenth century there were more slaves in the United States than in Brazil. The major factor explaining this outcome was the much higher mortality among slaves in Brazil due to disease and other factors. That high death rate required a constant replenishment with new slaves from Africa. As abolitionist efforts gradually closed down the slave trade to Brazil, the number of slaves there declined. In North America the disease environment was more forgiving and so required a much smaller number of new African slaves. In contrast to what happened in Brazil, the end of the slave trade into the United States in 1808 saw a rapid increase in the slave population.

It seems reasonable to assume that the higher the proportion of people born in Africa living in a part of the Americas, the stronger African beliefs, practices, and languages are likely to be. Conversely, the lower the share of African-born slaves, the lower the direct influence of African cultures is likely to be, since slaves born in the Americas learned the colonial language and were introduced to the dominant religion and culture of the colony. So it is not surprising that slave communities in the American South tended to develop culturally in quite different ways from those in Brazil or the Caribbean. In Virginia and South Carolina, for example, the African-born share of the slave population was already below 50 percent in the early 1700s. By the mid-1700s, African-born slaves were only a fifth of the total in Virginia and two-fifths in South Carolina. At the beginning of the 1800s, less than half a percent of slaves in Virginia were African-born and under 10 percent in South Carolina. The greatest increase in the number of slaves in the United States occurred after 1810 during a period when direct African influences were few and most slaves had several generations of American-born ancestors. Thus, it is ironic how much effort has gone

---

32. Paul E. Lovejoy, "The African Diaspora: Revisionist Interpretations of Ethnicity, Culture, and Religion under Slavery," *Studies in the World History of Slavery: Abolition and Emancipation* 2.1 (1997): 7. For a review and critique of these debates see David Northrup, "Igbo and Myth Igbo: Culture and Ethnicity in the Atlantic World, 1600–1850," *Slavery and Abolition* 21.3 (2000): 1–20.

into locating African survivals in the United States, a part of the Americas where the odds are most stacked against success.[33]

Studies of the Africanization taking place in Brazil and the West Indies during these centuries have exposed a second obstacle to finding cultures directly linked to Africa. Africa is an exceptionally large and diverse continent, so it is likely to expect mixtures of influences from different African societies, even among slaves who came from the same African region. In addition, the origins of slaves in every colony varied over time. For example, most slaves entering the port of Pernambuco in northern Brazil in the 1700s and 1800s were shipped from ports in West-Central Africa, whereas 60 percent of the slaves entering the port of Bahia in central Brazil in those centuries came from ports along the Bight of Benin in West Africa. Although these concentrations of regional influence are significant, the larger reality in Brazil was that newly arrived slaves and their descendants underwent a double process of acculturation: first they became Africans and then they became African Christians. The process was similar to what Du Bois believed happened in North America. While it may seem odd to say those newly arrived in Brazil from Africa had to *become* Africans, what this means is that the interactions among people from different African cultures made them aware that they were part of a much larger community than they would have encountered in their particular homelands. Those from different parts of West-Central Africa, for example, would have discovered beliefs and rituals that resembled their own, along with new beliefs and practices from other parts of Africa. In addition, they needed to learn the Portuguese language and were instructed in the beliefs and practices of Catholicism. Although this may sound like a jumble of disparate and incompatible pieces, the individuals involved seemed to have made sense of it. Slaves in Brazil perceived, for example, that the qualities of some Catholic saints resembled those of some African deities. The resulting mixture of religious traditions is called "syncretism" and was not confined to slave communities. An important study by historian James Sweet argues that a generalized version of West African rituals remained intact throughout the 1600s in Brazil, but thereafter the mix changed. However, he argues that up to 1770 "the impact of Christianity on Africans was no greater than the impact of African beliefs on Christians."[34]

Preserving distinctive aspects of any African culture is difficult when slaves came from different parts of Africa. However, in the last decades of the slave trade an unusually large concentration of people, who are now known as the Yoruba, arrived in Cuba

---

33. Philip D. Morgan, *Slave Counterpoint: Black Culture in the Eighteenth-Century Chesapeake and Lowcountry* (Chapel Hill: University of North Carolina Press, 1998), 61, 63.

34. Daniel Barros Domingues and David Eltis, "The Slave Trade to Pernambuco, 1561–1851," in Eltis and Richardson, *Extending*, tables 3.3 and 3.4; Alexandre Vieira Ribeiro, "The Transatlantic Slave Trade to Bahia, 1582–1851," in Eltis and Richardson, *Extending*, table 4.4; James H. Sweet, *Recreating Africa: Culture, Kinship, and Religion in the African-Portuguese World, 1441–1770* (Chapel Hill: University of North Carolina Press, 2003), 227–30.

and Brazil. The Yoruba before 1800 had several distinct kingdoms where particular dialects were spoken. These kingdoms shared religious traditions and other cultural traits, but not a common identity. As was mentioned earlier in this chapter, decades of warfare in the early 1800s destroyed the older Yoruba kingdoms, led to the formation of new kingdoms with more diverse cultures, and sent large numbers into the Atlantic slave trade. In parts of the Americas, the new pan-Yoruba identities began to incorporate Africans of other origins. A study by Oscar Maráguez shows that the number of slaves from ports on the Bight of Benin (many of whom would have been Yoruba) went from a few hundred in 1806–1820 to over 13,500 in the middle decades of that century. It is clear that the Yoruba had a strong cultural impact in Cuba, yet the author finds it puzzling that Yoruba influences were as large as they were since twice as many slaves arrived in Cuba from West-Central Africa in that period. The reasons, Moráguez concludes, "are likely to be complex and will require substantial additional research."[35]

Sorting out the complex processes taking place among Africans in the Americas continues to attract researchers. Although the results of such research confirm the importance of cultural continuity and change, as proposed by Mintz and Price, only in exceptional cases do they support the notion of entire African cultures surviving the passage to the Americas. Culture is dynamic not static, especially in difficult circumstances. However constrained by difficult circumstances, people sorted out their lives and made choices, sometimes preserving precious bits of an ancestral culture, borrowing aspects of fellow slaves, and learning from those with deeper roots in their new location. A final difficulty in seeking the survival of particular unified cultures in the Americas is that cultures and identities were also undergoing significant changes in Africa during this period, as the next chapter will discuss.

## Conclusion

The emotions understandably evoked by discussions of the Atlantic slave trade can make separating myth from reality a delicate and complex process. The first step is to establish the basic facts, such as how the trade was conducted, how many people were transported from Africa, and where they ended up in the Americas. Research is more successful when conducted with an open mind than when searching for evidence to prove a preconceived idea. It is also important to include the viewpoints of

---

35. Some of the many collections of studies of the Americas are Jacob K. Olupona and Terry Rey, eds., *Òrìsà Devotion as a World Religion: The Globalization of Yoruba Religious Culture* (Madison: University of Wisconsin Press, 2008); Kristin Mann and Edna Bey, eds., *Rethinking the African Diaspora: The Making of a Black Atlantic World in the Bight of Benin and Brazil* (London: Frank Cass, 2001); Isadore Okpewho, Carole Boyce Davis, and Ali A. Mazrui, eds., *The African Diaspora: African Origins and New World Identities* (Bloomington: Indiana University Press, 2001); Oscar Grandío Moráguez, "The African Origins of Slaves Arriving in Cuba, 1789–1865," in Eltis and Richardson, *Extending*, 195 and passim.

contemporary African participants in the trade, including those who were sold away. For a long time scholars dismissed the possibility of African cultures having survived the Middle Passage to the Americas. More recently scholars of the African diaspora have uncovered new evidence of such transmissions, but they have sometimes exaggerated the importance of such findings. Fortunately a happy medium is beginning to emerge. Whatever the proper balance between African roots and the acquisition of non-African culture, between continuity and change, the discussions have spurred important research. The next two chapters will explore identity formation and religious changes in Africa, themes that may help shed light on some of the topics discussed in this chapter.

# 5. CHANGE, CONTINUITY, AND IDENTITY:
## MERRIE OLDE AFRICA?

Africans are by nature "tribal" people and that "tribalism" is little more than an
irrelevant anachronism . . . deriving from the distant past of rural Africa.[1]
—*Leroy Vail, historian of Africa, describing the myth of African tribalism*

The Igbo peoples [sic] were a distinct ethno-historical group who shared a
distinctive set of ancestral traditions . . . a people whom modern scholars
can study as a separate "nation" in the transatlantic diaspora.[2]
—*Douglas Chambers, historian of Atlantic Africa*

Since 1800 Africans have changed enormously. They have assumed new ethnic identities (once called "tribal" identities) and built up new national identities within
boundaries largely drawn by outside colonizers. Large numbers have joined world
religions (both Islam and Christianity), learned new information and ways of thinking in modern schools, and mastered European languages. Many individuals have
moved temporarily or permanently to new cities and taken up new occupations. At
the same time, Africans have maintained links between their present and their past.
They consider their new identities to reflect old traditions and their new religions to
be informed by earlier beliefs and customs. Africans' new knowledge adds to traditional knowledge, rather than replaces it, just as their new second languages rarely
displace their ancestral languages. Finally, most urban Africans (including those who
have emigrated abroad) retain strong ties to specific rural homelands. Clearly change
and continuity are the yin and yang of modern Africa. Like the Chinese symbol, they
are both distinct and interdependent, one cradled in the other's arms.

Understanding the balance between continuity and change is challenging. Indeed,
it is even a problem to decide what one should call such identities. The words "tribal,"
"ethnic," and "national" have subtle differences in meaning, but the basic reality is
that "tribal" can imply backwardness when speaking of Africans, whereas "national"
tends to suggest monolithic modernity. To avoid biased language, scholars generally
speak of "ethnic" groups or, when addressing particular historical contexts, put the

---

1. Leroy Vail, ed., "Introduction" to *The Creation of Tribalism in Southern Africa* (Berkeley: University
of California Press, 1989), 2–3.
2. Douglas B. Chambers, "'My Own Nation': Igbo Exiles in the Diaspora," *Slavery & Abolition* 18
(1997): 73.

other terms in quotation marks. From the mid-1950s, scholarly attempts to make sense of transformations in Africa tended to stress the continuity of African cultures and the superficiality of new additions to them. However, in the 1980s, Harvard historian Leroy Vail critiqued what may be called the "myth of tribalism" that social scientists in the 1960s and 1970s had promoted in southern Africa. He identified three common, but faulty, theories about recent ethnic identities in the region. The first, was "that ethnicity was primarily the result of . . . 'divide-and-rule' tactics which colonial governments cannily employed." The second held that African "ethnicity was a recent phenomenon of the modern urban workplace in which boundaries and distinctions between peoples had been built up." The third theory was that modern African ethnicities were a kind of psychological "false consciousness" resulting from and reacting to unequal economic and social developments, a consciousness that was exploited by modern African politicians.

Vail argued that all three theories were partially true, but they were mythical rather than factual explanations because they left out major pieces of what was happening. The first omission was history, which shows that the formation of ethnic identities was more complex than the actions of colonial administrators and employers. The second, and even more important, omission was the input of Africans, who did not react in a mindless and muddled fashion to the actions of others but made decisions and choices about who they were and wanted to be. The third omission was the role of Christian missionaries, who offered Africans new visions of personal and group identity, as well as being the principal agents for spreading Western education. Missionaries' promotion of the standardization of African languages also had the effect of enlarging and standardizing ethnic identities. The process of identity formation that Vail analyzed in southern Africa was not exactly the same in all parts of Africa, but there were similarities in much of East Africa, West-Central Africa, and southern West Africa.[3]

Since the 1980s, another group of scholars, mostly Americans trained as historians, has embraced a second myth of African ethnicity, positing the transmission of identifiable African cultures to the Americas. As the previous chapter suggested, such a theory understates the complexity of cultural interactions in the Americas among Africans of different cultural and linguistic backgrounds. It also understates the importance of cultural interactions between those newly arrived from Africa and those born in the Americas, whether of African, European, or Amerindian heritage. As these authors are aware, there are many parallels between identity formation in the Americas and Africa, and there are also many differences. But the basic problem is that the Atlantic slave trade could not have transmitted fully formed African cultures to the Americas during the centuries before 1800 because the formation of the larger ethnic identities in sub-Saharan Africa largely took place after 1800. Historian Douglas Chambers, quoted above, may serve as an example. Chambers thesis would

---

3. Vail, *Creation of Tribalism*, 3–13.

be unassailable if he had written that the Igbo of southeastern Nigeria "are" an ethnic group, but, by stating that the various Igbo "peoples" shared a common identity before 1850 that facilitated their enslaved members in the Americas becoming a separate "nation," he is asserting the existence of a historical event that can more readily be disputed than proven.[4]

Identity change has been common everywhere in modern times, not just in Africa. People today commonly possess multiple identities. In twenty-first-century Europe, for example, people can simultaneously identify themselves as Europeans, members of defined nation-states, and members of sub-national ethnicities. They also have additional identities based on class, religion, and political views. If one considers the many immigrants who have settled in Europe, the complexity grows. In May 2016, for example, voters in London elected as their mayor, Sadiq Khan, a man born in Britain of working-class immigrants from Pakistan and the first Muslim to hold the post. People in Africa, like those in Europe and elsewhere, also possess multiple identities and sort out which is most significant depending on the circumstances.

Identity change is most obvious among people immigrating to a new country, but sometimes people living in the same place find their national identity being altered by boundary changes. One example is German identity since 1800. In the early 1800s, for example, numerous German states, large and small, were first incorporated into Napoleon's empire, and then reorganized in 1815 into a new confederation. Stirrings of pan-German nationalism sparked numerous failed revolutions in 1848 and then to the incorporation of most German states into a new German Empire under Prussian leadership in 1871. Defeated in World War I, the German Empire was reorganized as a republic that occupied a smaller territory, until Hitler created a third German Empire with greatly expanded boundaries in the 1930s. Following World War II, the defeated Germans were divided into four different zones of occupation, three of which combined to form a democratic West Germany, which, after the collapse of Soviet domination, annexed East Germany in 1990. In addition, Germany joined the European Community as well as the North Atlantic Treaty Organization (NATO). Even though no individual lived through all of these changes, they are indicative of how many permutations a single "nation" could have undergone in the past two centuries. African experiences have been complex, but they are not unique.

One reason for the complexity and diversity of change in Africa is that the continent is much larger than Britain, Germany, or Europe. Because it is impossible in this brief overview to be comprehensive, the chapter will identify general patterns and give illustrative examples. Changes are considered in chronological order, but it will be obvious that not every African society followed the same chronology. Political and economic factors are emphasized up through the end of European rule in most parts

---

4. Chambers, "Own Nation," 73. For a critique of Chambers' concepts and evidence, see David Northrup, "Igbo and Myth Igbo: Culture and Ethnicity in the Atlantic World, 1600–1850," *Slavery and Abolition* 21.3 (2000): 1–20.

of the continent. Religious change is considered more fully in the next chapter, and the examination of post-colonial changes are continued in the final chapter.

## Pre-Colonial African Identities and Dynamics

In the British Isles there once was a tradition of simplifying and romanticizing the past as "merrie olde England."[5] It was bad history. No one uses the phrase "merrie olde Africa," but many believe the myth that there was once a peaceful, happy, and rather uniform Africa of small villages and small ethnic identities that has been transformed into the nation-states of the present. Although it is certainly true that African identities have undergone tremendous enlargement of scale in the past two centuries, it has been anything but a straight-line progression.

In the early 1800s, Africans' primary identities were often smaller than the area of the language they spoke. The strongest direct evidence comes from research by S. W. Koelle, a missionary in Sierra Leone among Africans liberated from the Atlantic slave trade and resettled there during the early decades of the nineteenth century. In some cases Koelle found that a language had no common name, because those who spoke it identified only with their own dialect group, not with the language as a whole. One example was "Yoruba," a name some Sierra Leone missionaries used for several related dialects, but which Koelle rejected. His research had established that speakers of the dozen different dialects of the language used different names for it. "Yoruba" was the name used only in the northern kingdom of Oyo. Koelle called the language "Aku" (or Oku), the name other Africans in Sierra Leone had given to its speakers, based on a greeting common to all dialects. Similarly, in Cuba the Yoruba-speakers were called "Lucumi," and "Nago" (Nagu) in neighboring Haiti, since those who spoke the language had no common name for themselves.

Another people in Sierra Leone, who lacked a common name for their language and themselves are now called Igbo (or Ibo). Koelle noted, "In Sierra Leone certain [Africans] from the Bight [of Biafra] are called Ibos. In speaking to some of them respecting this name, I learned that they never had heard it till they came to Sierra Leone. In their own country they . . . know only the names of their respective districts," of which he recorded five examples. A third southern Nigerian language and people lacking a common name in Koelle's day were called "Kalaba" in Sierra Leone, but Koelle named them "Anang," the name of the westernmost district, perhaps because speakers of that dialect were most numerous in Sierra Leone. Although Koelle observed that all of them "speak nearly the same language," he recorded six different dialects, each with its own name and identity. In the mid-1800s, Scottish missionaries in Old Calabar (from which Kalaba derived) compiled a dictionary of the language, which they called "Efik," the name used by those in Old Calabar who

---

5. "Merry England," *Wikipedia*, http://en.wikipedia.org (accessed May 21, 2016).

spoke it. To this day the speakers of this language have not agreed on a common name for themselves and their language, even though they are well aware they can easily understand each other.[6]

The point of all this is that people often identify themselves quite differently from how outsiders name them. Put another way, people may well share the potential to hold a common identity, but realizing that potential is not inevitable, unless historical circumstances make such an enlargement of scale desirable. The nineteenth and twentieth centuries were a time when people in many places around the world found it desirable to enlarge their primary identities. The process sometimes involved expanding national boundaries, as was the case in Germany, Italy, and the United States in the 1800s. For most Africans the process of identity augmentation began at an ethnic level (as the previous chapter argued it did for Irish Americans and Italian Americans), but later assumed a larger territorial (or "national") dimension. Ethnic identities and expanding territorial membership sometimes appeared to be in conflict, as some examples will make clear.

As was mentioned in the previous chapter, the largest new state in West Africa in the 1800s was the Sokoto Caliphate, which was formed by conquests between 1804 and 1809. As the word "caliphate" indicates, it was an Islamic state whose formation reflected a reformist religious agenda. The religious aspects will be considered more fully in the next chapter; this chapter focuses on the process of ethnic consolidation. The leaders of the conquests were members of a minority group in the region, known locally as the Fulani. The Fulani (or Pula) were a pastoral people who had dispersed east across the savannas of West Africa over several centuries from a homeland near the Atlantic. After adopting Islam, some Fulani had specialized in clerical functions and become more urbanized. It was they who led the religious war (jihad) that led to the creation of the caliphate. The more numerous people in the region were the Hausa, an agricultural and commercial people, who shared a common language and culture (including Islam), but had traditionally organized themselves into separate city-states, which the Fulani jihadists and their allies conquered one by one. At the fringes of the empire, the jihadists also overran other peoples, many of whom they enslaved.

As the founders realized, the Sokoto Caliphate needed to be consolidated, if it was to survive. They divided the vast state administratively into a series of provinces, but the key change was the amalgamation of the Fulani ruling elite with the old Hausa rulers. The chronicle of the kings of the Hausa state of Kano gives a condensed account of this process. After Kano's forty-third Hausa ruler was driven out by Fulani jihadists, the victors objected to one of their own occupying the palace. If a Fulani leader entered Kano's palace, they argued, and begat children with Hausa wives, the children would look and act like the Hausa. Eventually the new ruler overcame this resistance, but as the years passed, the ethnic identity of the new ruling class did

---

6. S. W. Koelle, *Polyglotta Africana* (London: Church Missionary House, 1854), 5–6, 7–8, 18–19; Hugh Goldie, *Dictionary of the Efik Language* (Glasgow: Dunn and Wright, 1862).

indeed gradually alter. The chronicle explicitly identifies the two who ruled Kano from 1807 to 1846 as Fulani, but it does not so identify the next one, even though he had been named after the founder of the caliphate. Consolidation at the top was sufficient to hold on to political power, though the Hausa commoners in the city and their rural cousins remained distinct from the ruling class.[7]

In southeastern Africa (below the Limpopo River) new states were also formed in the early 1800s, probably due to rising population densities. After conflict broke out among the Northern Ngoni people, one leader emerged victorious, the young Shaka of the Zulu clan, who went on the found the most powerful state in the region. Shaka focused his attention on the young, drilling young men and women in the traditions of the Zulu. The men were also drilled in warfare that used new close-combat techniques that proved both deadly and effective. The discipline Shaka imposed both succeeded and backfired. On the positive side, his warriors made large conquests, forcing their neighbors to submit or flee, and those who were incorporated also came to identify themselves with the new Zulu nation, more than with their ancestral clans. However, the rigid discipline and annual military campaigns also convinced some Zulu that Shaka had become unhinged, especially after the death of his mother, to whom he was very attached. Some fled, employing the new fighting techniques to found new states and in time new ethnic identities. In 1828, Shaka was assassinated by his half brother, who succeeded in persuading the Zulu that this was for the best. The senior regiments were disbanded and their members were encouraged to marry and settle down. Although the Zulu were little more than a decade old, the cultural transformation and political centralization has struck a responsive chord. The Zulu were the most powerful and most populous state in southeastern Africa. In 1838, the young kingdom was challenged by a small force of whites who were in search of new lands to settle. As will be elaborated later in this chapter, the whites were mostly of Dutch ancestry and were seeking to escape from British rule. The Zulu first allowed them to settle to their south but then turned on the settlers, seizing thousands of cattle and sheep. Over the next few months there were repeated clashes between them, ending in a pitched battle in which the whites' firearms mowed down the Zulu as they charged. The defeat split the kingdom and the faction that allied with the whites made peace.[8]

Along with the new Yoruba identities developing in Cuba and Brazil mentioned in the previous chapter, two new Yoruba communities were emerging in West Africa. One was among those rescued from slave vessels by the British patrols and resettled in the small colony of Sierra Leone. The refugees from several different Yoruba kingdoms

---

7. H. R. Palmer, *Sudanese Memoirs* (Lagos: Government Printer, 1928), 3: 127–32; John Hunwick, "A Historical Whodunit: The So-Called 'Kano Chronicle' and Its Place in the Historiography of Kano," *History in Africa* 21 (1994): 127–46.

8. Carolyn Hamilton, *Terrific Majesty: The Powers of Shaka Zulu and the Limits of Historical Invention* (Cambridge, MA: Harvard University Press, 1998), provides a critical survey of the issues.

Anglican bishop Samuel Ajayi Crowther, a pioneering missionary in nineteenth-century West Africa, was rescued from a slave vessel and liberated in Sierra Leone. Source: Frontispiece in Jesse Page, *Samuel Crowther: The Slave Boy who Became Bishop of the Niger* (1888), Princeton Theological Seminary Library. Wikipedia Commons, public domain.

there quickly developed a pan-Yoruba identity and elected a "king," although no pan-Yoruba king had existed back in the homeland. At the same time that the speakers of various dialects of Aku were discovering a common identity in Sierra Leone, many of them were also receiving a formal education, learning English, and becoming Christians.

As the long civil war back in the Yoruba homeland came to an end, new communities and customs were also in formation. The frontiers and residents of the new kingdoms were quite different from those the fighting had destroyed. As peace returned, some Yoruba began returning home from Sierra Leone and the New World, including a number of Christian missionaries. To aid in proselytizing, Bishop Samuel Ajayi Crowther compiled a dictionary of the spoken language that he decided to call "Yoruba." Anthropologist John Peel has carefully documented the complex paths that led to the acceptance of education and Christianity in parts of the Yoruba homeland, along with a new pan-Yoruba identity. But Peel warns against crediting these changes to external agents. The missionaries, he argues, were only the "midwives" in the birth of a pan-Yoruba nation. In 1897, a Yoruba named Samuel Johnson, whose parents had been liberated from the slave trade in Sierra Leone, completed a massive *History of the Yorubas*, which became the charter of the new nation. Johnson also argued that the fall of the old Oyo kingdom had been part of a divine plan to bring the Yoruba to Christianity. New nations need new myths. Crowther helped give them a common name; Johnson gave them a spiritual destiny. The pan-Yoruba identity that Africans brought from Sierra Leone may have planted the seed for national identity formation; but, just as among the Yoruba in the diaspora, the assent and participation of the local communities over several generations was essential for the new nation to come about.[9]

One could multiply examples, but the larger point seems clear: during the course of the 1800s, enlargements of scale in identity were taking place in many places in

9. David Northrup, "Becoming African: Identity Formation among Liberated Slaves in Nineteenth-Century Sierra Leone," *Slavery and Abolition* 27 (April 2006): 1–21, analyzes the transformations in Sierra Leone, and J. D. Y. Peel, *Religious Encounter and the Making of the Yoruba* (Bloomington: Indiana University Press, 2000) carries the story from there to the homeland. Samuel Johnson, *The History of the Yorubas* (Lagos: CMS Bookshops, 1921).

sub-Saharan Africa. The causes varied from inter-African conflicts (Zulu) to religious influences both Muslim and Christian (Sokoto, Yoruba).

## Changes and Responses during European Colonial Rule

The rapid extension of European colonial rule in the late 1800s, from a few coastal enclaves to almost the entire continent, stimulated, reframed, or deflected the movements toward cultural and political amalgamation that were under way. Political changes were the most obvious and widespread. Within the colonies' fixed boundaries pre-existing African empires and kingdoms were either broken up or became subordinate units of the colonial state. In addition, the amalgamation of culturally similar small societies into colonial administrative districts often stimulated the formation of larger ethnic identities. Another arena of change was economic and technological. Trade and population movement became easier due to the suppression of local wars (a phenomenon known as the "colonial peace") and the building of railroads and motor roads. Other newly introduced technologies also broadened horizons. A third arena of change was cultural and intellectual, which was notable in the new cities as well as in rural areas where Christian missions operated. Generally acting independently of the colonial state, the missionaries introduced basic education and modern medical services along with their religious message. These European actions were obviously important, but it was the African responses to them that did most to create new African identities.

The colonial takeover in Africa moved quickly. Africans generally found it impossible to resist for long the better-armed, European-led forces. Small-scale communities were subjected to harsh punishments if they continued to resist, which usually persuaded others to surrender without a fight. Large states were capable of more prolonged resistance. After the French destroyed the larger kingdoms of the Western Sudan, an upstart leader named Samori Touré (ca. 1830–1900) organized the fight against them. Although it was impossible to halt the French force, Samori used one army to slow their advance from the west, while employing a second to expand his area of control to the east. He also held a third force in reserve. Samori trained his forces in the use of firearms that he bought from British traders and also attempted to forge alliances with neighboring African states. He made overtures to the ruler of the Tukulor Empire to his north to coordinate their resistance to the French, arguing, "If you continue to make war on your own, the whites will have no trouble in defeating you." Though Samori was a fellow Muslim, Amadu Tall (ca. 1835–1898), the Tukulor ruler who was descended from a learned and distinguished family, refused to ally with a man he regarded as a mere adventurer. Later Samori attempted to ally with the Asante kingdom to the south, but the rulers there, already fighting British advances, feared they had more to lose from antagonizing the French than from gaining an African ally.

While European imperialists are often accused of pursuing policies of "divide and rule," the sad truth evident in this example is that divisions among Africans also facilitated their conquest and sometimes halted developing political identities. The French completed their conquest of the Tukulor Empire in 1893, with Amadu Tall dying while fleeing to the Sokoto Caliphate. In 1895, the British sacked Asante's capital and sent the young King Prempeh (1870–1931) into exile, from which he was not allowed to return until 1924. The French captured Samori in 1898 and sent him into exile in Gabon, where he died of pneumonia.[10]

The colonial takeover was followed by a less violent period of administrative consolidation, during which Africans variously responded to the changing circumstances by acquiescing as well as by resisting. The realms of Samori and Amadu were dissolved and incorporated into French West Africa. Asante became a part of Britain's Gold Coast Colony but was given a special protected status and King Prempeh was restored to his throne in 1926. The British preference for imposing a level of administration on top of defeated and submissive African institutions is also evident in their disposition of the Sokoto Caliphate. Although the largest and most populous state in pre-colonial West Africa, the caliphate had kept a decentralized administration, largely based on the earlier Hausa states. Just as the Hausa states has fallen one by one to the Fulani jihadists, Sokoto's autonomous administrative districts fell one by one to the British forces. In addition to the absence of a centralized military command, there was also a split between the Hausa-Fulani ruling elite and the Hausa masses. A Hausa woman recalled, "We Habe [Hausa] wanted [the Europeans] to come; it was the Fulani who did not like it. When the Europeans came the Habe saw that if you worked for them they paid you for it, they didn't say like the Fulani, 'Commoner, give me this! Commoner, bring me that!'"[11] This recollection is colored by post-conquest events, but it still makes the point that, although common people (and slaves) might see improvements in their lives, British rule in the new colony of Northern Nigeria depended on preserving the old African elites and political structures in order to govern through them. With significant modifications the Islamic institutions of the Sokoto Caliphate survived, but such continuity was accompanied by an ossification that contrasts with the dynamic changes taking place among the Igbo of Southern Nigeria and the Kikuyu of Kenya, to whose histories we now turn.

The British became so devoted to the idea of ruling through existing African authorities ("indirect rule") that colonial officials often created chiefs in societies that lacked such hierarchical organization. This provoked interesting confrontations from the Igbo of southeastern Nigeria and the Kikuyu of western Kenya. Though

---

10. John D. Hargreaves, *West Africa Partitioned*, vol. 2, *The Elephants and the Grass* (Madison: University of Wisconsin Press, 1985); Michael Crowder, ed., *West African Resistance: The Military Response to Colonial Occupation*, rev. ed. (London: Hutchinson, 1978), 19–79, 111–41. Michael Crowder's, *West Africa under Colonial Rule* (London: Hutchinson, 1968), remains a balanced and readable overview of the whole period.

11. Mary F. Smith, *Baba of Karo: A Woman of the Muslim Hausa* (New Haven, CT: Yale University Press, 1981), 67.

unrelated, far apart, and inhabiting different environments, these two peoples shared many qualities. Both farmed land held by kinship groups and distributed among member families. Both had a tradition that they once had had kings but had overthrown them, which was likely a myth that justified their preferences for decentralized and democratic systems of governance. Igbo and Kikuyu men had greater authority than did women, and elders held more authority than the juniors, but women's rights and those of the young adults were still respected. Finding no rulers to govern through, the British appointed government chiefs over Igbo and Kikuyu communities. In the absence of any checks from below, government chiefs tended to become autocratic and corrupt. For that reason and because they lacked any traditional mandate, the chiefs became unpopular.

Though unhappy with the government chiefs and with the system of taxation imposed on adult males, Igbo men lacked the ability to organize on a large scale to oppose them and had learned to fear the power and violence of the police whom the chiefs could summon. However, in 1929 when a rumor spread that women were also to be taxed, there was a different response. Women in southeastern Nigeria were deeply involved in the market networks that blanketed their area. Women brought small surpluses to sell in the market, bought other things, and had plenty of time to befriend each other. The rumored new tax became the talk of the markets, where the women worked out a plan to deal with it through direct action. Mobs of angry women sacked stores, set local courthouses on fire, and attacked unpopular chiefs. The women reasoned correctly that the British and the appointed chiefs would be reluctant to retaliate against them as readily as they would have against the men, although in one instance police fired on a violent crowd killing or wounding sixty-three people. Eventually the waves of violence wore themselves out, but the "Women's Riot" or "Women's War" of 1929 had had its effect. Following the recommendations of a special commission that investigated the causes of the riots, the government-appointed chiefs were removed and replaced with a system of local government that was closer to the pre-colonial system. This innovation was accepted and worked much better.

The Kikuyu were also challenging the European order in 1929, but their focus was not directly on the government-appointed chiefs. In the background of their protests was resentment of the privileged position of white settlers. The Kenyan government had set aside large tracts of land adjacent to the Kikuyu for European settlement and was promoting European agricultural at the expense of African farmers. In the foreground of Kikuyu protests was their desire to have more control over their lives and livelihoods. Even though many Kikuyu had become avid Christians and were enthusiastic about modern education, they resented attempts by some white missionaries to change other aspects of their lives. In 1924, leaders had formed the Kikuyu Central Association to promote education, address economic grievances, and promote Kikuyu unity. A talented young Kikuyu named Jomo Kenyatta (1891–1978) became head of the KCA in 1928. Kikuyu complaints in 1929 focused on two issues: controlling their schools and defending their custom of female genital cutting (clitoridectomy), then called female "circumcision." The latter was an issue because some missionaries (especially Presbyterians) had condemned it. The Kikuyu felt strongly that the decision to continue old customs or promote useful new practices was theirs to make. Of course, not all Kikuyu thought alike. Some stayed with the Presbyterians, while others joined a new African Independent Pentecostal Church. Some stayed in the mission schools, while others attended new "independent" schools, which followed the same curriculum but were African-run. Presbyterian parents mostly chose to abandon the ritual of genital cutting; Roman Catholics continued the custom but often had the operation performed in a Catholic mission hospital under sterile conditions.[12]

The Igbo were as enthusiastic about schooling for their children as the Kikuyu, but, with no white settlers to complicate relations, generally welcomed with the missionaries' educational efforts. Igbo communities invited Christian missions to build primary schools and provided the land on which to erect them and the funding to pay the teachers, all of whom were Africans. There were a handful of government-run secondary schools in Nigeria, but too few to satisfy the rising demand among the Igbo for more education. Most students paid tuition to attend mission-run, single-sex boarding schools, which competed for the best students. As was true in Kenya, instruction in upper primary and secondary schools was in English, in part to accommodate students who spoke different first languages and in part because advanced studies in science, geography, mathematics, and history needed to use English-language textbooks. As a result, secondary school graduates were sufficiently proficient in English to attend British and American universities.

As the Igbo moved out of their homeland in search of other opportunities, they began to form ethnic associations for fellowship and support. Associations in distant cities of Lagos and Kano were soon mirrored by associations in the different sections of the Igbo homeland and then by the formation of an Igbo State Union in 1948, which had the dual goal of uniting the various Igbo-speaking peoples and using their unity to gain greater political autonomy from the British. The key individual was Nnamdi Azikiwe (1904–1996), born and raised by Igbo parents in Northern Nigeria and educated in mission schools and American and British universities. He rose to prominence as an outspoken journalist, orator, and political organizer.

The two colonies followed different paths to majority rule. In Nigeria the transition to African rule was orderly, beginning with regional elections (Azikiwe becoming the chief executive of the Eastern Region) followed by national elections. After independence in 1960, Azikiwe replaced the last British governor-general while a

---

12. For overviews see Simon Ottenberg, "Ibo Receptivity to Change" in *Continuity and Change in African Cultures*, ed. William Bascom and Melville J. Herskovits (Chicago: Phoenix Books, 1965), 130–44; and Jomo Kenyatta, *Facing Mt. Kenya: The Tribal Life of the Gikuyu* (New York: Vintage Books, n.d.). Two novels vividly describe these events: T. Obinkaram Echewa, *I Saw the Sky Catch Fire* (London: Penguin, 1992) for the Igbo; and Ngugi wa Thiong'o, *The River Between* (London: Heinemann, 1965) for the Kikuyu.

northern leader held the post of prime minister. In Kenya an underground movement led by the Kikuyu to regain their land rights from the white settlers disrupted the last years of British rule. To overcome the struggle, which the whites called "Mau Mau," the British imprisoned 80,000 Africans (mostly Kikuyu, including Jomo Kenyatta) and imposed a state of emergency. In the conflict 13,000 African lost their lives, compared to the deaths of fewer than 130 white settlers and soldiers. The central issue was access to farmland. Kenya's African population had doubled between 1921 and 1954, reaching 5.7 million, while the number of white settlers grew from fewer than 10,000 in 1921 to nearly 50,000 in 1954. Once peace was restored, Kenyatta won the election for president in 1964.[13]

Writing in the later 1950s, anthropologist Simon Ottenberg expressed the view that under colonial rule, of all Nigerian peoples, the Igbo "have probably changed the least while changing the most."[14] Something similar could be said of the Kikuyu in East Africa. Over the course of the first six decades of the twentieth century, both societies formed larger ethnic identities based on language and customs in addition to traditional kinship-based identities. By the 1950s, new national identities were also forming within the boundaries of colonial Nigeria and Kenya. The Igbo and Kikuyu retained historic customs and languages, while adding fluency in English, Christian beliefs, and Western education. Ottenberg argued that the Igbo applied their traditional value of personal achievement in sports, farming, and war to new activities as times changed. School degrees and success in business became new expressions of the drive to succeed. While details were different, the Kikuyu also became noted for their adherence to traditional values their embrace of new values borrowed from the West.

How typical were the colonial experiences of these two peoples? As Ottenberg suggests, the Igbo were exceptionally adept in taking up new things without losing a sense of continuity with the past. But it can also be argued that, if the fervor and speed with which the Igbo and Kikuyu embraced both continuity and change were exceptional, other African peoples followed similar paths, if a bit more slowly or less smoothly. In 1962 Colin M. Turnbull, a respected anthropologist of Africa, wrote a sobering book called *The Lonely African* that detailed the harm and dislocation that rapid changes brought to some people, but he also concluded that, for all the problems he identified, "no suggestion is meant that Africa would have been better left alone."[15] Therefore, it is useful to look more closely at some reasons for change other than colonial boundaries and policies.

---

13. David Anderson, *Histories of the Hanged: The Dirty War in Kenya and the End of Empire* (New York: W. W. Norton, 2005); Caroline Elkins, *Imperial Reckoning: The Untold Story of Britain's Gulag in Kenya* (New York: Henry Holt, 2005).

14. Ottenberg, "Ibo Receptivity," 142.

15. Colin Turnbull, *The Lonely African* (New York: Simon and Schuster, 1962), 241.

## Social, Cultural, and Economic Change

The fact that ethnic identities in Africa generally grew larger and more important was due only in part to newly imposed colonial boundaries and administrative districts. As was true among the Igbo and Kikuyu, missionaries could be another powerful force for change, not just in offering Africans new beliefs and educational systems but also in expanding language areas. Foreign missionaries normally relied on African interpreters to preach their message and on African teachers to instruct students in the vernacular in the early years of schooling, but some missionaries also sought to master African languages so as to provide accurate translations of scriptural and liturgical texts. To that end the missions compiled vocabulary lists, dictionaries, and grammars, in the process producing "standard" versions of African languages that could be used in churches and schools. Eventually standardized linguistic usage and spelling were used for radio broadcasts, newspapers, and other publications. As people became familiar with the standardized version of their language, they were more apt to identify with the larger language community.[16]

Actions taken by Africans were even more important than colonial regimes and missionaries in shaping the development of ethnic identities. The choices that individual Africans made in pursuit of their own welfare help explain the wide variations in developments during the colonial era. Decisions to migrate for work, attend school, and join ethnic, religious, political, and labor organizations also broadened the horizons of personal identity.

For some African trading groups identity horizons had been expanding well before the colonial era. For example, over many centuries the Juula trading community had dispersed southward from their Western Sudanese homeland. Hausa traders had set up similar connections within the Central Sudan and beyond, and the Aro traders of Arochukwu had established a powerful trading network in what is now southeastern Nigeria. During the 1800s, Swahili traders from the East African coast had forged commercial ties with inland trading connections of such intensity that the Swahili language became widely used as a regional lingua franca over a wide area. What had begun in pre-colonial times expanded much more during the 1900s, greatly affecting individuals' identities and perspectives.[17]

Rapid population growth in Africa during the middle half of the twentieth century was another major change that influenced identity formation. Africa's population grew by an average of 275 percent between 1925 and 1975, faster than the rates for Asia and Europe. Growth was somewhat slower than that average in the relatively poor colonies of French West Africa, the Belgian Congo, and Portuguese Mozambique, though populations there still more than doubled. Populations in the British territories of Nigeria,

---

16. For an example of this process among the Yoruba see Peel, *Religious Encounter*, 283–95.
17. Philip D. Curtin, *Cross-Cultural Trade in World History* (New York: Cambridge University Press, 1984), 34–59.

South Africa, Uganda, and Kenya grew substantially faster than average. Such rapid growth was primarily due to improved health care, including drugs to treat infections, inoculations against common diseases, and improved infant care.

Population pressures in rural areas drove some younger men seek work in mines and cities. Other rural Africans found ample employment in their own areas from "cash crops," that is, crops grown, harvested, processed, and transported to markets for sale. Aided by new motor roads, Africans in southeastern Nigeria continued to increase their production of palm oil, which had begun in the 1800s, and of palm kernel oil. New railroads to the coast enabled northern Nigerians and Senegalese to become major exporters of peanuts, another commodity valued for its oil. Africans in the Gold Coast and southwestern Nigeria created a profitable new economy based on cacao, which employed migrant African labor. Individuals from smaller groups often associated themselves with the dominant ethnicity from their area, even if they did not share the same mother tongue.[18]

Other parts of Africa lacked the resources and adequate transportation infrastructure to pursue cash crop production. In these cases colonial administrators resorted to forms of poorly remunerated coerced labor or unpaid forced labor. This was true of the rubber economy of the Congo Free State and early Belgian Congo, inland parts of French West Africa, as well as the Portuguese colonies. Where there were white settlers, as in Kenya, Algeria, and southern Africa, colonial policy often greatly favored their cash crops and imposed limits on African export crops in order to push Africans in the labor market working for white settlers. In southern Africa where there was a high demand for miners and farmworkers colonial governments promoted labor migration. While labor migration mixed people from different backgrounds, it also tended to strengthen larger identities based on a common language. The push of overpopulation in rural areas decreased the need to use coercion to get an adequate labor force.

Although movement to commercial and administrative centers grew slowly at first, urbanization was an increasingly important phenomenon from the 1940s. By the early 1950s, many cities in West Africa were twice as large as they had been a decade earlier. The same was true elsewhere. From its founding in 1900, Kenya's capital city, Nairobi, grew to be home to 222,000 people by 1957. The population of South Africa's largest city, Johannesburg, also less than a century old, was over 900,000 in 1951. Until the 1960s, African men tended to outnumber African women in the newer cities, both because it was male labor that was in greatest demand and because many single men migrated in order to earn enough money to get married back in their home villages. Some migrants became permanent urban residents, but before 1940 most shuttled back and forth between city and village. In South Africa segregation was strictly enforced and legislation in the 1950s made family life increasingly difficult for migrants who

---

18. Immanuel Wallerstein, "Ethnicity and National Integration in West Africa," in *Africa: Social Problems of Change and Conflict*, ed. Pierre L. van den Berghe (San Francisco: Chandler Publishing, 1965), 472–82.

had not resided for fifteen years in the urban area where they lived. Ironically, the apartheid government was attempting to maintain the myth of migratory labor in the part of the continent where African had the deepest roots in urban areas.[19]

Besides those whose horizons were broadened by migration, other Africans who remained closer to home became more aware of the larger world as the result of access to bicycles, books, and broadcasts. Bicycles were a new invention that found a growing market in colonial Africa. The new "safety" bicycle of the late 1800s had two equal-sized wheels, pedal-powered chain drive, front steering, and, by the 1900s, pneumatic rubber tires. Although a single seat was standard, add-ons included a platform over the rear wheel (for passengers or cargo) and a basket over the front wheel. For most Africans the bicycle's purchase price was high, but its versatility and durability made it a valuable investment for moving goods and people more rapidly and easily than by walking. Farmers could move produce to market more quickly and easily, with the added advantage of making family excursions. It was rare for women to peddle bikes.

Other newly available products broadened mental horizons without the need to travel far. Schools brought literacy and books, at first mostly textbooks and Bibles, but in time a whole range of texts were available from mission-sponsored and private bookstores. Newspapers had appeared in sub-Saharan Africa in the 1800s, first in Cape Town, Sierra Leone, and Liberia and then in the Gold Coast. The *Lagos Daily News*, West Africa's first daily paper, edited by Herbert Macaulay (1864–1946), Bishop Crowther's grandson, voiced political demands beginning in the 1920s, and by the 1950s many African nationalists were also making very effective use of newspapers to reach and arouse followers. For those with electricity, there were radio broadcasts in local languages as well as short-wave broadcasts from overseas. The first radio broadcast appeared in the 1920s and 1930s in settler colonies in eastern and southern Africa (though anyone could listen). Broadcasts in African languages were common by the 1950s when the transistor radio, with small batteries that provided enough power for longer periods, opened this medium to the masses. Even before that, some Africans and schools had power-hungry vacuum tube radios and, of course, word of mouth spread news, too.[20]

19. J. D. Y. Peel, "Social and Cultural Change," in *The Cambridge History of Africa*, vol. 8, *From c. 1940 to c. 1975*, ed. Michael Crowder (Cambridge: Cambridge University Press, 1984), 142–91; Kenneth Little, "The Role of Voluntary Associations in West African Urbanization," in *Africa: Social Problems*, ed. Van den Berghe, 325–45; David Welsh, "The Growth of Towns," and Leo Kuper, "African Nationalism in South Africa, 1910–1964," in *The Oxford History of South Africa*, ed. Monica Wilson and Leonard Thompson (New York: Oxford University Press, 1971), 2: 172–243, 424–76; Luli Callinicos, *Working Life: Factories, Townships, and Popular Culture on the Rand, 1886–1940* (Braamfontein, SA: Raven Press, 1987).

20. Simon McBride, "Communications Media" in *The Cambridge Encyclopedia of Africa*, ed. Roland Oliver and Michael Crowder (Cambridge: Cambridge University Press, 1981), 403–4; Mark R. Lipschutz and R. Kent Rasmussen, eds., *Dictionary of African Historical Biography*, 2nd ed. (Berkeley: University of California Press, 1986), 128–29.

## Race and Identity in Southern Africa

John L. Dube (1871–1946) was a preacher, educator, and political activist in South Africa. Two years after this photograph was taken in 1910, he founded the black civil rights organization later known as the African National Congress of South Africa. Source: Wikimedia Commons, public domain.

In most cases, as Chapter 7 recounts, the transition to majority rule was completed fairly peacefully and democratically between 1956 and 1968. However, in colonies with significant white settler populations, independence was delayed by prolonged, violent struggles, because equal rights for all would mean a loss of white privilege. We have already touched upon the struggle in Kenya, which ended early. Also over in the early 1960s was the violent struggle in Algeria, which France fought for eight years to protect the privileged position of European settlers. However, in southern Africa a bloc of settler states strongly resisted the transition to majority rule for many decades.

Because of South Africa's importance as the anchor of white supremacy in the region. let's begin with an overview of its history. From its origin in 1652 at Cape Town as an outpost of the Dutch East India Company, Dutch settlers had spread across the inland areas as farmers and herders. By the time Great Britain took over the Cape Colony from the Dutch in 1806 the white settlers there numbered about eighteen thousand and thought of themselves as Africans, "Afrikaners" in their language. Although the colony continued to be a stopping point on the way to trading outposts in the Indian Ocean, the arrival of British rule brought new settlers, a new language, and laws against slavery, which aroused opposition from some of the older white settlers in rural communities. In the 1830s growing numbers of these white "Afrikaners" began moving outside Cape Colony along with their cattle and slaves, sometimes engaging in conflicts, as was seen earlier, with the Zulu and other Africans. In the 1850s they founded two new states on the high plains, the Transvaal Republic and the Orange Free State. Initially, the British had been reluctant to extend the colony's frontiers, but their policies changed after the discovery of gold in the Transvaal Republic and Germany's founding of African colonies in the mid-1880s. The British first annexed African lands to cut the Afrikaner republics off from the sea, including the Zulu kingdom in 1887 and the Rhodesias to the north in 1890. A bungled British attempt to provoke British gold miners in the Transvaal into rebellion had ultimately led to the bitter South African War (1899–1902), during which the Afrikaner republics were defeated and later joined the English in a new self-governing Union of South Africa in 1910. The Union gave equal rights to all whites but few rights to Africans and other "non-whites."

This uneasy alliance of English and Afrikaner whites spurred African leaders to promote a united African front. The new African leaders were the product of mission-run schools and study abroad, which brought them into contact with the parallel struggle for equal rights for blacks in the United States. In 1911 black leaders in the United States had formed the National Association for the Advancement of Colored People (NAACP); the next year black South Africans formed the African National Congress (ANC) of South Africa. The ANC's first president, the reverend John L. Dube, had studied in the United States and was influenced by Booker T. Washington's educational efforts at Tuskegee (see Chapter 4). After visiting Tuskegee in 1903, Dube established a similar training school in his native Zululand. In a statement after being elected ANC president in 1912, Dube emphasized the need for unity across African ethnic lines, declaring, "We are one people. These divisions, these jealousies, are the cause of all our woes and all of our backwardness and ignorance today." Mohandas K. Gandhi and the Indian National Congress, which had a branch in South Africa from 1894, had also influenced the ANC commitment to non-violent protest.[21]

As the rest of Africa moved toward equality and independence after World War II, southern Africa was moving in the opposite direction. The victory of the right-wing Afrikaner National Party in the South African election of 1948 led to a far more radical program of separation by race, known as *apartheid* (separation), disenfranchisement of the small number of black voters, and a program of separate development to promote African ethnic nationalism to blunt the pan-African unity advocated by Dube and the ANC. Peaceful protests by black South Africans were met with bullets, imprisonment, and loss of citizenship. When, in response, the ANC turned to low-level violence, Nelson Mandela and other ANC leaders were accused of treason and sentenced to indefinite detention at hard labor in 1962.[22]

As John Dube had said in 1912, the root cause of African weakness in South Africa was that they were divided along ethnic lines. His implication was that intra-ethnic divisions were a greater obstacle than divisions between whites and blacks. In the decades that followed African cooperation across ethnic lines increased, but the older divisions did not disappear. Well aware of how important it was to keep black Africans divided along ethnic lines, apartheid governments promoted separate development and restricted entry into the cities where cross-cultural integration had been growing. Thus, it is ironic that the policies of white supremacy became such a great force for unifying South Africa's diverse peoples, although one needs to keep in mind that African identities were also products of other historical forces. In the nineteenth century Africans had built new kingdoms and political institutions in southern Africa. Some exceptional leaders in the 1800s managed to broaden their horizons even more by getting a good education in missionary schools, which involved learning English,

---

21. J. D. Omer-Cooper, *History of Southern Africa*, 2nd ed. (London: James Currey, 1994); Leonard Thompson, *A History of South Africa*, 3rd ed. (New Haven, CT: Yale University Press, 2001); George M. Frederickson, *Black Liberation: A Comparative History of Black Ideologies in the United States and South Africa* (New York: Oxford University Press, 1995). For more about Dube, see "John L. Dube: A Biographical Sketch," Oberlin College, http://www.oberlin.edu/external/EOG/Dube/Dube.htm.
22. Thompson, *History*, 204–20.

a language that became the means of communication among opponents of white supremacy. Until apartheid laws ended mission schooling, more and more Africans managed to become educated. Some of these African leaders adapted to their circumstances strategies being used by people elsewhere. The struggles under way for equal rights in the United States and British India provided one set of models. Christian teachings also became powerful forces in the long struggles for unity and equal rights.

## Conclusion

Even this selective overview must make clear that the notion of unchanging African identities is a myth. Continuity is an important theme in African history, but so too is change, and never more than in the nineteenth and twentieth centuries. Parts of Africa in the 1800s saw the emergence of major new political units accompanied by changes in ethnic identities. Some of these new states were destroyed by the advancing European colonial frontier (notably in French West Africa). The colonial era ushered in new political frontiers, along with expanding economies, new technology, and great new cultural institutions. In Algeria, Kenya, and much of southern Africa, the power and privileges of white settlers both retarded and promoted African unity. Elsewhere settlers were not a significant factor. Overall, African responses to colonial rule varied. Some sought to shield themselves from foreign influences, while others embraced the new possibilities to improve their lives individually, expand their identity horizons, and regain control over their lives.

# 6. Is Islam More Authentically African Than Christianity?

The Mohammedan Negro is a much better Mohammedan than the Christian Negro is a Christian, because the Muslim Negro, as a learner, is a disciple, not an imitator.[1]

—*Edward Wilmot Blyden, Afro-Caribbean educator and Christian minister, 1876*

When [the Negro] is bragging about being a Christian, he's bragging that he's a white man, . . . the religion of Islam [is] designed to undo the type of brainwashing that we have had to undergo for four hundred years at the hands of the white man.[2]

—*Malcolm X, Black Muslim leader, 1962*

In essays first published in 1875 and 1876, Edward Wilmot Blyden (1832–1912) argued that Islam was a religion better suited to Africans than the Western versions of Christianity then entering sub-Saharan Africa. Blyden came to this conclusion by a curious and personal path. He was born in the Virgin Islands in the West Indies to free people of pure African heritage, who traced their roots to the Igbo people in what is now southeastern Nigeria. Refused admission to a seminary in the United States and fearing enslavement if he stayed there, he sailed from Baltimore at the age of eighteen to the African American colony of Liberia in West Africa, where he completed secondary school, was ordained a Presbyterian minister, and took over as principal of his former school. Blyden had a passion for learning languages. He mastered Spanish as a boy living in Venezuela and taught himself Italian and French along with Latin and classical Greek. In the 1860s, he accepted a position as professor of classical languages in Liberia College (a small but intellectually ambitious institution of higher learning), became Liberia's secretary of state, and traveled to Egypt, Lebanon, and Syria to learn Arabic.[3]

A learned man and a keen observer of Africa, Blyden's views have long commanded respectful consideration. His conclusions about the aptness of Islam for black Africans were based on his personal explorations in West Africa in 1872 and 1873, during which Blyden concluded that Islam was superior to West African

---

1. Edward W. Blyden, *Christianity, Islam and the Negro Race*, 2nd ed. (London: W. B. Wittingham, 1888), 44.

2. Malcolm X, "Black Man's History," ed. Imam Benjamin Karim, http://www.malcolm-x.org.

3. Hollis R. Lynch, *Edward Wilmot Blyden, Pan-Negro Patriot, 1832–1912* (London: Oxford University Press, 1967); Barbara Celarent, review of 1994 reprint of *Christianity, Islam and the Negro Race, American Journal of Sociology* 120.4 (January 2015): 1285–93.

Edward Wilmot Blyden, 1904. Source: Internet
Archive, Public Domain.

traditional religions (which he called "Paganism," a designation he respectfully capitalized). On his explorations, he observed Muslims being more devout and subdued than non-Muslims and presenting a loftier moral atmosphere in contrast to their non-Muslim neighbors' noisy dancing and other amusements. In a later essay he added abstinence from alcohol to the list of Muslim virtues.

Even though Blyden considered Christianity to be superior to Islam in principle, he judged that the Christianity of African Americans was inferior in practice to West African Islam. West Africans, he argued, had converted to Islam "at home in a state of freedom and independence." Inspired by the preaching and teaching of North African Arabs and local Muslim traders, they had embraced Islam "from choice and conviction." But West Africans had also created a satisfying new version of Islam, rather than being Arabized and totally abandoning their earlier beliefs and customs. In Blyden's words, this blending was "not, as is too generally supposed, by a degrading compromise with Pagan superstitions, but by shaping many of its traditional customs to suit the milder and more conciliatory disposition of the Negro." He contrasted this peaceful adaptation of Islam in West Africa with the forced imposition of Christianity on Africans brought in earlier times to plantation economies in the Americas. Christianity, he wrote,

> came to the Negro as a slave, or at least as a subject race in a foreign land. Along with the Christian teaching, he and his children received lessons of their utter and permanent inferiority and subordination to their instructors, to whom they stood in the relation of chattels. Christianity took them fresh from the barbarism of the ages, and forced them to embrace its tenets.

In a second essay, published in 1876, Blyden drove home his point: "The Mohammedan Negro is a much better Mohammedan than the Christian Negro is a Christian, because the Muslim Negro, as a learner, is a disciple, not an imitator." Blyden's argument was situational and pragmatic: under existing circumstances Islam was a better fit for black people. A black African could be a devout disciple of Islam, but a black American could not readily escape being a poor imitator of a Christianity distorted by slavery and inequality.[4]

---

4. Blyden, *Christianity, Islam,* 6–7, 13–14, 44, 201.

The key historical question examined in this chapter is whether Blyden's argument is factually accurate not which religion is theologically superior. The issue is important to explore not just because of Blyden's influence, but also because a similar thesis about Islam being superior to Christianity for black people was put forward in the mid-twentieth century. The thoughts of Malcolm X (1925–1965) quoted at the beginning of the chapter are remarkably similar to Blyden's but seem to have arisen independently. The embrace of Islam or Christianity is a living issue among modern Africans as well as among modern African Americans.

Blyden could not have not foreseen the explosive growth in the number of African Christian adherents that was coming. As historians of Africa have observed, "To an impartial observer living in the year 1400 Africa would have seemed inevitably destined to join the world of Islam."[5] Four and a half centuries later, Blyden sensed the same religious destiny was unfolding. Yet in Africa today, Christians outnumber Muslims.[6] The number of Muslims hasn't shrunk; they have also increased rapidly. It is the number of Africans practicing traditional religions that has plummeted. It is possible to draw a line from west to east across Africa roughly dividing lands that have a Muslim majority from those that have a Christian majority. In the northernmost parts of Africa nearly 100 percent of the population is Muslim. In southernmost Africa most people are Christians.

Blyden may be excused for not foreseeing the rapid rise of African Christianity. His argument is flawed because he failed to see that Africans could make Christianity their own as successfully as he knew they had Africanized Islam in West Africa. This chapter argues that Blyden's thesis is mythical not only in its flawed vision but also in its factual errors about the histories of Christianity and Islam in Africa.

## African Christians before 1800

Early Christianity put down deep roots in Africa. Despite the Roman persecutions, North Africa became largely Christian during the third century, a time when only pockets of Christians could be found in Europe. The Christian thinkers of Alexandria put an indelible mark on the theology of their native Egypt and of the whole Eastern Church. Saint Augustine of Hippo (354–430), born in western North Africa, similarly shaped the theology of the Western Church for more than a millennium. Christianity also spread among Africans south of the Sahara well before it spread among Europeans north of the Alps. It became the court religion of the rulers of Aksum in

---

5. Roland Oliver and Anthony Atmore, *The African Middle Ages, 1400–1800* (New York: Cambridge University Press, 1981), 5.

6. The World Christian Database estimates that in 2015 48.4 percent of Africans were Christian and 41.7 percent were Muslim, http://www.worldchristiandatabase.org; Philip Jenkins, "How Africa Is Changing Faith Around the World," *Trust*, Pew Charitable Trust, July 5, 2016, http://magazine.pewtrusts.org.

the Horn of Africa by the mid-fourth century. A century later, Christianity was a force in the Nubian kingdoms south of Egypt, where it would flourish for the next eight centuries. These ancient Africans adapted Christianity as they adopted it, much as Blyden observed West Africans doing in the case of Islam. The early Egyptian Church was based on monasteries and a rigorous asceticism. In western North Africa ecclesiastical authority was in the hands of bishops like Saint Augustine, and a puritanical tradition known as Donatism flourished among Christian Berbers during the fourth and fifth centuries. Likewise, to the east, the distinctive cultural imprint of Ethiopians and Nubians remained evident in their religious art and churches.

Following the Arab conquests in the seventh century, however, most North Africans gradually abandoned Christianity in favor of Islam. For the most part this transformation was peaceful. Islam tolerated Christians and Jews as "people of the Book" (the Bible). Arab rulers accorded a measure of protection to Egyptian Christians, known as Copts, although authorities later banned building new churches or repairing the old ones. Nevertheless, social and economic circumstances led many other people to embrace Islam.

For some time the Christian communities in Nubia and Ethiopia remained unaffected by the rise of Islam because they lay outside the territories the Arabs had conquered. As Chapters 1 and 2 recounted, the Ethiopian crown undertook massive church construction under King Lalibela and others in the late 1100s and early 1200s, carving the buildings out of solid rock. Ethiopians had long enjoyed special protection from Muslim rulers because of their protection of early Arab Muslims, but, as Chapter 2 detailed, between 1527 and 1543 much of Ethiopia fell to the onslaught of a Somali Muslim known as Ahmed Gragn, who destroyed most churches except for the stone ones of Lalibela. A Portuguese expedition sent from India managed to kill Gragn and rescue the Ethiopian rulers. Meanwhile, Nubian Christian kingdoms had been extinguished. After a vigorous period of church building in eleventh century, the Nubians had fallen to nomadic Arab bands in the early fourteenth century. The new Muslim rulers forcibly suppressed the practice of Christianity and turned Nubian churches into mosques.[7]

As Chapter 2 also related, Portuguese aid to Ethiopia was part of a second wave of Christian expansion that was taking place in sub-Saharan Africa. It was a smaller wave in comparison to what was to come, but it was significant. Like the surviving community of Ethiopian Christians, the new converts in West and West-Central Africa represented distinctive indigenous Christianity, which was free from the associations with slavery that Blyden believed tainted Christianity in the Americas.

---

7. W. H. C. Frend, "The Christian Period in Mediterranean Africa, *c.* AD 200 to 700," in *Cambridge History of Africa*, vol. 2, *From c. 500 BC to AD 1050*, ed. J. D. Fage (Cambridge: Cambridge University Press, 1978), 410–89; Peter Garlake, *Early Art and Architecture of Africa* (Oxford: Oxford University Press, 2002), 66–71, 88–95.

This second wave of Christian expansion also provides individual examples of why Africans chose to convert—and sometimes of why they abandoned their new faiths. The modern idea of a "separation of church and state" made no sense to African rulers in earlier times. To be powerful and to secure the well-being of their kingdoms, rulers believed they needed to obtain the cooperation and support of supernatural forces through proper prayers and sacrifices. To a large degree Portuguese Christian monarchs thought the same way. The voyages they sponsored along the coast of Africa from the fifteenth century onward had a combination of religious, economic, and political motives. In part they were continuing the crusading tradition that had expelled the Muslim conquerors of their Iberian homeland. Failing to find any Christian princes in West Africa, the Portuguese sought to persuade African rulers to become Christians and thereby become potential allies against the Muslim dominions in North Africa. Most likely, African rulers would have assumed that the Portuguese's powerful firearms, valuable trade goods, and splendid ships were in some way connected to the supernatural force of their faith. The Portuguese efforts to secure African allies were not disappointed.

One prospective ally the Portuguese found was the *oba* (king) of Benin, who ruled a powerful state above the Niger Delta. Curious about the strange visitors who came to him from the sea in 1486, the *oba* sent an ambassador back to Portugal, where he was feted and shown the best features of that Christian kingdom. The ambassador returned with rich gifts for the *oba*, along with missionaries to teach about Catholicism and traders to organize Benin's profitable trade in pepper. In 1514 another *oba* of Benin sent a new delegation to Portugal to discuss trade, conversion, and the sale of firearms. When new missionaries arrived in Benin, the king took them to a battlefront where they presumably were directed to use their spiritual powers to secure victory over the enemy. The outcome was satisfactory enough that in 1516 the *oba* directed his sons and important noblemen to become Christians and a church to be built in his capital city. Many of the records from this era were lost in the earthquake that destroyed Lisbon in 1755, so it is not until 1538 that we can pick up the story. Three missionaries who arrived in Benin that year met with the new *oba*, who had been baptized as a child and had learned to speak Portuguese. He made it clear that he had no interest in further discussion of religion. Although the Christian experiment failed in Benin, it succeeded in the smaller, neighboring kingdom of Warri, whose rulers remained Christian until the 1800s.

While the rulers of Benin were trying out Catholic Christianity, a similar experiment was under way in the kingdom of Kongo south of the Equator that would be longer lasting. The parallels are remarkably close: an African embassy to Lisbon, the dispatch of missionaries whose powers were tested in an ongoing war, and the political elite's acceptance of baptism (in 1491). What is different is that the new faith continued, despite some disagreements over the unceremonious destruction of pre-Christian religious objects and the missionaries' condemnation of plural marriage. When the first Christian king of Kongo died, the resulting succession contest was between the Catholic party and a traditionalist party. With some Portuguese support the Catholic party won.

The new king, Afonso (r. 1506–1543), set out to consolidate his power by strengthening the position of the Christians and by Africanizing the new religion. He sent a son named Henrique to Portugal to be trained as head of Kongo's Catholic diocese. Pope Leo X issued special exemptions so Henrique could be ordained a priest and consecrated as a bishop. In 1521 Bishop Henrique and four newly ordained Kongo priests returned to their African homeland. The Catholic experiment in Kongo survived, despite new succession disputes, but the kingdom would be weakened by warfare between the Portuguese and Dutch and with rival African kingdoms. For a time the inland kingdom of Ndongo also adopted the Catholic faith.

As had earlier been the case in northeastern Africa, the adoption of Christianity by the rulers of Benin and Kongo was voluntary and peaceful, even though military considerations played a role. However, when the Portuguese encountered Muslim states, their response could be violent. In 1415 the Portuguese had attacked Morocco, continuing their long crusades to drive medieval Muslim conquerors out of their homeland. Participating in that expedition was the young Prince Henry, later known as "the Navigator" for his sponsorship of voyages down the Atlantic coast of Africa. After passing into the Indian Ocean in 1497, several Portuguese fleets attacked Muslim city-states along Africa's eastern shores, known as the Swahili Coast.[8] Although these attacks had a religious component, they were not intended to foster conversion, for the Portuguese knew from long experience that few Muslims would convert. As the next section narrates, the spread of Islam in Africa also had peaceful as well as militant components.

The third wave of Christian expansion in Africa, which began in the nineteenth century, was led by Protestants and was linked to the anti-slavery movement. As Chapter 4 mentioned, the British had resettled tens of thousands Africans rescued from the Atlantic slave trade in Sierra Leone, a colony originally founded for free blacks from Britain, North American colonies, and Jamaica. Missionaries were drawn there to tend to the physical, spiritual, and educational needs of these liberated Africans. To the south of Sierra Leone another new Christian community was developing in Liberia, a colony founded by the American Colonization Society in 1821 as a refuge for free blacks from the United States. Although some settlers, like Blyden, hoped Christianity would expand from Liberia to other parts of West Africa, in fact, as Chapter 5 mentioned, the more important push came from Yoruba-speaking Christians returning to their homeland (in what is now Nigeria) both from Brazil and Cuba, and, in greatest numbers, from Sierra Leone. It was led by Bishop Samuel Ajayi Crowther (1809–1891), himself rescued as a child from a captured slave vessel. At first, most Yoruba residents were more interested in their traditional religion or in Islam than in

---

8. For more detail see David Northrup, *Africa's Discovery of Europe, 1450–1850*, 3rd ed. (New York: Oxford University Press, 2014), 25–53.

the new Christian message. Gradually, however, the Christian community won over new adherents. Meanwhile, another Christian front had been opened in southern Africa. Inspired by the idea of bringing Christianity to Africa and stopping the Indian Ocean slave trade, a Scottish medical doctor named David Livingstone (1813–1873) had gone as a missionary to southern Africa in 1841. He soon embarked on extensive journeys through southeastern and eastern Africa, writing lengthy descriptions of slave trading, geography, biology, and Christian possibilities. Livingstone seldom stayed in any one place long enough to start a congregation, but his books were best sellers and inspired followers from different branches of Western Christianity. In 1910 there were 10,000 foreign evangelizers in Africa, and by then the Catholics among them had become more numerous than the Protestants. The new wave of Christian expansion was cresting, and it would make a big splash.[9]

## The Spread of Islam in East and West Africa

After the Arab conquests across North Africa in the seventh and eighth centuries, the spread of Islam to the south was largely the work of pious traders. As was seen in Chapter 3, the Moroccan traveler Ibn Battuta wrote vivid descriptions of the commercial, cultural, and religious life of both the Swahili Coast and the Western Sudan in the 1300s. Arab and Persian Muslims had been trading for some time with the African people along coast of the Indian Ocean they called the Swahili ("shores" in Arabic). Probably most of these foreign traders returned home at the end of the trading season, but some became permanent residents, marrying African wives and raising families that in a few generations became African in appearance if not in culture. In his account of his visit to the Swahili Coast in 1331, Ibn Battuta noted the dark complexions of rulers and described without criticism their customs and their practice of Islam. At the city of Mogadishu the Muslim scholar was warmly welcomed and greeted by the sultan in Arabic, though the ruler's mother tongue was Somali.

Ibn Battuta was similarly lavish in his praise of piety of the Muslim inhabitants of Mali, which he visited in 1351–1352. But he was also more critical of them, perhaps because he found more to criticize or perhaps, being twenty years older, he had become less tolerant—or both. He famously drew up a balance sheet of the Malians' good and bad qualities. On the positive side, he noted that the land was peaceful and the people were honest and wore clean white garments when they went to prayers in the mosque. Ibn Battuta also praised Mali's Muslims for faithfully observing the Muslim prayer schedule, for disciplining their children to make them observe religious

---

9. Adrian Hastings, *The Church in Africa, 1450–1950* (Oxford: Clarendon Press, 1994), 242–393; J. D. Y. Peel, *Religious Encounter and the Making of the Yoruba* (Bloomington: Indiana University Press, 2000), 152–277.

duties, and even for chaining up their sons until they completed learning passages from the Qur'an by heart. His greatest disapproval was directed at the nakedness of girls and adult female servants and slaves in the sultan of Mali's palace. He also criticized Malians for continuing the pre-Islamic custom of sprinkling dust on their heads when greeting the sultan and for eating meat from animals that Muslims considered "unclean" or that had not been butchered according the Muslim laws. A more tolerant observation might be that the Malians had adopted the main beliefs and practices of Islam but had not in the process abandoned traditional customs they thought acceptable, even if a puritanical old North African might object to them.[10] As Blyden had argued, Islamic societies in West Africa were not carbon copies of those in Arab lands.

Ibn Battuta did not visit the kingdom of Kanem-Bornu in the Central Sudan, where the process of Islamization had moved more rapidly than in the Western Sudan. Trading connections were an obvious reason why a ruler of the older kingdom of Kanem chose to become a Muslim around 1070. By the mid-thirteenth century, the majority of the inhabitants of Kanem may have been Muslims, and the ruler at that time was the first to make the pilgrimage to Mecca. Shortly thereafter, another ruler, likely enjoying the support of a Muslim majority, attacked and destroyed the central shrine of the traditional religion. Not surprisingly this outraged the non-Muslim population, producing conflicts that led the rulers to move their capital to Bornu, west of Lake Chad. Bornu became a center of Islamic scholarship and proselytization. From Bornu, Islam spread west to the Hausa states in the fourteenth century.[11]

One of the best-known examples of tolerance and cooperation between Muslim traders and non-Muslim Africans are the Juula. The Juula's ancestors had migrated south from the Mali Empire, perhaps in the 1200s, to trade for gold and other things. Although living outside the Muslim dominions, the Juula preserved a strong devotion to Islam, while also accommodating themselves to the non-Muslim majority around them. Beyond setting good examples of Islamic life, the Juula did not attempt to spread their faith, because aggressive preaching against "pagan" customs would have upset their non-Muslim trading partners. At the same time, the Juula were being changed by living outside the Muslim-ruled zone. Most significantly, Juula men often chose wives from within their host community. The wives were required to become Muslims, but their children grew up familiar with their mother's language and non-Islamic customs, a familiarity that was naturally useful in trading with their hosts. People in the host community often bought leather pouches from the Juula containing written texts from the Qur'an, which they wore as talismans, believing they had powers superior to local charms. Thus, the Juula used Islam as a way of preserving a distinct identity within these host communities, but they did not attempt to spread

---

10. Said Hamdun and Noël King, *Ibn Battuta in Black Africa*, rev. ed. (Princeton, NJ: Markus Wiener, 1994), 15–25, 58–59.

11. Timothy Insoll, *The Archaeology of Islam in Sub-Saharan Africa* (Cambridge: Cambridge University Press, 2003), 273–78, 289–93.

their religion, except in the case of people (including wives) who wished to become Muslims.[12]

Blyden described how traders such as the Juula spread Islam peacefully and benevolently in sub-Saharan Africa, but other observers reported that Islamic expansion could be violent as well. Ibn Battuta mentioned without comment that the sultan of the city-state of Kilwa at the southern end of the Swahili Coast was much devoted to holy war (jihad) against the non-Muslim Africans on the mainland, whom the Arabs called Zanji. His account of what was done with the goods and people obtained during these raids shows an admixture of piety and plunder. The sultan of Kilwa put aside a fifth of the plundered goods for good works in accordance with Islamic teaching, reserving a share for gifts to *sharifs*, that is, the descendants of the Prophet Muhammad, who might come visiting from Iraq, Saudi Arabia, or elsewhere. Another passage mentioned that the sultan's generosity also included "fine slaves," presumably captives from the mainland. As we have already seen, slavery was common in West Africa both in Muslim and non-Muslim lands. Ibn Battuta wrote matter-of-factly about slaves, including his own concubines and servants, both female and male. The Moroccan traveler also mentioned the existence of slave markets.[13]

Ibn Battuta's passing mention of slave markets opens a door that Blyden left closed. Slaves were not just bought for domestic use but were also sold away. The size of the domestic market is very hard to calculate, but rough estimates have been made of the magnitude of the slave trades across the Sahara and into the Indian Ocean. One respected study estimates that Muslims traded a total of over three million black Africans across the Sahara during the eleventh through fourteenth centuries. In the same period there was also a smaller Islamic slave trade from eastern Africa. The export trade in slaves from sub-Saharan Africa into the Muslim world generally grew larger during the five centuries after 1400. In Blyden's day about eighteen thousand enslaved men, women, and children a year embarked on the perilous forced march across the desert. Blyden was aware of the fact that Muslims enslaved non-Muslims, but he made the surprising claim that, in the *Bilad as-Sudan* (the land of the blacks), "the slave who embraces Islam became free." Although devout slave owners, both Muslim and Christian, sometimes did emancipate slaves, among Muslim West Africans the practice of freeing slaves who became Muslims seems to have been no more common in the 1800s than freeing slaves who became Christians was in the Americas.[14]

---

12. Ivor Wilks, "The Juula and the Expansion of Islam into the Forest," in *The History of Islam in Africa*, ed. Nehemia Levtzion and Randall Pouwels (Athens: Ohio University Press, 2000), 93–112; David Robinson, *Muslim Societies in African History* (Cambridge: Cambridge University Press, 2004), 55–58.

13. Hamdun and King, *Ibn Battuta*, 22–25, 47, 52, 56, 58, 61–62, 68–70.

14. Ralph A. Austen, "The Trans-Saharan Slave Trade: A Tentative Census," in *The Uncommon Market: Essays in the Economic History of the Atlantic Slave Trade*, ed. Henry A. Gemery and Jan S. Hogendorn (New York: Academic Press, 1979), tables 2.8 and 2.9; Blyden, *Christianity*, 202. For

Besides being wrong about slave emancipation in West Africa, Blyden also errs in asserting that Islam generally spread peacefully. Across the vast region below the Sahara known as the Sudan, three major Islamic states were created in the nineteenth century, all under the banner of jihad and all tied to massive increases in slavery and slave trading. Blyden may not have been aware of what was taking place in the distant Eastern (or Nilotic) Sudan, but it is difficult to imagine that events in West Africa could have escaped his attention.

Chronologically the earliest Muslim conquest state was the Sokoto Caliphate, founded by Usuman dan Fodio (1754–1817) in the Central Sudan. As was explained in Chapter 4, the Sokoto Caliphate was vast in size and densely populated. The jihadists took very large numbers of people prisoner, most of whom were enslaved on the grounds that they were unbelievers (*kafiri*) or that they were insufficiently orthodox in their practice of Islam to be considered true Muslims. Insight into these events comes from the letters that an official named al-Kanemi (1776–1837) of the state of Bornu wrote in protest to Muhammad Bello (r. 1817–1837), the son and successor of Usuman dan Fodio. As the jihadist armies were overrunning Bornu, whose rulers, this chapter showed earlier, had been Muslim for a many centuries, al-Kanemi penned these calm and reasoned words:

> Tell us therefore why you are fighting us and enslaving our free people. If you say that you have done this to us because of our paganism, then I say to you we are innocent of paganism. . . . If praying and giving alms, knowledge of God, fasting in Ramadan and the building of mosques is paganism, what is Islam? These buildings in which you have performed the Friday prayer, are they churches or synagogues or fire temples? If they were other than Muslim places of worship, then you would not pray in them when you capture them. Is this not a contradiction?

Al-Kanemi conceded that individuals might have fallen short of perfection in their practice of Islam, but denied that such human lapses justified launching a jihad against them. In his reply, Bello refused to back down but referred only to rumors of pagan practices. In the end al-Kanemi's armies were able to drive the jihadists out of Bornu. Perhaps in this case the politics of jihadists were stronger than their theology.[15] Unfortunately, there was no learned man like al-Kanemi to defend the illiterate non-Muslims who were taken captive by the jihadists. Their fate was, however, described

---

the perils of the trans-Saharan slave trade in the 1800s see David Northrup, "Overseas Movements of Slaves and Indentured Workers," in *The Cambridge World History of Slavery*, vol. 4, *AD 1804–AD 2016*, ed. David Eltis, Stanley L. Engerman, Seymour Drescher, and David Richardson (Cambridge: Cambridge University Press, 2017).

15. For Usuman dan Fodio's call for jihad, Al-Kanemi's rebuttal, and M. Bello's reply see Thomas, Hodgkin, ed., *Nigerian Perspectives: An Historical Anthology*, 2nd ed. (Oxford: Oxford University Press, 1975), 247–49, 261–67.

at mid-century by German explorer Heinrich Barth, the first European to visit the caliphate. His description of the quasi-independent eastern frontier province of Adamawa is all the more chilling because Barth lists the facts without indulging in moral outrage:

> Slavery exists on an immense scale in this country; there are many private individuals who have more than a thousand slaves . . . the governor of the whole province [M. Lowel] has all his slaves settled in *rumde* or slave villages, where they cultivate corn [grain] for his use or profit. . . . I have been assured also that Muhammad Lowel receives every year, besides horses and cattle, about five thousand slaves, though this seems a large number.[16]

Barth noted that some of the governor of Adamawa's lieutenants forced already conquered villagers to supply them with food so they were able to employ their slaves in raiding for more slaves. By these means, more people were enslaved than could be employed locally. There is no firsthand evidence from those sent across the Sahara, but some details survive from the few dozen fortunate to be rescued from the Atlantic slave trade and resettled in Sierra Leone. For example, a man named Sisi, who was known in Sierra Leone as John Cole, related that he had been taken in war by the Fulani, "who had come from afar on horses, and had conquered many countries, spreading terror before them on account of their poisoned weapons, by the mere touch of which they killed their enemies." Despite the thousands sold away, historian Paul Lovejoy estimates that half of the Sokoto Caliphate's population in the 1850s may have been slaves. After the emancipation of slaves in the United States in 1865, Sokoto may have had the largest slave population of any state in the world.[17]

Blyden lacked firsthand knowledge of the situation in Sokoto, but he had traveled in the Western Sudan where Umar Tall (1797–1864) had created a large state on the model of Sokoto. Umar's passion for Islam had driven him to make the pilgrimage to Mecca three times in 1828–1830, and on his return journey he spent six years in the Sokoto Caliphate, partly as the guest of Muhammad Bello. While there, al-Hajj Umar became captivated with the idea of launching a similar jihad to rid his homeland of unbelievers. Between 1855 and 1861 his forces seized the main centers of the Bambara kingdoms along the upper Niger, for which he was celebrated by other West African Muslim leaders. However, when Umar attacked the Muslim state of Masina, his initial success was reversed (much as happened in Bornu) and he was killed. As in Sokoto, the wars of Umar and his successor reduced large populations to slavery. Lovejoy estimates that slaves outnumbered free persons in many parts of Umar's empire and that in both empires the numbers of slaves did not diminish in

---

16. Heinrich Barth in Hodgkin, *Nigerian Perspectives*, 330–31.
17. Sisi's account is in Koelle, *Polyglotta Africana* (London: Church Missionary House, 1854), 12; Paul E. Lovejoy, *Transformations in Slavery: A History of Slavery in Africa*, 2nd ed. (Cambridge: Cambridge University Press, 2000), 201–8.

This Zanzibar-based Muslim trader, known as Tippu Tip (ca. 1837–1905), helped spread Islam inland within his vast trading empire. Of Swahili, Arab, and East African descent, he wrote an autobiography in Swahili. Source: Wikimedia Commons. Public domain.

the decades after the conquests, as Blyden's account of manumission after conversion to Islam would have suggested. The reason is likely the same in West Africa as it was in the Americas: the slaves were the principal labor force on profitable plantations and thus too valuable to set free.[18]

In the Eastern Sudan (south of Egypt) holy war and enslavement occurred in reverse order. Under Ottoman rule in Egypt in the 1800s, the age-old trade in slaves from the south expanded to unprecedented proportions. As Lovejoy writes, "By 1838, an estimated 10,000 to 12,000 slaves were arriving in Egypt each year" from black "pagan" lands.[19] Those sold away were only a part of the destruction, as the British explorer Samuel Baker reported of the early 1860s. A prospective Arab slave trader borrowed enough money to hire boats, sign up one hundred to three hundred men, and buy large quantities of guns and ammunition. When the slaving expedition reached the south, it formed an alliance with a local African chief who had a score to settle with a neighbor. The expedition surrounded the neighboring village, set it afire, shot the men, and seized the fleeing women and children, along with cattle herds and other items of value. Baker reported that dividing the spoils of a raid "generally leads to a quarrel with the negro ally, who in his turn is murdered and plundered by the trader—his women and children naturally becoming slaves." The cattle were exchanged for ivory and the enslaved women and children were tied together and transported down the Nile to the slave markets further north, where they were sold and the money used to pay off the financiers and hired help. Accounts such as Baker's helped spur British intervention to stop the Nile slave trade. However, a British presence in Sudan provoked a Muslim named Muhammad Ahmed to holy rebellion. In 1881, after Muhammad Ahmed proclaimed himself the Mahdi (the savior foretold in Muslim tradition), his followers drove out the British, the Ottoman Turks, and the Egyptians. The Mahdi's revolt was not against the enslavement of black pagans but against the presence of outsiders, the Ottomans as much as their agents, the British. Therefore, slavery continued.[20]

---

18. David Robinson, "Revolutions in the Western Sudan," in Levtzion and Pouwels, *Islam in Africa*, 140–43; Lovejoy, *Transformations*, 194–99, 220–24.

19. Lovejoy, *Transformations*, 154.

20. Baker's account is in Robert O. Collins, ed., *African History: Text and Readings* (New York; Random House, 1971), 312–17. Paul E. Lovejoy and Jan S. Hogendorn, *Slow Death for Slavery: The Course of Abolition in Northern Nigeria, 1897–1936* (Cambridge: Cambridge University Press, 1993), 1; Jay Spalding, "Precolonial Islam in the Eastern Sudan," in Levtzion and Pouwels, *Islam in Africa*, 125–27.

The 1800s were also a time of commercial and religious expansion inland in East Africa from the large island of Zanzibar, to which the sultan of Oman had moved his capital in 1840 from Arabia. A trader known as Tippu Tip (1837–1905), who was half African and half Arab, negotiated and fought his way inland from Zanzibar in his quest for ivory and slaves and then across the Great Lakes, building an empire in what became the eastern Congo. Tippu Tip and other Zanzibari traders introduced their Islamic faith to the populous inland kingdom of Buganda beginning in the 1840s, where they received a warm welcome from rulers interested in Islam's revelations and customs. At the royal court of Buganda, the king, some of his chiefs, and their student pages began learning and following Muslim customs as a new state religion, although some found the requirement of circumcision repugnant.

Islam's initial successes in East Africa, however, were eclipsed by the arrival of European Christian missionaries, explorers, and colonizers. On a visit to Buganda's capital in August 1875, the Anglo-American explorer Henry Morton Stanley (1841–1904) wrote admiring of King Mutesa's intelligence, military prowess, and intellectual curiosity. To Mutesa's delight, Stanley had selections from the Bible translated into the Swahili language, which many of the Ganda people had learned from Zanzibari traders. According to Stanley, Mutesa was impressed that his European visitors refused to deal in slaves, unlike the Muslims from the coast and from Sudan. As Anglican and Catholic missionaries began to gain support at the royal court, the stage was set for a major confrontation that would be triggered by political events. In 1890 Great Britain declared a protectorate over Zanzibar and four years later staked a similar claim to Buganda and neighboring states, which became known collectively as Uganda. Meanwhile, with British support Ganda Christians had defeated the Muslim party, whose followers retreated to the north of the kingdom. Rather than becoming an extension of the Islamic stronghold at the coast and to the north, Uganda went on to become a Christian stronghold.[21]

## Islam and Colonial Rule

The period of European colonial rule witnessed the greatest expansion of Christianity in sub-Saharan Africa that had even taken place. But those inclined to assume that Christianity's expansion was due to an active European policy of spreading the Gospel might be surprised to learn that Islam also saw its greatest period of growth during that same period. Aside from colonies of Belgium and Portugal, where policies favored Catholicism, colonial policy in Africa was officially neutral in matters of religion. In practice, most colonial administrators viewed religion in Africa much as Blyden had: Islam was better suited to African societies than Western Christianity.

---

21. Robinson, *Muslim Societies*, 153–68; David. C. Sperling and Jose H. Kagabo, "The Coastal Hinterland and the Interior of East Africa," in Levtzion and Pouwels, *Islam in Africa*, 273–97; Henry M. Stanley, *Through the Dark Continent* (New York: Dover Publications, 1988), 1: 233–55.

Therefore, most administrators did not support Christian evangelization, whether because, in the French case, they were anticlerical or because they doubted black Africans were capable of becoming practicing Christians. As a practical matter, French and British officials in Muslim areas catered to the desires of Muslim leaders, whose support they needed. Thus, while colonial policies undoubtedly shaped the context of this transformative period, one must look deeper into what was happening to discover the root causes for this growth of Islam and Christianity.

Let us begin with the *Dar al-Islam*, the lands where Islam dominated. As the chapter has already described, Islam first became dominant in North Africa, and by the eleventh century had spread down the Swahili Coast of eastern Africa and across the Sahara into northern West Africa. In the 1800s, the commercial penetration of East Africa from Zanzibar and the reformist revolutions in the Western and Central Sudan had brought millions of Africans into the Islamic fold whether by example or through enslavement. The twentieth-century expansion of Islam was largely within these zones where the religion already had a strong presence. In North Africa the growth of Islam was largely due to population increase. In the Sudanic zone, Muslim expansion came from population growth as well as from large numbers of new converts. Along the Swahili Coast, Islam remained a dominant force, but its spread inland was countered by the expanding Christian frontier in inland East Africa and the Congo. The gains Islam had made among the Yoruba in the 1800s were offset by an expanding Christian presence. Finally, a growing Muslim presence in coastal Atlantic cities where Muslim merchants were active was partly balanced by an African Christian migration into cities in the Sudanic belt and North Africa.

European colonial policies were quite favorable to Muslims in lands where their religion was already well established. Echoing Blyden's views on the suitability of Islam for Africans, one official with wide experience wrote in 1922, "To the British official or trader in West Africa, there is little doubt that the Mohammedan Negro . . . is a more likeable, attractive personality than the Christian Negro." Another British official opined that Islam was "eminently suited to the native," spreading trade, civilization, and "a much more decent life." Such admiration for African Muslims was genuine enough, though it must be considered in the context of the low esteem in which many Europeans held Africans. However, as was seen in the previous chapter, European administrators also had good reasons to be apprehensive about Muslim power and cohesion. Even after defeating and dismantling the empires of Samori and al-Hajj Umar's son in the Western Sudan, the French still needed to cultivate the support of powerful Muslim leaders, both to carry out colonial directives and to check rebellions, such as the one in Algeria in 1871. For their part, the British had not dismantled the Sokoto Caliphate after a quick conquest, preserving its institutions in a classic example of how indirect rule could be effective and cost-efficient.[22]

---

22. Michael Crowder, *West Africa under Colonial Rule* (London: Hutchinson, 1968), 69–143, quotations 359.

For such cooperation with Muslim leaders to work, colonial authorities had to avoid offending Muslim sensibilities. To this end, the British banned Christian missionary activity in northern Nigeria and in their Somali colony. Both France and Britain offered the sons of the Islamic elite access to government schools that were carefully supervised to exclude topics that might give offense. In Zanzibar the British established a "dual mandate," recognizing the autonomy of the Arab sultan in return for his acceptance of a British protectorate over his lands. The French negotiated an analogous arrangement with the sultan of Morocco. In both territories, however, actual administration came to resemble colonial rule elsewhere. Nevertheless, despite the eroding of Islamic authority over time in many places, such collaborative relations worked fairly well for both sides. Even in the once rebellious Anglo-Egyptian Sudan, the Muslim elite became loyal supporters of the colonial rulers. In return Muslim leaders gained respect and power, and limited the inroads of Western education and culture among the masses. As seen in Chapter 5, Muslims (and non-Muslims) in French West Africa and Nigeria also benefited from economic opportunities brought by the construction of railroads to carry goods to the Atlantic.[23]

In the early years of colonial rule when the support of Islamic societies was uncertain, colonial authorities dragged their feet in keeping the pledge they'd made at the Brussels Conference of 1889–1890 to abolish the institution of slavery. A presence in many African societies, including Christian Ethiopia, slavery's largest concentrations were in Muslim North Africa, in the empires of the Western and Central Sudan, and in the sultan of Oman's former empire in East Africa and the eastern Congo. The slow process of emancipation is easiest to trace in the legal record, although it is important to keep in mind that passing laws making slavery illegal in colonies did not mean that it suddenly ceased to exist. Local colonial officials feared moving too quickly against an economically and socially important institution still sanctioned by Islam. Thus, in the expanded colony Sierra Leone that incorporated many Muslims, the legal status of slavery was abolished in 1896 (meaning no owner could to sue to recover possession of runaway slave, for example), but the institution of slavery became illegal only in 1928. In Zanzibar a British decree abolishing slavery in 1897 exempted the large number of concubines and required former slaves to present themselves to often-reluctant Muslim authorities in order to register as free persons. Out of an estimated 120,000 slaves only 10,000 had completed the emancipation process by 1909, when a new decree gave slave owners more incentives to comply. Similarly, actual emancipation advanced slowly in northern Nigeria, despite a British decree in 1900 that ostensibly freed the million or more slaves there. Individual emancipations by courts and other means occurred over the next two decades but not until 1936 was there a blanket ordinance against slavery, and even then some royal slaves and concubines

---

23. Ludwien Kapteijns, "Ethiopia and the Horn of Africa," in Levtzion and Pouwels, *Islam in Africa*, 258; Ira Lapidus, *A History of Islamic Societies*, 2nd ed. (Cambridge: Cambridge University Press, 2002), 606–12, 772–74.

were exempt. In a situation where slavery was tolerated but not legal, many slaves fled, knowing that their masters could not easily re-enslave them.[24]

Because British and French administrations in the Western and Central Sudan recognized Islamic law and Muslim authorities, adherents of traditional religions in these locales became convinced that adopting Muslim practices and clothing might be to their advantage. Urbanization also favored the world religions. People who moved to a town often turned to the universalism of Islam or Christianity because the religious rituals and practices of their native villages seemed unable to provide them with spiritual security in the new location. Muslims in the city of Ibadan in southwestern Nigeria, for example, rose from 35 percent to 60 percent of the population between 1913 and 1952, while the number of Christians went from 1 percent to 32 percent. As Blyden had recognized, Africans often found Islam more familiar and less disruptive than Christianity, at least initially. New converts' knowledge and understanding of Islam or Christianity could be quite superficial at the outset but over time grew deeper.[25]

Slaves generally adopted their masters' religion soon after entering Islamic societies (or even while on the journey across the Sahara), and it appears that most of those who were liberated by courts, manumission, or decree continued to adhere to that religion. Islam served as a refuge from the changes going on around them. Just as slaves emancipated in the Americas generally retained an adherence to Christianity, slaves of a Muslim master were unlikely to blame their status on their owner's religion. Indeed as historians have noted, both enslavement and the "freeing of slaves was built into Islamic understanding."[26] Freed black slaves in North Africa largely remained in the same communities and the large numbers of freed female slaves in sub-Saharan Africa generally did so as well, since they were in no position to flee even when their homeland was only a few days travel away.

Because literacy rates were lower in Muslim areas, documented examples of the spread of Islam are fewer than are records of Christian conversion. It is not surprising that one of the best-known expansions in the twentieth century concerns a Sufi brotherhood, since these religious communities had long been common in sub-Saharan Africa. Like most Muslims in Africa, the Murid Sufi Muslims of Senegal were Sunni Muslims, but they followed a particular tradition of special practices that in some ways resembles the religious confraternities joined by pious Catholic lay people. The Murids' founder was Amadu Bamba Mbacke (ca. 1853–1927) who, although he

---

24. Lovejoy, *Transformations*, 273–74, 294; Lovejoy and Hogendorn, *Slow Death*, 30, 287–304; Michael Lofchie, *Zanzibar: Background to Revolution* (Princeton, NJ: Princeton University Press, 1965), 60–61.

25. William F. S. Miles, "Religious Pluralisms in Northern Nigeria," in Levtzion and Pouwels, *Islam in Africa*, 209–15; Crowder, *West Africa*, 361–63; J. Spencer Trimingham, *The Influence of Islam upon Africa* (New York: Praeger, 1968), 103–110, 137n3.

26. John Hunwick and Eve Troutt Powell, *The Africa Diaspora in the Mediterranean Lands of Islam* (Princeton, NJ: Markus Wiener, 2002), 165.

came from a politically important Muslim family in the Wolof kingdom, chose the pursuit of piety over power, a path that would put him in conflict with the French administration of Senegal. After exploring some other Sufi orders, he decided that the troubled times of Senegal in the late 1800s required a new approach.

Though Bamba urged his followers to flee the things of this world, the French suspected wrongly that he was another jihadist and exiled him. However, exile strengthened Bamba's conviction that he had a special role to play. Bamba's letters encouraged his followers to persist in the way of life he had taught, which was to avoid the colonial system and concentrate on cultivating peanuts and millet on large communal farms. A second exile convinced Bamba to assure the French that he had no objection to their rule so long as they permitted the Murids to practice their farming and praying. Like other Muslim leaders, he banned the establishment of Western schools near his people. The pact worked. The Murid order expanded greatly after Bamba's death in 1927, becoming dominant in the production of peanuts for export, which new railroads made profitable. By 1960 the Murid numbered some 400,000, one-eighth of Senegal's population.[27]

## Christianity and Colonial Rule

The rapid European colonization of Africa in the quarter century after 1885 had also facilitated the growth of Christian missionary activity. Early colonial statistics are notoriously unreliable, but in 1910 there were probably fewer than ten million Christians in Africa, well under a tenth of the population. By 2000 African Christians numbered something like 380 million, nearly 47 percent of the population. That was a phenomenal change. Since then the number of Christians has increased by another 200 million, but the percentage increase is only slightly higher than the rate of population growth.

Scholars have used the term "mass movements" to describe the rapid spread of Christianity in the early 1900s, although it can be difficult to identify the common factors behind these movements. As historian Adrian Hastings has pointed out, the rate of Christian conversion in Africa in these early years was well beyond the resources and expectations of the foreign missionaries. Hastings provides ample evidence that Africans were the primary agents behind the mass conversions. Most of these Africans had some contact with foreign missionaries from whom they gained a zeal for the Christian message and some basic education. Some were "catechists," Africans employed to teach catechism (a simple statement of Christian beliefs) and often other school subjects. Some became free agents, preaching on their own, at times with astonishing success. It is worth noting that Hastings' emphasis on the African role in

---

27. Robinson, *Muslim Societies*, 182–96, 742–43; Jean-Louis Triaud, "Islam in Africa under French Rule," in Levtzion and Pouwels, *History of Islam in Africa*, 169–82.

The preaching of William Wade Harris (ca. 1860–1929) in the 1910s inspired many West Africans to become Christians. Source: Wikimedia Commons, CC-Zero.

spreading Christianity bears a strong resemblance to Blyden's account of the role African traders played in the earlier spread of Islam in West Africa.

Some mass conversions to Christianity occurred within missionary-led denominations. For example, among the Ganda people of modern Uganda, as we saw earlier, both Christianity and Islam had taken root before colonial rule, and in the 1890s traditional chiefs had encouraged their people to join the Anglican and Roman Catholic missions. As Chapter 5 recounted, the rush to become Christian among the Kikuyu of Kenya a few decades later led to the rapid growth of mission denominations as well as of independent African churches and schools. Among the Igbo people of southeastern Nigeria in the early 1900s, a mass movement occurred within the Roman Catholic community, which in twelve years jumped from 5,000 to 74,000 members, along with a growth in the number of Catholic churches and schools from 24 to 355. Here the key instrument was an army of 550 mission-trained Igbo catechists. Rejecting the idea that a few Irish clergy could have brought about this "miracle," Hastings insists that the Igbo "converted themselves." Methodist and Anglican Christianity spread nearly as fast among the Igbo in these years, as was also the case in Southern Rhodesia, where, Hastings argues, "the pace was clearly being set by African demand rather than missionary hard work."[28]

If dedicated catechists were midwives of growth in the larger mission denominations, in some cases popular movements that started within such denominations grew into separate churches. William Wade Harris (ca. 1860–1929) was a native Liberian who had been imprisoned for his opposition to the rule of African American settlers there. While in prison, he had a vision of the Archangel Gabriel, who told him that he was to be a prophet. Drawing on his Methodist upbringing, Prophet Harris preached a fairly standard version of Protestant Christianity, except for his approval of polygamy. Within a few months in 1914 his preaching led an estimated 200,000 Africans in the neighboring colonies of Ivory Coast and the Gold Coast to abandon traditional religions in favor of a Christian vision. In response to the influenza pandemic of

28. Hastings, *Church in Africa*, quotations 451, 452.

1918 in Nigeria, some Yoruba Anglicans formed prayer societies to promote spiritual healing and gain protection from the disease. As the influenza epidemic waned, other groups prayed for protection against witchcraft, which was widely feared. These *Aladura* (Yoruba for "praying people") spread into non-Christian rural communities and became a major Christian force separate from the mission churches. In the Belgian Congo, Simon Kimbangu (1887–1951), originally a Baptist, began a prophetic healing mission that grew into a separate church. Initially Kimbangu had resisted the visions that came to him in dreams but accepted his prophetic destiny in 1921. During a few short months he attracted an immense following, including many from the Baptist community. His preaching and healing mission was cut short by Belgian authorities, who tried him for disturbing the public order and sentenced him to death. Although the king of Belgium commuted this harsh sentence, Kimbangu spent the rest of his life in prison. By keeping a low profile, Kimbangu's followers survived, and, after restrictions on their activities were eased, the movement again spread widely. Today the Church of Jesus Christ on Earth by His Envoy Simon Kimbangu has an estimated 5.5 million members and is a member of the World Council of Churches.[29]

Throughout southern Africa, where Protestant missions had found many African converts in the 1800s, African-led congregations and churches were also spreading rapidly. African-run churches that broke away from the Protestant missions there have been called "Ethiopian" churches, in reference to the ancient black African Christians mentioned in the New Testament. Scholars distinguish these theologically conservative "Ethiopian" churches from more radical "Zionist" churches, whose African leaders incorporated new prophetic visions and spiritual healing inspired by traditional African practices. "Zionist" churches achieved great success among Africans like the Zulu, who had resisted white-run mission churches.

In other instances African religious leaders founded congregations inspired by non-traditional Protestant churches in the United States. In southeastern Nigeria, for example, Africans who had read the teachings of the American prophet Joseph Smith (1805–1844), founder of the Church of Jesus Christ of Latter-day Saints (popularly known as the Mormons), formed their own Mormon congregations in the 1940s. At that time, Mormon leadership in the United States had no enthusiasm for African followers and clergy, so the importance of African initiatives is especially striking.[30]

The challenge of African-led Christian movements in sub-Saharan Africa led large missionary churches to consider Africanizing their denominations by ordaining African clergy and adding African cultural usages in their religious services, but changes came slowly. By the 1950s, both Catholic and Protestant missions already depended heavily on African catechists to preach, conduct religious services, and teach in schools,

---

29. Hastings, *Church in Africa*, 443–68; Richard Gray, "Christianity," in *The Cambridge History of Africa*, vol. 7, *From 1905 to 1940*, ed. A. D. Roberts (Cambridge University Press, 1986), 140–90.

30. D. Dmitri Hurlbut, *Nigerian Converts, Mormon Missionaries, and the Priesthood Revelation: Mormonism in Nigeria, 1946–1978* (Boston: Boston University African Studies Center, 2015).

but they were generally quite cautious in ordaining African clergy. Experiments in the nineteenth century, such as the Anglican use of African priests among the Yoruba and similar Roman Catholic efforts in Uganda, had not been continued. There was some talk of incorporating African culture into church services, but little meaningful action. Conservative church leaders in Europe tended to believe that to become good Christians Africans needed to be Westernized and found few Africans "suitable" for ordination. Foreign missionaries were also concerned about the "excesses" of Zionist movements. Protestant missions had long promoted Bibles and services in African languages, but Catholics did not feel so strongly about the vernacular, as their own services were still in Latin until the 1960s. Colonial officials were equally slow in Africanizing their administrations.

However, African initiatives became as important in changing the churches as it was in decolonizing politics. The earliest and most widespread African initiative was in the rapid spread of Western schools, mostly operated by the churches. As Chapter 5 explained, education became a high priority for African parents, who paid fees to have their children educated. For their part, the pupils accepted that the effort to learn the colonial language and other forms of Western culture was a small price to pay for the opportunities that literacy opened up. As best their budgets permitted, colonial administrations, especially the British, subsidized schools that could meet accreditation requirements. Some Protestants resisted government "interference" in their schools, but Catholics and others embraced such financial support. The papal delegate to British African colonies in the 1920s urged his missionaries to cooperate fully, even if it meant neglecting "your churches to perfect your schools."[31]

This education policy and continuing growth in the number of missionaries enabled Catholics to become the leading Christian denomination in Africa after World War II. Over the course of the colonial period the number of Catholics in sub-Saharan Africa went from under 2 million to 34 million. In 1900 the major Protestant denominations had had a somewhat greater membership, but their growth to 21 million members in 1965, while certainly impressive, was not as fast as that of the Catholics. And yet the movement was just getting up a head of steam. The number of African Christians would increase nearly 500 percent during the last thirty-five years of the century.[32] Although one often reads that Protestants are more numerous than Catholics in Africa, that statement is misleading because Catholics belong to a single institution whereas the broad definition of "Protestants" that is commonly used in such counts includes more than 11,000 separate denominations, "the vast majority of which," in the words of a noted authority, "are completely unknown in

---

31. Kevin Ward, "Christianity, Colonialism and Missions," in *The Cambridge History of Christianity*, vol. 9, *World Christianities c.1914–c.2000*, ed. Hugh McLeod (Cambridge: Cambridge University Press, 2000), 77–78.

32. Hastings, *Church in Africa*, 540–92; Philip Jenkins, "How Africa Is Changing Faith around the World," *Trust*, July 5, 2016, Pew Charitable Trust, http://magazine.pewtrusts.org.

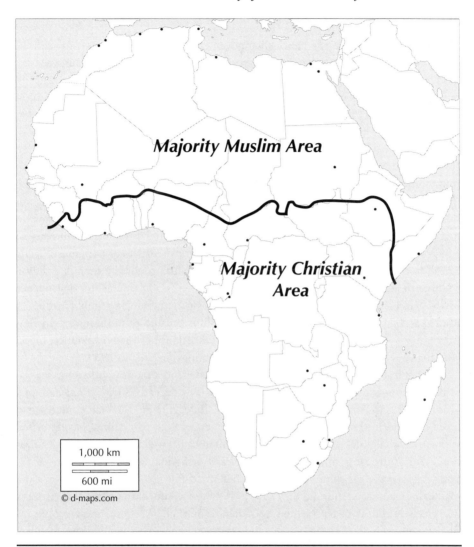

Muslim and Christian areas of Africa.

the West, and whose ecclesiastical and theological roots skirt completely the story of European Christendom and its various reformations."[33] It would be more meaningful to distinguish the denominations that trace their roots to the Reformation from those that arose later and, has been argued above, are better seen as a distinct African branch of Christianity.

33. Jonathan J. Bonk, "Ecclesiastical Cartography and the Invisible Continent," *The Dictionary of African Christian Biography*," Council on African Studies and the MacMillan Center African Studies Lecture Series, October 15, 2008, updated October 19, 2009, http://www.dacb.org/xnmaps.html.

## Nationalism and Indigenization

As Chapter 5 suggested, the nationalist movements for independence in Africa were led by well-educated men, often with degrees from European or American universities. With a few exceptions, especially in North Africa, this meant that the leaders had initially gone to schools in Africa run by Christian missions. It also meant that Muslims had to cooperate with or support Christian nationalists, because they had fewer leaders of their own. This imbalance was offset by the fact that most nationalist leaders favored secular governments that were neutral in matters of religion, although Muslims did not always see things that way. Muslims had accepted colonial rule in return for protection from outside interference, but often found themselves at a disadvantage in competing in democratic elections. Senegal and the Ivory Coast, for example, had more Muslims than Christians, but their first African rulers after independence were Christians. In practice these leaders and others worked hard to balance the interests of their Muslim and other citizens. Elsewhere in West Africa, the African leaders of populous Nigeria agreed to split power between Christian south and Muslim north. Nnamdi Azikiwe, a Christian, assumed the more ceremonial office of governor general at independence in 1960 and then president (1963–1966) when Nigeria became a republic, while Sir Abubakar Tafawa Balewa (1912–1966), a Muslim, became prime minister. In East Africa, newly independent Tanganyika (mostly Christian) negotiated a political union with the largely Muslim island of Zanzibar, becoming Tanzania in 1964.

Besides dealing with new political elites after independence, the world religions had to build better bridges to the African masses. As Blyden had argued, Islam had long been adapting to African cultures, and the new independent Christian churches had taken the lead in transforming the Christian message into something that resonated with African religious sensibilities, a process often called indigenization or Africanization. With a deeper commitment to traditional orthodoxy and a longer denominational history, the mainline mission churches could not move quite so far down the road to indigenization, nor did they have to. A great measure of their appeal to Africans was precisely that they represented a modern (if formally Western) message, but, as Blyden had realized, that did not preclude certain changes that would leave theology intact while appealing to African religious and cultural sensibilities. As colonial rule was ending, African clergy began to replace Europeans in the Roman Catholic and the major Protestant denominations. Given the size of the Christian population, the process took time. For example, less than 25 percent of Catholic bishops in Tanzania were Africans in 1984, but by 1996 all twenty-nine of them were. Protestants had led the way in Africanizing church services, but the Catholic Church caught up after the Second Vatican Council (1962–1965), which had both affirmed Catholic doctrine and permitted liturgical reforms that had great appeal in Africa. The Latin Mass was dropped in favor of services in the vernacular, that is, the language people normally spoke. The door was also opened to using vestments made from local designs as well as using indigenous music and art. The rapid increase in African clergy enabled religious services to be conducted in local African languages, although English, French, Portuguese, or Swahili were often used in the multilingual cities and towns.

Sometimes indigenization involved accommodating African cultural traditions. For example, African Christians always seated themselves in church by sex, men on one side, women on the other. After some initial hesitation, the major Christian denominations chose to use the same word for God in translations of the Bible and vernacular services that traditional African religions had used for the Creator. Other times indigenization was a break with tradition, reflecting changing standards. For example, among Catholics in many places the number of African women joining religious orders grew even faster after independence than did the number of male clergy. Both the empowerment of women and the commitment of both priests and nuns to celibacy were departures from tradition. The bottom line was that Africans were free to define religious practice as they saw fit.[34]

The themes of indigenization, differentiation, and consolidation that characterized Christianity in independent Africa have their counterparts in the history of African Islam. Just as there are many branches of Christianity, both old and new, Islam in Africa is also highly diverse. In the words of historian Ira Lapidus, "While Islam is in principle a universal religion, . . . in Africa it takes on an infinite variety of local forms."[35] Such diversity illustrates how indigenized or Africanized Islam has become, but diversity is also a product of poverty, isolation, and limited education, which have weakened the universalism of the Islamic appeal. Efforts to better inform Muslim adherents can lead in different directions. Some Muslims have promoted translations of the Qur'an into African languages, much as Protestants have promoted translations of the Bible. Others have promoted reformist Islam, Islamic universities, and the traditional Islamic law code known as Shari'a, or engaged in more destructive activities.

Shari'a is fully applied only in Mauritania and Sudan (where it led to the country splitting along Muslim and Christian lines). Several other African countries allow Muslims to use Islamic courts in limited social contexts, such as for personal and family matters. Since 1999 a dozen states in northern Nigeria have adopted Shari'a in whole or in part, often in defiance of the Nigerian constitution, which is secular. Some ill-educated Islamic jurists have tarnished Shari'a's reputation by imposing sentences such as stoning or mutilation that were common in medieval times but are generally rejected by modern Muslim states. The Nigerian federal government's policy of universal primary education introduced in 1976 provoked some extreme reactions in the northern part of the country, where many Muslims believed public schools were intrinsically Christian, even though the Nigerian school curriculum is secular and encourages religious knowledge classes that reflect the religious beliefs of the students. The law does not

---

34. David Maxwell, "Post-colonial Christianity of Africa," in McLeod, *Cambridge History of Christianity*, vol. 9, 409–11.
35. Lapidus, *Islamic Societies*, 784.

require parents to send their children to public schools, and many Muslims have refused to do so, restricting the new generation's future employment opportunities.

The distinguished Tanzanian political scientist Ali A. Mazrui (1933–2014), born in Zanzibar, has written that Africans like himself have a triple heritage: African, Muslim, and Western. The Western element refers particularly to education and language, and Mazrui had a distinguished career using English in teaching, writing scholarly works, and making a major television series about Africa. However, many other Muslims, such as the Murids, have rejected Western education and culture. Africans who became Christians in the late 1900s seem to have found blending African, Christian, and Western traditions an easier task. Outside as well as inside Africa, many Muslims continue to find the reconciliation of religion, history, and modern Western cultural primacy a vexing task.[36]

## Conclusion

Blyden was correct in seeing the appeal of Islam to Africans, but, understandably, failed to anticipate how great the appeal of Christianity would become. He understated the importance that conquest and enslavement had had in the spread of Islam in sub-Saharan Africa, and his sense of how much slavery had distorted Christianity in the Americas led him to underestimate how differently Africans would respond to the forms of Christianity that came to Africa from different backgrounds, whether from liberated Africans, European missionaries, or new African prophets. Western colonial rule also came largely by conquest, but the French and British also introduced a strong tradition of separation of church and state, whereas the older Islamic conquests established a union of political and religious authority. Islam and Christianity both had the appeal of universal religions and both brought literacy. Literacy opened the doors of learning, which, as an educator, Blyden well understood. He had even opened a school for Muslims in Lagos (now in Nigeria) in 1896, which followed a Western curriculum. However, Christians have been much more likely to become literate in European languages and explore a Western curriculum that included secular subjects as well as religion. Islam has a rich tradition of learning, including secular subjects. For example, Muhammad Bello of Sokoto was delighted when Heinrich Barth presented him with an Arabic translation of Euclid's *Geometry*, for the copy in his library had been destroyed in a fire. Islamic universities in North Africa have carried on this broad approach to education and expanded its availability to more than just the elite. In general, ordinary Muslims in sub-Saharan Africa have been less likely to have access to such learning. Those who went to Qur'anic schools rarely mastered more than prayers and the Arabic text of the Qur'an. As will be explored in more detail in the next chapter, the number of Muslims who attended Western schools

---

36. Ali A. Mazrui, *The Africans: A Triple Heritage* (New York; Little Brown, 1986).

operated by colonial authorities was small, and fewer Muslims than Christians have attended such schools since independence.

The shortcomings that Blyden found in Western Christianity for black people has had an interesting parallel in the emergence of a Black Muslim movement in the United States. Although not directly influenced by Blyden, the Nation of Islam (NOI), founded in Detroit in 1934, echoed Blyden's views that Christianity's association with slavery and racism rendered it unsuitable for black people. Despite an early history troubled by internal disputes and arrests, by 1959 the NOI operated fifty temples in twenty-two states. Black Muslims at that time were distinguished by virtues Blyden had lauded among African Muslims: sobriety, piety, diligence, and serious focus. They dressed modestly and the men wore dark suits, white shirts, and neckties. After a serious split in the movement, both factions attracted celebrated converts, such as Malcolm X and the boxer Muhammad Ali, and more infighting occurred. By 2010 the U.S. Bureau of the Census estimated that 25 percent of Muslims in the United States were African American. However, only 1 percent of African Americans are Muslim, while 83 percent remain Christian.[37]

---

37. "America's Changing Religious Landscape," Pew Research Center, May 12, 2015, http://www.pewforum.org.

# 7. COMPETING MODERN MYTHS:
## AFRICA RISING? AFRICA FAILING?

Seek ye first the political kingdom, and all things shall be added unto you.[1]
—*Kwame Nkrumah, West African known as the "Father of African Nationalism"*

The usual images [of Africa] are painted in the darkest colors. . . .
Africa is a nightmarish world where chaos reigns. Nothing works.
Poverty and corruption rule. War, famine and pestilence pay
repeated calls. The land, air and water raped, fouled, and polluted.
Chronic instability gives way to lifelong dictatorship. Every
nation's hand is out, begging aid from distrustful donors.[2]
—*Malinda S. Smith, Canadian political scientist, describing Afropessimism*

The statement of African nationalist aspirations, quoted above, by Kwame Nkrumah (1909–1972) in the 1950s is open to misinterpretation. At first reading the promise that all wants can be solved by capturing political power can sound impossibly idealistic (like the statement of Jesus about seeking the Kingdom of Heaven that it echoes). In fact, it is more of a slogan than a plan of action. Gaining control of the state was an obvious first step to transforming colonial arrangements, but Nkrumah and most other successful African nationalists of that era were not naive about the difficulties that would come next. They knew that re-directing the colonial political system to African ends would be a big task, as would be harmonizing African traditions with modern democratic and egalitarian institutions.

Mainstream nationalists largely agreed on what they wanted to do once in power. They would replace the authoritarian European rulers with democratically elected African leaders, who would use the state to promote economic and social equality. Because they associated colonial rule with capitalism, they called their agenda socialism, a term that Asian nationalists who had come to power during the first decade of decolonization after World War II had also used. While often sympathetic with the Marxist critique of capitalism, Asian and African nationalists generally were less admiring of the authoritarianism of Soviet and Chinese Communism. African leaders adapted their program for democratic socialism to the particular

---

1. Kwame Nkrumah, *Ghana: The Autobiography of Kwame Nkrumah* (New York: International Publishers, 1957), 164.

2. Malinda S. Smith, "Representations of Postcolonial Africa," in *Globalizing Africa*, ed. Malinda S. Smith (Trenton, NJ: Africa World Press, 2003), 16.

circumstances of their countries. In Ghana, which became independent with a relatively strong economy and comparatively high literacy, Nkrumah envisioned government programs for economic growth and the equitable distribution of benefits. In much poorer African countries, such as Tanzania and Mozambique, leaders put greater emphasis on primary education, basic health care, and grassroots economic development.

Most African nationalists were thus realistic in their goals and expectations. However, as will be explained later, several circumstances caused their agendas to take on mythical qualities. One cause was the revolution of rising expectations among the African masses, who grasped the basic slogans but were impatient with the necessarily slow and complex process of transformation. Changes in the post-war global economy also forced economic transformations in Africa to proceed more slowly than expected. In addition, during the era of the Cold War against the spread of communism some Western capitalist countries tried to block changes in African countries whose socialist rhetoric alarmed them. Finally, when white supremacist regimes blocked the non-violent transition to African rule, many African nationalists there turned to more radical agendas to inspire their supporters.

As the years of independence passed the myth of "Africa rising" came to be replaced by an opposite myth about "Africa failing." The name "Afropessimism" has been given to an extreme form of this myth that news from Africa is invariably bad. This pessimistic tendency has many causes. In the first place, it must be said, African news often has been bad. Independent Africa has had more than its share of corrupt or inept leaders, civil wars, and even genocides. Africans are among the poorest people in the world, so even small failures or problems can have horrific results. In the semi-arid regions of the continent, a bad harvest can lead to famine and starvation. In tropical Africa, life-threatening diseases that can be prevented cause debilitating illnesses, suffering, and premature death. If unaddressed, the effects of rapid population growth and global climate change threaten new misfortunes.

Besides the bad news from within Africa, the negative news also results from how outsiders view the continent. As earlier chapters of this book have demonstrated, bad news from Africa has a long history. A saying common in Greco-Roman antiquity, "there's always something new out of Africa," invariably meant something unpleasant or abnormal. As the Introduction detailed, Pliny the Elder populated the unknown parts of Africa with imaginary monsters and freaks, though strange animals and plants might also be included among African novelties. This tradition of bad news was reborn in modern times when the history of Africa was reduced to the slave trade and imperial exploitation. Both eras brought many misfortunes, but, as Chapters 3, 4, and 5 related, exaggerating them distorts the larger realities. Racism has played its role as well: when Africans are viewed as inferior and deserving enslavement and discrimination, then warfare, corruption, and disease reinforce racist expectations.

Although some causes of the negative portrayal of Africa are mean-spirited, others stem from more prosaic causes. Bad news makes better headlines than good news in every region of the world. A destructive storm is a front-page story; a thousand successful harvests are not. One maniac on a killing spree can dominate the news for a week, but ten thousand hardworking students earning college degrees rarely merit a mention. Two other factors exaggerate bad news from Africa. First, because so few Americans (or Europeans or Asians) care much about Africa, only the biggest stories (by definition the worst stories) get wide circulation. Second, in general news accounts Africa tends to be considered as a single place, even though it is the second largest of the continents, so that reporters mine the bad news from dozens of countries to come up with the worst stories. This treatment is unique to Africa. When things happen in Asia (or Europe or South America), the news is reported by country not continent: a flood is in China, a famine in India, a nuclear meltdown in Japan.

The Internet has made good news from Africa available—just google "Africa good news" or "Africa rising" and see. But, unless the breaking news is of the magnitude of Nelson Mandela being released from prison after a quarter century, one has to search hard for the good news. One has to work even harder to separate the particular news of each African country from broader trends. Because the purpose of this chapter is to correct the myth of all news from Africa being bad, it will not try to summarize all the bad news. As readers of the previous chapters will have learned, the way to correct a distorting myth is not to proclaim its opposite, but to place facts in a balanced perspective. The bad news from Africa, while mostly true, needs to be combined with important and more positive facts about the continent's slow, if painful, progress.

This chapter first examines the struggles against colonialism and white supremacy that fed the African-rising myth. Then it turns to the more positive trends in independent Africa that can be buried by the deluge of pessimistic news. The chapter tries to be balanced, but in a short chapter it would be tedious to survey the continent country by country. For the historian, the large trends are the main story. That Africans are living longer and achieving more may not make the headlines, but it does make a huge difference to the people experiencing it. Africans as a whole are struggling hard to make their lives better, despite the efforts of some to benefit themselves at the expense of the majority. Short-term trends are no guarantee for the future.

## Rising to Self-Rule

In a famous essay published at the end of the 1960s, Jacob Ajayi (1929–2014), a highly respected Nigerian historian, made the provocative suggestion that one should view the period of colonial rule as "an episode in African history." The colonial era brought many changes, Ajayi admitted, but in most of Africa it was a brief period in the broad sweep of the African past. Post-colonial issues, he argued, derived as much (or more) from pre-colonial trends as they did from the colonial changes. Ajayi does not have the last word on the subject, but his observations are a useful reminder that

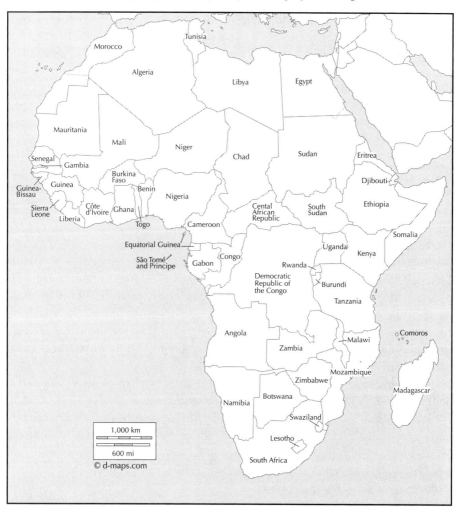

African States and Boundaries, 2017.

the foreign colonial rule did not mean that Africans ceased to be in control of the larger patterns of their lives. As Chapters 5 and 6 argued, most changes in the colonial era, as earlier, resulted from Africans' choices rather than being imposed from above. African actions and aspirations continued to dominate the ending of colonial rule and building of modern African nations and societies. Africans largely own both the successes and the failures.[3]

3. J. F. A. Ajayi, "Conclusion: An Episode in African History," *Colonialism in Africa, 1870–1960,* ed. L. H. Gann and Peter Duignan (Cambridge: Cambridge University Press, 1969), I: 497–509.

Even so, the colonial era did bring many enduring changes. As Ajayi recognized, fixed political boundaries were going to be a key legacy of colonial rule. The half century since he wrote has confirmed how enduring the political boundaries imposed by colonial rulers have been and are likely to remain. For African nationalists generally, fixed political boundaries were not so much a blessing or a curse as an opportunity to build new nations and identities. Some Africans' dreams of creating a giant United States of Africa or large regional states have remained largely unrealized.

The fixed colonial boundaries presented Africans with a way to get rid of the colonial rulers. Following the devastation of World War II in Europe, the idea of preparing colonies for greater independence had gained favor in Britain and (to a lesser extent) in France. The change of attitude partly reflected widespread doubts about the legitimacy of empires and partly was due to pragmatic considerations, notably that colonies were unprofitable, especially when they contained well-organized nationalist movements. The first wave of decolonization had swept across Asia, the Middle East, and North Africa in the 1940s and 1950s, but European leaders generally believed that sub-Saharan African colonies needed many more decades to be ready for self-rule. African nationalist leaders hastened the pace of change by organizing effective political movements and winning elections. The movements for self-rule also had the effect of strengthening the sense of common identity within the colonial boundaries.

Nationalist organizations took good advantage of new representative legislative bodies and administrative posts that some colonial powers, notably Great Britain, opened to Africans. In addition to appointing Africans to advisory posts, some colonies permitted the election of Africans to offices with real authority, such as the regional premierships in Nigeria mentioned in Chapter 5. Once the door to African representation was opened a little, nationalists pushed hard to expand their roles and ultimately to replace European rulers.

To win the prize of political power African nationalists needed to forge strong new alliances within the existing political boundaries. New elites provided the leadership and stirred support among the masses. Unlike the older elites who came from royal and noble African families or held religious offices, the new elites depended on modern education and leadership in labor, political, economic, and social organizations. In the struggles for independence the new elites generally gained ground over the old hereditary elites, who were closely wedded to the colonial regimes.

The new elite leaders were remarkably well educated in the 1950s. Schools had expanded rapidly during the colonial era, but mostly at the primary level. By 1950, a few colonies such as Kenya and the Belgian Congo had managed to attract a quarter to a third of youth into primary education, but many more resembled Senegal and Tanganyika in enrolling 10 percent or fewer. In most of Africa less than 1 percent of African teenagers were enrolled in secondary schools in 1950, and those who completed that level usually needed to go abroad for college.[4] Thus, the fact that many of the leading African nationalists had earned university degrees made them quite exceptional in sub-Saharan Africa. Despite their elite status, the nationalists were remarkable in their ability to win over the support of the masses. Rather than being jealous of the leaders' educational achievements, large segments of the population saw the leaders' success as embodying their own aspirations for themselves and their children.

The nationalist elites had to work hard to mobilize popular support into disciplined movements. Members of labor unions and organizations of teachers and market women were disproportionately important in building political movements. Those who had completed primary school also stood out in the movements. But until election campaigns began to be held, it was anyone's guess how much of a colony's population would unite behind a national candidate.

Kwame Nkrumah's success in the prosperous British colony of the Gold Coast in West Africa showed what could be done. Despite a modest family background, Nkrumah had earned several advanced degrees in the United States and Britain before returning home after the end of World War II. He soon attracted widespread attention as a dynamic speaker and political organizer. When the British offered some new political rights to Gold Coast Africans, Nkrumah won a large popular following, both by denouncing the offer as half a loaf and by organizing assemblies of common folk and pushing a program of boycotts, strikes, and demonstrations that led to his arrest. However, after his party won the first colony-wide election in 1951 by a landslide, the Gold Coast's governor released Nkrumah from prison so that he could become the colony's new prime minister. After six years of learning the ropes, Nkrumah led the campaign for independence in 1957. To remind the world that Africans had an old history of self-rule, Nkrumah renamed the newly independent country "Ghana," a name for the ancient empire of Wagadu far to the north. The name Ghana also focused attention away from the country's ethnic divisions.

Ghana's smooth and peaceful transition to independence forced European colonizers to rethink their belief that independence in the rest of sub-Saharan Africa was a long way off and encouraged Africans in other colonies to mount their own campaigns. A French plan to maintain close ties with their vast African territories in West and Equatorial Africa by offering Africans there more rights faltered when African voters in French Guinea in 1958 rejected such an association in favor of complete independence. In a gesture of pan-African solidarity, Ghana formed a loose political union with Guinea. In short order the French moved to grant independence to most of their African colonies. The major exception was Algeria, where a million white settlers' interests prevailed for a time.

The movement of a score of African countries to independence in 1960 was a watershed for African independence. Nigeria contained the most people, but the devolution of the extensive French empire made the biggest impression on the map.

---

4. J. D. Y. Peel, "Social and Cultural Change," in *The Cambridge History of Africa*, vol. 8, *From c. 1940 to c. 1975*, ed. Michael Crowder (Cambridge: Cambridge University Press, 1984), 180.

(See map, p. 131, and the chronology below.) As the cascading wave of independence swept toward the Belgians' vast empire in Central Africa the government rushed to grant independence to the Belgian Congo, Rwanda, and Burundi. A baker's dozen of other African independence celebrations followed over the next eight years.

---

### A Chronology of African Independence from Colonial Rule

Pre-1925   Liberia (1847), Union of South Africa (1910), Egypt (1922)

1951–1958   Libya, Eritrea, *Morocco, Tunisia*, Sudan, Ghana, *Guinea–Conakry*

1960   *Mauretania, Senegal, Mali, Niger, Burkina Faso, Ivory Coast, Benin, Chad, Congo-Brazzaville, Central African Republic, Gabon, Togo,* Cameroon, Nigeria, Somali Republic, Congo–Kinshasa, *Malagasy Republic*, Burundi, Rwanda.

1961–1968   Sierra Leone, Tanzania, *Algeria*, Uganda, Kenya, Malawi, Zambia, Botswana, Lesotho, Swaziland, Equatorial Guinea (from Spain), Mauritius

1974–1980   **Cape Verde, Guiné–Bissau, São Tomé and Principe, Angola, Mozambique,** *Comoros*, Seychelles, *Djibouti*, Zimbabwe

1990   Namibia

*Note:* Former British territories are underlined; former *French* territories are in *italics*; former **Portuguese** territories are in **boldface**; former Italian territories are in small caps. After World War I the former German colonies of Togo, Cameroon, Burundi, Rwanda, and Namibia were placed under the supervision of the League of Nations and then of the United Nations, in whose name they were administered variously by Britain, France, Belgium, and South Africa. Congo-Kinshasa was a former colony of Belgium. The American Colonization Society founded Liberia for African American settlement.

---

Some of the individual transitions to independence were heroic, some pragmatic, a few tragic. In the resource-poor British colony of Tanganyika in East Africa, Julius Nyerere (1922–1999), the first Tanganyikan to earn a collage degree, managed to win the support of his ethnically diverse countrymen in the elections in 1958 and 1960. Gaining independence in 1961, Tanganyika needed a strong national movement to unite the members of its hundredfold, small ethnicities. Not content with that achievement, Nyerere negotiated a union with the former British territory of Zanzibar, creating the new nation of Tanzania in 1974.[5]

---

5. Thomas Hodgkin, *Nationalism in Colonial Africa* (New York: New York University Press, 1957) remains a readable and reliable overview of the period. David Birmingham, *Kwame Nkrumah:*

Tanganyika and several other territories that gained autonomy had once been German colonies and were placed under the supervision of the League of Nations and its successor the United Nations but were administered by colonial powers. Most of the British and French administered zones of Cameroon reunited as a new nation. Voters in the French zone of Togo chose independence, while the British zone chose to join Ghana. The Somali people on the Horn of Africa agreed to unite the former British and Italian territories as the Somali Republic (also known as Somalia). An effort to provide independent Ethiopia with a seaport by joining it with another Italian colony led to lengthy conflict and the eventual independence of Eritrea as a separate nation.

The hastily prepared independence of the former Belgian Congo was tragically unsuccessful. The colony was so vast that the Belgians had administered it as a series of regions. The transition to independence showed Congo's lack of unity as well as the acute shortage of well-educated African leaders and the power of Belgian mining interests. The new African prime minister who came to power in 1960, Patrice Lumumba (1925–1961), lacked the higher education of his West and East African counterparts, had only a few months to learn the ropes rather than their several years, and faced strong opposition at home and abroad. Lumumba was soon assassinated due to regional rivalries and foreign opposition to his radical politics. Much more successful, at least initially, were the politicians who first built an ethnic base from which they went on achieve national victories.

The African experience in nation building was impressive but not unique. The experience of people in many parts of the modern world attests that artificial national boundaries do not necessarily lead to artificial nations. Germany, Italy, and the United States formed diverse new nations in the nineteenth century, as did scores of new Asian countries in the twentieth. Some boundary changes have occurred in Africa, most recently the separation of South Sudan from Sudan. However, most independent African nations that have been torn by bloody civil wars have survived these crises intact. Within a couple of years of the end of the Nigerian Civil War (1967–1970), for example, both sides became reconciled to reunification as the best prospect for the future.

## Delays in Southern Africa

The successful transitions to majority rule in sub-Saharan Africa between 1957 and 1968 gave Africans and their outside supporters hope that the process of decolonization would continue, but "the wind of change" blowing through Africa, as one world leader put it, had halted at the white-ruled states of southern Africa, where opposition

---

*The Father of African Nationalism*, rev. ed. (Athens: Ohio University Press, 1998), and Chambi Chachage and Annar Cassam, eds., *Africa's Liberation: The Legacy of Nyerere* (Oxford: Pambazaka Press, 2010) provide brief overviews of key leaders.

to majority rule was high. As South Africa clamped down on African protest in the 1960s and 1970s, hope for change switched to the five "frontline states" to the north: the Portuguese colonies of Mozambique and Angola, the British colony of Southern Rhodesia (where whites had gained self-government in 1923), and the South African–administered United Nations Trust Territory of South West Africa.

The struggle against the white minority had two effects on African consciousness. First it brought Africans closer together, though unity proved difficult to achieve. Second, it pushed African resisters to embrace leftist "liberation ideologies" of a type that had earlier motivated revolutions in Russia, China, Cuba, and Vietnam. American, British, and other European governments' support for the enemies of change reinforced this movement to the left. Partly these Western governments feared the spread of "communism." Partly they were motivated by a mistaken pragmatism based on the belief, as President Richard Nixon's National Security Council head put it in 1969, that "the whites . . . were there to stay."[6]

It took years of painful struggle within the region and massive international campaigns to achieve, but white minorities were too small and vulnerable in the frontline states to hold out for long. The first to fall were Portugal's giant colonies of Angola and Mozambique. Fighting the determined African resistance movements was consuming half of Portugal's national budget, and military conscription had become very unpopular there. Moreover, as many senior Portuguese military officers had come to see to see, the political rights that Africans were fighting for were also denied to Portuguese citizens at home. In 1974 military officers who were veterans of the African wars ousted Portugal's undemocratic government. The next year a new democratic government in Portugal granted independence to Angola and Mozambique. Most of the white settlers in the former Portuguese colonies chose to leave rather than accept majority rule, often destroying everything they could on their way out.

The independence of Mozambique made it much more difficult for neighboring white-ruled Rhodesia to continue evading the sanctions that the United Nations had imposed in 1965. Independent Mozambique also provided guerilla fighters with convenient bases from which to attack white Rhodesia. The guerillas said they were fighting to liberate "Zimbabwe," adopting the name of the medieval capital city and rejecting the name John Cecil Rhodes had given the colony he had seized by force in the 1890s. Despite maneuvers that included a unilateral declaration of independence from Britain, white Rhodesians were eventually forced to agree to a transition to majority African rule. In elections in 1980, the Zimbabwe African National Union (ZANU) party, headed by Robert Mugabe, won a substantial majority of the African votes, and he became president of independent state of Zimbabwe. Initially, most white settlers stayed on.

---

Mohamed A. El-Khawas and Barry Cohen. eds., *The Kissinger Study of Southern Africa: National ·ty Study Memorandum 39* (Westport, CT: L. Hill, 1976), 105–6.

The struggles in Angola, Mozambique, and Zimbabwe faced modest white set-tler populations. However, South Africa's white settler minority was much larger and more deeply entrenched, having controlled the country's government since 1910. As Chapter 5 recounted, the South African government had also been actively construct-ing a system known as apartheid (separation), which divided the black population not only by color but also by ethnicity and restricted entry to "white" areas. However, the successes just to the north inspired many in South Africa to believe they could also win equal rights. A new generation of Africans risked their lives in renewed protests. In 1976, the year after neighboring Mozambique's independence, students in the African township of Soweto, outside the city of Johannesburg, challenged curriculum changes that would have retarded their advancement in school. The student protests spread to the city of Cape Town. Later that year black trade unions staged the largest work stoppage in South African history, and in the decade that followed the unions grew ever larger and more militant. The white government countered with violent crackdowns and states of emergency that suspended legal rights. It maneuvered to split urban and rural Africans, and tried to co-opt the Indian and "Coloured"[7] popu-lations with token political rights.

Appalled at the continuing conflict, Christian clergymen (including prominent whites) preached against the violence and injustice. As opponents of the regime in Europe and the United States withdrew their investments from South Africa and imposed boycotts on the country's exports and other sanctions, pragmatic white leaders chose to abandon apartheid and make other concessions. South Africa relin-quished its hold on the UN Trust Territory of South West Africa, permitting demo-cratic elections in 1990, which brought an African majority to power in what was renamed Namibia. That same year the South African government released Nelson Mandela and other leaders of the banned African National Congress (ANC) from prison, lifted the state of emergency it had imposed, began repealing apartheid legisla-tion, and moved to hold democratic elections. In 1994 the ANC won 63 percent of the popular vote, and Nelson Mandela became the first non-white president of South Africa and appointed the first multi-racial administration. White flight, which had been common during the years of violent protest, slowed.[8]

The new majority governments in southern Africa shared the high hopes that had been evident elsewhere in Africa after independence and went through many

---

7. In South Africa "Coloured" referred to the descendants of slaves imported from Indian Ocean islands, indigenous Khoekhoe, and other people of mixed race.

8. Leonard Thompson, *A History of South Africa*, 3rd ed. (New Haven, CT: Yale University Press, 2001), 221–96; James Duffy, "Portuguese Africa, 1930 to 1960," in *Colonialism in Africa, 1870–1960*, ed. L. H. Gann and Peter Duignan (Cambridge: Cambridge University Press, 1982), 2:171–93; W. G. Clarence-Smith, "Capital Accumulation and Class Formation in Angola," and Ian R. Phimister, "Zimbabwe: The Path of Capitalist Development" in *History of Central Africa*, ed. David Birmingham and Phyllis Martin (New York: Longman, 1983), 2:163–250, 251–382.

of the same difficult learning experiences. Indeed, parts of southern Africa struggled through far worse situations. Angola and Mozambique were plagued by violent civil wars between different political factions, though these ended in the 1990s as support from the Cold War powers and apartheid South Africa evaporated. In Zimbabwe, Robert Mugabe slowly transitioned from a liberating hero to a despot, who has retained power since his first election in 1980. South Africa went through a remarkable process of truth telling and reconciliation and a series of democratic elections. Mandela and the white former president, F. W. de Klerk, shared the Nobel Peace Prize for 1993. As elsewhere in sub-Saharan Africa, gaining the political kingdom was only a key first step in building more equal societies.

## Political and Economic Trends in Independent Africa

At independence African states faced many challenges. Their new leaders governed nation-states whose ethnic and regional divisions strained the bonds that united their new nations. Political leaders embraced democratic institutions but struggled to balance conflicting interests that could be destabilizing. In choosing to strengthen the political center, many leaders erred on the side of authoritarianism. Election crises and military coups were distressingly common in the 1960s and 1970s. In the former Belgian Congo, Mobutu Sese Seko (1930–1997), who came to power in 1965, rescued a state as large as all of Western Europe from the infighting of the early years of independence. He promoted African clothing styles and other symbols of what he called "authenticity," but also became a dictator who stayed in power until his death and looted the treasury for the benefit of himself and his supporters. In neighboring Uganda Idi Amin (r. 1971–1979) did worse, gaining a reputation as "the butcher of Uganda." In comparison, the more stable and better governed states looked very good indeed.

Besides building nation-states, African governments also sought to institutionalize pan-African cooperation. The Organization of African Unity (OAU), founded in 1963, lacked power to act decisively. It became a forum where African heads of state could discuss common problems, but it ignored the most egregious failings of member states. The African Union, the OAU's successor in 2002, has proven more effective in addressing political problems.[9]

To explain away their failures or lack of successes, it became convenient for modern African leaders to blame their problems on the legacies of colonial rule and neocolonial exploitation, even as the decades of African self-government passed. Such mythmaking exaggerated external forces, while unfairly demeaning Africans' abilities to take charge of their lives. UN Secretary-General Kofi Annan told his fellow

---

Frederick Cooper, *Africa Since 1940: The Past of the Present* (Cambridge: Cambridge University 2002), 156–87; Paul Nugent, *Africa Since Independence: A Comparative History*, 2nd ed. (New Palgrave Macmillan, 2012), 109–263.

Kofi Annan of Ghana was Secretary General of the United Nations, 1996–2007. He was the first sub-Saharan African to hold that post. Source; photo by Harry Wad, Creative Commons Attribution 2.5 Generic license.

Africans in 1998 that blaming problems on the colonial past should be replaced with accepting responsibility for problems and solving them. On a visit to Ghana in 2009, President Barack Obama made a similar statement. The larger reality is that, for the most part, African countries have chosen to retain the boundaries they inherited and have greatly expanded the use of languages and educational systems introduced in the colonial era. As in societies elsewhere, African leaders have struggled to reform unequal economic and social systems, with varying degrees of success.[10]

In some respects political realities have improved in the twenty-first century. Referencing the state of affairs up to 2011, historian Paul Nugent noted that military coups "were increasingly seen as an aberration" and that "the vast majority of governments were now elected to office, despite the many imperfections." Improvements have continued. Referencing the decade 2006–2015, the highly respected Ibrahim Index of African Governance reported, "70% of African citizens live in a country that has seen improved governance. 37 countries improved their Overall Governance score and the continental average score for Overall Governance has improved by one score point between 2006–2015, from 49.0 to 50.0." In addition, "78% of African citizens live in a country that has improved in Participation & Human Rights" and "43 countries, home to 87% of African citizens, registered progress in Human Development." Echoing Nugent, the report stressed that Africa was a complex place with more than fifty separate countries, which varied considerably from each other. On a scale of 100 points, there was a difference of 70 points between the score of the highest ranked country, Mauritius, and the lowest, Somalia. Still, improving trends are good news.[11]

African rulers inherited economies only partly modernized by a few decades of European rule. Fluctuations in global markets that Africans sold into could throw even the best-laid plans for a loop. Of course, not all development plans were well made. Nkrumah's government, for example, spent heavily on lavish buildings even while income from cocoa exports fell due to growing international competition. Some

---

10. Barbara Crossette, "Stop Blaming Colonialism, U.N. Chief Tells Africa," *New York Times*, April 17, 1998; Alex Spillius, "Barack Obama Tells Africa to Stop Blaming Colonialism for Problems," *The Telegraph*, July 9, 2009.

11. Nugent, *Africa since Independence*, 446; Yannick Vuylsteke, "The 2016 Ibrahim Index of African Governance: Key Findings," Mo Ibrahim Foundation, October 4, 2016, http://mo.ibrahim .foundation.

countries, such as Nigeria, gained large revenues from petroleum exports in the 1970s and afterward, but failed to invest enough of the money in building a modern economy.

In the twenty-first century, even as petroleum prices have tumbled, some African countries have been doing better. Every year the giant multi-national professional services company known as Ernst & Young (or EY) publishes summaries of various large trends that might be of interest to its corporate clients. Its African Attractiveness Program report for 2016 indicates that sub-Saharan African economic growth will be slower for the foreseeable future than it had been during the previous ten or fifteen years, but emphasizes that slowing is not stopping. Sub-Saharan Africa, it predicts, "will remain the second-fastest growing region in the world for the forseeable [sic] future, after emerging Asia." The report docsn't need to tell its sophisticated readers that African economic growth can be faster than the world average because less developed economies have more potential for improvement than fully developed ones. But it does stress that growth rates will vary considerably in different African countries, and provides a ranking of countries based on how their political and legal systems, as well as their economic momentum, will affect performance. The top five mainland countries in order are geographically diverse: South Africa, Morocco, Egypt, Kenya, and Ghana. The report notes that Nigeria, whose economy is Africa's largest and one of its most resilient, is "somewhat surprisingly" ranked fifteenth overall, due to internal problems—and, it might be added, the current low price commanded by petroleum, its most important export.[12]

Poverty in African countries has many causes, but raising productivity (output per worker) is at the heart of finding a solution. Some 60 percent of Africans work in agriculture, which is generally not a very productive sector, in part because the export prices of African agricultural products, such as cocoa, palm oil, and coffee, keep falling due to competition from more efficient growers elsewhere in the world. Moving out of agriculture might be a solution for some, but growing higher-quality crops that can command better prices is also proving to be a solution. In the early years of independence, many women in Kenya turned to growing tea for export and reaped a good living. Today tea is the country's largest export. More recently other Kenyans have turned to another promising crop—fresh flowers. The flowers need to be grown in special greenhouses and require careful tending. Most critical is flying freshly cut flowers to markets, generally in Europe. Since 1988, flower farming has grown more than tenfold in Kenya. Every day an average of 360 tons of flowers are dispatched overseas from Nairobi's airport. Neighboring Ethiopia has also begun to grow flowers, but its promotion of manufacturing is another promising strategy. Carefully crafted government policies and substantial foreign investment have led Ethiopian manufacturing to grow an average of over 10 percent a year since 2006. At first, manufacturing was concentrated in industries such as textiles and leather products, that took

---

Ernst & Young, "Africa Attractiveness Program, Africa 2016: Navigating Africa's Current Uncer-
'es," http://www.ey.com, PDF, 3, 9. In the country rankings, the Indian Ocean nation of Mau-
nks ahead of Ghana.

advantage of Ethiopia's low wages, but the country has begun to attract pharmaceutical companies, whose better-educated employees will command higher wages.[13]

For the rates of economic growth to improve more widely, African governments need to address some crippling underlying structural problems. New technologies can help. Until recently in most of Africa telephone service was unreliable or unavailable. However, the development of cellphone service tied to satellite communication systems has produced revolutionary improvements. Africans can now communicate with family members as well as check market prices, and even take out small loans over their phones.

A second infrastructure weakness is that too little electricity is produced for industrial and domestic use. As populations have exploded in Africa, overall electricity production per capita has actually declined. For example, Nigeria has the largest population and the largest economy in Africa, but it generates less electricity than North Korea. Because power outages are so common, businesses must install their own generators to ensure a reliable supply of electricity. Here again technology is beginning to turn things around by making electricity from a resource Africa possesses in greater amounts than any of the other continents: sunshine. In 2016 South Africa's operational solar plants were capable of generating 1,400 megawatts (MW) of power, and simple passive solar heating devices promise to deliver hot water to thousands of homes. In April 2016 a Chinese company opened a 20 MW facility in Ghana, whose capacity it plans to double. Several other countries are also moving in this direction. Morocco plans to have 2,000 MW of solar electricity operational by 2020.[14]

No quick technological fix is possible for Africa's inadequate and crumbling transportation infrastructures. In some places railroads built during the early colonial period have been allowed to decay to the point where they are unusable, along with their outdated and broken rolling stock. African motor roads have not kept up with population and traffic growth, with deadly consequences. The proportion of people dying in traffic accidents in Malawi is double the global rate and is nearly as bad in Liberia, Congo, Tanzania, and Kenya. Traffic mortality rates are lower in South Africa and Nigeria but still double those in Europe. Indeed, more Africans die of traffic accidents each year than die of malaria.[15]

Bad roads are also a serious impediment to internal and external trade. Except in southern Africa, transporting goods in Africa can cost twice as much as in China,

13. "Kenya's Flower Trade: Leaving on a Jet Plane," *The Economist*, February 6, 2016, 46; "Special Report: Business in Africa," *The Economist*, April 16, 2016, 8; "Industrialization in Africa: More a Marathon Than a Sprint," *The Economist*, November 7, 2015, 41; "Djibouti: The Superpowers' Playground," *The Economist*, April 9, 2016, 49.

14. "African Entrepreneurs: Opportunities Galore," *The Economist*, June 2, 2016, 39–40; "The 1.2 Billion Opportunity; Special Report: Business in Africa," *The Economist*, April 16, 2016, 3–11; "Solar Power in Africa," and "Solar Power in South Africa," *Wikipedia*.

15. "Road Deaths in Africa: Worse Than Malaria," *The Economist*, October 24, 2015, 45.

Brazil, or the United States. Farmers can't get their produce to market efficiently, and so fail to produce as much as they could if better and cheaper transport were available. Transportation into and out of ports is so poor that one study concluded that African port cities bore more resemblance to islands than hubs. As a consequence, trade within Africa represents only 11 percent of the continent's total trade, compared to 50 percent in Asia and 70 percent in Europe. Improvements are being made in some places, but much more needs to be done. The growth of manufacturing in landlocked Ethiopia has led to the construction of a new railroad to the port of Djibouti on the Gulf of Aden. Other eastern African countries, including Tanzania and Rwanda, have also begun to reap the rewards of manufacturing, and Kenya Railways Corporation has built a new railroad to the coast and plans many new rail links to neighboring countries.

The pace of economic development in Africa is such that some observers are beginning to speak of an emerging African "middle class," although that term means something different from what it means in developed countries. The African Development Bank has used a definition of middle class that includes a third of the continent's people, namely those with cash incomes between $1,460 and $7,300 a year.[16] The expanding middle class is the product of improving economic opportunities, rising educational levels, and, of course, individual efforts. Spending by those in the middle class promotes further economic growth, whether the expenditures are on education and health care or luxuries such as tobacco, alcohol, cars, and fashionable clothes because such spending creates jobs and generates profits for others.

## Population and Health Trends

Persistent myths of African depopulation that are associated with the slave trade accounts have been reinforced by stories of colonial and post-colonial exploitation. The impression of a faltering population is also reinforced by news stories about deadly diseases. Past injustices and ever-present diseases are real, but the larger reality is that populations in Africa are growing rapidly. This is due to dramatic decreases in infant and childhood mortality and steady reductions in deaths from once common diseases.

The United Nations Human Development Index (HDI) ranks countries around the world based on their combined scores in life expectancy, educational attainment, and per capita income. The highest score is 1.0, which only the most developed countries approach. Norway has been at the top of the list for many years. Within Africa only three North African states get a "high human development" ranking (above 0.7) and the rest of North Africa, along with much of southern Africa and Ghana, follow in the middle category (above 0.55). Most African countries are in a lower human development category (0.35 to under 0.55) with Kenya, Angola, Tanzania, Nigeria, Cameroon, and Zimbabwe rated in the upper part of that category. The rankings

---

16. Ian Bremmer, "These 5 Facts Explain the Good News about Africa," *Time*, March 3, 2016.

might seem bad news, but Ernst & Young's attractiveness report emphasizes some positive trends. Although Ethiopia ranks low globally, it scores twice as high as it did twenty-five years ago. Rwanda, recovering from Africa's worst genocide, does nearly as well, and HDIs in Angola and Zambia are now a third higher. The EY report points out some continental trends: the poverty rate in Africa has been falling steadily since 1995, as have child mortality rates, while average adult literacy rates have gone from 52 percent in the 1990s to almost 65 percent today.[17]

The EY report cites Africa's high rate of population growth as a positive sign for the future. As historian Michael Brett observes, "The paradox is that despite all such threats to life and limb, the population of the continent is now *five times* larger than in the mid-twentieth century, turning Africa from the second least, after Australia, into the second most populated continent in the world after Asia." It is certainly good news that the scourges of warfare, poverty, and disease have not interrupted overall growth in Africa, but population growth is not benign. Rapid population increases can diminish or cancel the benefits of economic growth. Unlike other parts of the world where birthrates have fallen as incomes rose, birthrates in Africa have generally stayed high, although they are beginning to fall in some African urban areas, such as Addis Ababa, Ethiopia.[18]

African population growth also reflects another positive trend: the decline of premature deaths. United Nations figures show that infant mortality rates (deaths before the first birthday) in sub-Saharan Africa have fallen dramatically, from 156 per thousand births in the early 1960s to 64 per thousand in the early 2010s. In part because of fewer deaths at a young age, life expectancy at birth in sub-Saharan Africa has risen sharply in that same half century, from forty-one years to fifty-seven years. Life expectancy in Africa is still well below other parts of the world, but these improvements are encouraging. In some parts of the continent gains have come even faster. According to World Bank figures, between 2006 and 2010 childhood mortality rates (deaths before the fifth birthday) declined by 10 percent in Senegal and Rwanda and between 6 and 8 percent in Kenya, Uganda, and Ghana. Such rapid improvements are due to relatively simple measures like distributing insecticide-treated mosquito nets and expanding medical access, measures that other countries should be able to duplicate.[19]

A second cause of rising longevity in Africa is the decline in premature deaths due to disease. Scientists distinguish between communicable diseases that can spread among persons, either directly or through intermediaries, and conditions, such as cancer and heart disease, which are not contagious. Worldwide at the end of the twentieth century

---

17. United Nations Development Programme, *Human Development Report 2015*, http://hdr.undp.org; Ernst & Young, "African Attractiveness," 8.

18. Michael Brett, *Approaching African History* (Rochester, NY: James Currey, 2013), 305; Mertule Mariam, "African Demography: The Young Continent," *The Economist*, December 12, 2015.

19. United Nations Department of Economic and Social Affairs, Population Division, "World Population Prospects, the 2015 Revision: Key Findings and Advance Tables," https://esa.un.org/unpd/wpp; "African Child Mortality: The Best Story in Development," *The Economist*, May 19, 2012.

about 30 percent of deaths were due to communicable diseases, but in Africa that percentage was higher. Tropical Africa has long been home to a number of debilitating and deadly infectious diseases, spread by mosquitoes or other vectors. The good news is that communicable diseases are generally cheaper and easier to prevent and cure than noncommunicable conditions, since their spread can be reduced by targeting transmitters such as mosquitoes, by immunization efforts, and by rendering acquired diseases less deadly through drug therapies. Massive efforts on this front in recent years have led to sharp reductions in deaths from communicable diseases worldwide as well as in Africa.

Mass campaigns to inoculate people against particular diseases have proven successful in curbing their spread because vaccinated individuals not only cannot get the diseases but they also cannot transmit them to others. Isolating those who do become infected also blocks disease transmission from one person to another. In the 1990s, the very deadly smallpox disease was eliminated through mass vaccination programs and isolating the last cases in Ethiopia until they were no longer contagious. Efforts to eliminate polio by the same methods have been highly effective, except for a small area in northern Nigeria, where violence and local opposition have prevented immunization. There was no immunization available against the deadly Ebola virus when a major outbreak occurred in West Africa in 2014, nor was any successful treatment then available. About half of those who contracted the disease died, but those who recovered from the infection appear to have acquired lifetime immunity. Nevertheless, efforts to block the spread of Ebola were successful both within West Africa and worldwide. Medical professionals protected by special clothing isolated those with Ebola symptoms so that the disease could not spread. In late 2015, with the active help of local village leaders, the epidemic was halted.[20]

Isolating people is not possible in the case of some contagious diseases against which immunization is impossible. Controlling the spread of sexually transmitted diseases (STDs) has long been difficult, both because people who are infected might display no obvious symptoms and because it is difficult to get people to curtail their sexual activity, although campaigns to encourage abstinence and fidelity or to promote the use of prophylactics have had some success. The use of antibiotics to cure STDs such as syphilis and gonorrhea has proven the most effective approach of preventing their spread (by reducing the number who are infected). That approach also halted the development of advanced stages of diseases, which are more life threatening.

The disease known as Acquired Immune Deficiency Syndrome (AIDS), caused by the Human Immunodeficiency Virus (HIV), that appeared in the 1970s was in many cases a fairly typical STD in that it was difficult to pass on except through sexual contact or via transmission of other bodily fluids such as during blood transfusions. Initially, AIDS was unusual in terms of the speed and frequency with which it caused death. AIDS broke out in many places, but by the late 1990s 70 percent of the world's new infections were in Africa, as were 80 percent of the deaths.

---

20. "Ebola in Sierra Leone: Hail to the Chiefs," *The Economist*, August 20, 2015, 38.

At that time the disease was most common in southern Africa, but instead of becoming more evenly distributed over time, the incidence of HIV has remained regionally variable in Africa. In the 2010s the infection rate in southern Africa was over 15 percent of the population and over 10 percent in eastern Africa but under 5 percent in the rest of the continent. The reasons for the variations within Africa are not well understood, but the greater risk of uncircumcised men acquiring the infection has led to an increase in voluntary adult circumcision. The initial fears about dying from AIDS have declined as effective treatments have been developed to prevent HIV infection from developing into full-blown AIDS. The most effective treatment is with antiretroviral drugs. As the result of major public health efforts, the number of HIV-positive Africans receiving the drugs rose by 700 percent between 2005 and 2012, while the number of deaths due to AIDS fell by a third. The number of new infections has also continued to fall. AIDS is no longer a death sentence.[21]

Other contagious diseases are not transmitted directly from person to person, but need an intermediary. This is true of malaria, a debilitating disease common in much of Africa. Mosquitoes transmit the parasitic organism that causes malaria when they ingest the blood of an infected person and then spread it to others they bite. Although it has long been known that regular doses of a quinine-based drug can prevent malaria, getting people who feel well to pay for a weekly preventative dose has been a hard sell. Worse, taking preventative doses of a drug irregularly has resulted in parasites becoming resistant to it, requiring new compounds that are usually more expensive. At the end of the twentieth century, something like a million Africans died annually from malaria, and many more recovered from its flu-like symptoms yet still harbored the parasite that caused debilitating relapses. Because children are particularly vulnerable to malaria, anti-malaria campaigns in Africa since 2000 have made protecting the young a top priority. Just using insecticide-treated bed nets to protect sleeping children from mosquito bites has reduced deaths among children by 71 percent. Although there is still a long a way to go, these results are quite encouraging. The Bill and Melinda Gates Foundation, an American charity that supports this campaign, estimates that malaria deaths and illness have been a major drain on African economic growth. In 2015 Mr. Gates pledged an additional $5 billion to aid Africa.[22]

Disease prevention programs in Africa have become a high priority and achieved great success. Not only does reducing diseases enable people to live longer, but, by reducing debilitating sickness, it also makes people more productive throughout their lives. As people in other parts of the world have increased longevity, they have decreased the number of children they have, thus reducing the negative effects of rapid population growth. So far, except in some cities, African birthrates have remained high.

---

21. AVERT, "HIV and AIDS in Sub-Saharan Africa: Regional Overview," updated April 25, 2016, http://www.avert.org "HIV/AIDS in Africa," *Wikipedia.*
22. World Health Organization, *World Malaria Report 2015*, http://www.who.int; "Eradicating Disease," *The Economist*, October 10, 2015.

## Educational and Cultural Trends

A high birthrate and falling infant mortality rate have given Africa a rapidly growing school-age population. As a result, African governments are devoting a larger proportion of their budgets to education than any other part of the world. Since 1990, the number of pupils in African primary schools has nearly tripled, and African secondary school enrollment has seen the most rapid expansion in the world. Although the proportion of Africans receiving higher education is smaller than in other continents, African investments in universities have also grown substantially. Overall, the Africa-America Institute's 2015 report on education in Africa gives the continent grades of C for the level of enrolment and overall quality of education, although it does give primary schools a B+.[23]

A significant factor that the report does not mention is that most upper primary and post-primary education in Africa is conducted in an international language, which allows African students to communicate within the continent as well as globally. French, Arabic, and Portuguese are used, but the broadest trend is to learn English because it has become the de facto global language. Some twenty-six African countries use English as their official language or one of their official languages. Most of these were British colonies, and one, Liberia, was founded by black Americans. Others without historic connections to English-speaking countries have chosen to adopt English. Ethiopia did so after being freed from Italian rule during World War II, and Rwanda, once a Belgian colony, added English as an official language in 2000. Neighboring Burundi followed suit in 2014; South Sudan made English its official language after breaking away in 2011 from Sudan, where Arabic was the official language. Several countries that were once French colonies and teach in French, such as Gabon, now promote English as a second foreign language. Countries that use Arabic and Portuguese officially often have English-medium universities or programs in English. Sometimes the choice of English language education comes from below, as in South Africa, whose 1997 constitution accorded equal standing to eleven languages (not just English and Afrikaans), but in practice African students have preferred to be taught in English, forcing great changes in the curriculum and structuring of higher education. An indication of the growing importance of the English language in Africa is the volume of free books distributed by the American charity Books for Africa, which in recent years (2010–2015) has shipped 1.5 to 2.4 million books a year, plus half a million e-books in 2015.[24]

Not only have Africans broadened their educational horizons, but, as Chapter 6 demonstrated, they have also been broadening their religious horizons. The

---

23. Africa-America Institute, "State of Education in Africa Report 2015," http://www.aaionline.org.
24. Patrick Plonski, Asratie Teferra, and Rachel Brady, "Why Are More African Countries Adopting English as an Official Language?" (paper presented at African Studies Association Annual Conference, Baltimore, November 23, 2013), PDF downloaded from www.booksforafrica.org; David Northrup, *How English Became the Global Language* (New York: Palgrave Macmillan, 2013), 99–103, 138.

Desmond Tutu, Anglican Archbishop of South Africa. Source: Photograph by Benny Gool, 2004, public domain, Wikimedia Commons.

phenomenal spread of Christianity and Islam in recent decades has altered the global distribution of those faiths. There are now more Muslims in West Africa than in the traditional heartland of North Africa, and more Muslims in sub-Saharan Africa than in the Middle East (excluding Egypt). There are also more practicing Christians in Africa than in Europe. Some African religious leaders have achieved notable success; for example, Desmond Tutu, who was then the Anglican bishop of Cape Town, won the Nobel Peace Prize for 1984, the second black South African to do so. Roman Catholic leaders in Africa are regularly considered likely candidates to become pope. Judaism is even spreading in parts of Africa. Africans have also become missionaries overseas. The evangelical Redeemed Christian Church of God, started in Nigeria in 1952, has over 750 congregations in North America and is adding a hundred congregations a year worldwide. African Muslims are also influential in the United States. The Senegalese Murids (see Chapter 6) are such a strong presence in New York City that their founder's feast, "Amadu Bamba Day," has been celebrated there since 1989.[25]

Africans have also achieved renown in the arts. Many successes have come in the music industry both within Africa as well as abroad, where "Afropop" is spreading.

25. "Who Wants to Be a Jew?" *The Economist*, May 28, 2016, 42; John Burnett, "Nigerian Church Spreads African-Style Zeal Across North America," *Weekend Edition Sunday*, National Public Radio, May 18, 2014; David Robinson, *Muslim Societies in African History* (Cambridge: Cambridge University Press, 2004), 193.

African novels gained popularity during the colonial period, and the number of successful writers of note continues to grow. The novels of Nigerian Chinua Achebe have achieved great success in Africa and abroad. Fellow Nigerian Wole Soyinka won the Nobel Prize in Literature for 1986.[26]

Another way Africans have sought to better themselves is by moving somewhere else. African migration patterns fall into three basic categories: rural to urban migration within their home country, regional migration within sub-Saharan Africa, and emigration from below the Sahara to North Africa and overseas. The influx of people from rural hinterlands gives Africa the fastest rate of urbanization in the world. There were no cities in sub-Saharan Africa with over a million people in 1950; today there are close to fifty. The largest share (63 percent) of African migrants who move across national borders do so within their region of origin. Much intra-regional migration is economic and may be short term (seasonal) or long term. Thus the prospering West African nation of Ivory Coast receives migrants from its poorer northern neighbors Mali and Burkina Faso. Similarly, many migrants from Zimbabwe and Mozambique go to neighboring South Africa in search of work. The number of intra-regional refugees varies; at the moment there are over half a million refugees in Kenya, mostly from war-torn Somalia, some of whom have been there for more than a decade. The Kenyan government would like to close down the camps and send the refugees home.

The third category, international migrants, is smaller, but because of the distances involved they are likely to be better off. From Egypt many migrants (both Egyptian and non-Egyptian) go on to Saudi Arabia and most migrants leaving Algeria and Morocco seek to enter Europe. Many sub-Saharan Africans who migrate to North Africa hope to continue on to Europe in search of jobs, but, because they lack visas or refugee credentials, their efforts to sneak across the Mediterranean in overcrowded boats and rafts is perilous and can be deadly. Many who reach southern European countries alive are disappointed and, lacking legal status, spend months or years in crowded migrant camps or are deported back where they came from.

There has been a growing legal migration from Africa to the United States that includes refugees, students, and permanent residents. From about 80,000 in 1970 the number of African-born migrants in the United States grew to over 880,000 in 2000 and to over two million in in 2015. Many African countries are represented, with the largest numbers coming from West Africa (Nigeria and Ghana), Egypt, and Ethiopia. The influx of Africans into the United States since the 1990s has been larger than during all the decades of the Atlantic slave trade.[27] Aside from the refugees, many of these Africans are well educated and speak good English. A number of them

---

26. There are many lists of notable African musicians and writers on the Internet.

27. World Bank, *Migration Factbook*, 2011; "African Cities: Left Behind," *The Economist*, Sep. 17, 2016, 45; "Kenya Says Go Home," *The Economist*, May 14, 2016, 40–41; Marie-Laurent Flahaux and Hein De Haas, "African Migration: Trends, Patterns, Drivers," *Comparative Migration*

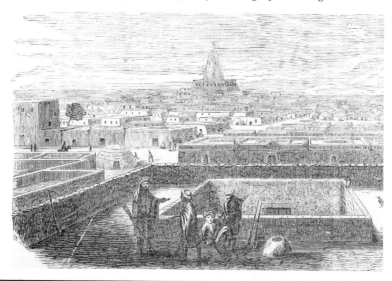

The city of Timbuktu has been a center of trade, learning, and Islam for many centuries. This view from the mid-1800s is dominated by a great mosque built entirely of earth reinforced by wood, straw, and fiber. In its present form the mosque has three inner courts and a pillared space capable of accommodating two thousand for prayers. Source: Internet Archive book image in the public domain from Heinrich Barth, *Travels and Discoveries in North and Central Africa* (1859).

have become college professors, for example, Harvard historian Emmanuel K. Akyeampong of Ghana, Congo-born Salikoko Mufwene, who holds an endowed chair in linguistics at the University of Chicago, and Gambia-born Lamin Sanneh, who is professor of comparative religion at Yale University. Dr. Ayo Ajayi, who earned his M.D. from the University of Ibadan in his native Nigeria, went on to study and teach at Boston University and now heads the African Team at the Bill and Melinda Gates Foundation, overseeing its extensive programs in sub-Saharan Africa. Architect David Adjaye, born of Ghanaian parents in Tanzania and now a British resident, was the head designer of the new National Museum of African American History and Culture in Washington, DC. His design incorporates influences from both Yoruba sculpture and an iron grillwork made by a South Carolina slave. The son of a Kenyan student at the University of Hawaii even became president of the United States.[28]

Sometimes the term "brain drain" is used to describe the departure of talented people from a developing country to a developed one. This can be an aspect of the situation, but it is not the whole story. For example, Nigeria invested in Dr. Ajayi's

*Studies* 4.1 (2016); Monica Anderson, "African Immigrant Population in U.S. Steadily Climbs," *Pew Research Center Facttank*, February 14, 2017, www.pewresearch.org.

28. Simon Alison, "The Most Notable African You've Never Heard Of," *Daily Maverick* (South Africa), July 15, 2015. In addition to articles on "David Adjaye" and "Barak Obama Sr.," *Wikipedia* has annotated lists of notable "Africans in Europe" and "Africans in the United States."

education, but Nigeria is not worse off by having him administering a multi-billion-dollar aid program for Africans. Unhindered movement is a fundamental principle of modern societies, so migrants are normally as free to return to their home countries as they were to leave. Many Ghanaians who moved to the United States, for example, have chosen to return in recent years as Ghana's economy and political climate have improved. Most arriving refugees and economic migrants would love to be able to return to their homes when conditions improve, but if they cannot, they may put down roots that can be hard to pull up. On the whole, African migrants and their families become better off overseas, whether they were pushed to leave home by intolerable conditions or drawn away in search of improved opportunities. Because international money transfers can now take place easily, remittances from relatives abroad have become vitally important to family members back home in Africa. Although it can be a wrenching experience for the individuals involved, migration can also lead to improvements in their lives. It can be good for the host country as well.

Making global connections can have unexpected benefits. The modern country of Mali provides an interesting example. The medieval city of Timbuktu was a center of Islamic learning in the fourteenth century and was recognized as a UNESCO World Heritage Site because of its large collections of manuscripts and historic buildings. However, in 2012 the city was captured by Saharan invaders and soon fell into the hands of Islamic extremists, who banned Western music and sports and, it was feared, would soon target the manuscripts. Indeed, when French troops liberated the city in January 2013, it was widely reported that the precious collections had disappeared. Though a few texts had been burned, the most precious manuscripts had been spirited away under the direction of Timbuktu-born scholar Abdel Kader Haidara. Dr. Haidara organized a plan that eventually moved 370,000 manuscripts clandestinely from forty-five Timbuktu libraries to safety in Mali's capital, Bamako. Using his connections to secure funding from foreign governments and private donors, he sent cars loaded with manuscripts four hundred miles south over the bumpy roads to Bamako. When the jihadists closed the roads, manuscripts were smuggled away in boats up the Niger River. In addition to saving the heart of the collection, Dr. Haidara has been making high-quality photocopies of the manuscripts with the help of Catholic monks from Minnesota who were experienced in this process. Never again can the Timbuktu collection be threatened with total loss.[29]

## Conclusion

"No condition is permanent," a saying commonly stenciled on Nigerian transport vehicles, might be taken to suggest that things will improve or that one's good fortune

---

29. Joshua Hammer, "The Brave Sage of Timbuktu: Abdel Kader Haidara," *National Geographic*, April 21, 2014, http://news.nationalgeographic.com; "Faith's Archivist," *The Economist*, December 19, 2015, 63–65.

today may take a turn for the worse tomorrow. In the nationalist campaigns of mid-twentieth-century Africa, optimism for the future was high, in many cases so unrealistically high as to seem mythical. The disappointments of the early independence decades led expectations among Africans and the wider world to swing to the opposite extreme. However, a recent wave of moderate optimism has begun to displace the prevailing pessimism in news stories about Africa. The phrase "Africa Rising" has been the title of a book by a celebrated business school professor in 2008 and a series in the *Wall Street Journal* in 2011, cover stories in *The Economist* in 2011 and in *Time* magazine a year later, and the theme of an International Monetary Fund conference held in Mozambique in 2014. This good news is welcome, but it is not universal or necessarily a permanent condition. It is still possible in 2016 for a major newspaper like the *New York Times* to publish a story suggesting that "Africa Reeling" might be a better description of the continent's present state, even if to illustrate its thesis it had to mix events as diverse as political unrest in Ethiopia, an economic crisis in Nigeria, and protests over university tuition in South Africa.[30]

Picking and choosing diverse themes from the dozens of African countries may create a coherent story, but it cannot be an adequate summary of the lives of a billion people. This chapter has tried to suggest there is good news from Africa without denying that much of the news could be better. It has separated the trends in different sectors. Politics is inherently volatile, especially in Africa, and the character of those in power can affect trends in other sectors. It is welcome that, on the whole, African governments are growing more democratic. Authoritarian rulers in Africa have sometimes been benevolent forces, but many of them have done a lot of harm. Economic trends in Africa tend to be more stable than political ones. Africans have yet to achieve the economic leap forward that has transformed large parts of Asia in the last half century, but there are some encouraging long-term trends.

Social trends in Africa are also improving. Literacy, longevity, and population growth have all made impressive gains since independence, though they pose great challenges too. The best African schools turn out brilliant graduates and provide opportunities for advancement for all, but it has been difficult for educational systems to keep up with the rising population. Population growth could seem a less positive trend if economic gains and ecological improvements cannot keep pace with the number of people. Culturally, Africans have made impressive advances in becoming citizens of the larger world, practicing versions of world religions and communicating in international languages. At the same time, they have preserved their traditional languages and infused historic values into new institutions.

---

30. Vijay Mahajan, *Africa Rising: How 900 Million African Customers Offer More Than You Think* (New York: Pearson Prentice Hall, 2008); cover stories in *The Economist*, December 3, 2011, and *Time*, December 3, 2012; Jeffrey Gettleman, "'Africa Rising?' 'Africa Reeling' May Be a More Fitting Slogan These Days," *New York Times*, October 18, 2016, 45.

# Suggested Reading

## General

Cordell, Dennis D., ed. *The Human Tradition in Modern Africa*. Lanham, MD: Rowman and Littlefield, 2010.

Ehret, Christopher. *The Civilizations of Africa: A History to 1800*. Charlottesville: University Press of Virginia, 2002.

Gilbert, Erik, and Jonathan T. Reynolds. *Africa in World History: From Prehistory to the Present*. 3rd ed. Upper Saddle River, NJ: Pearson Prentice Hall, 2011.

Howe, Stephen. *Afrocentrism: Mythical Pasts and Imagined Homes*. London: Verso, 1988.

Lefkowitz, Mary. *Not Out of Africa: How Afrocentrism Became an Excuse to Teach Myth as History*. New York: Basic Books, 1996.

Mamigonian, Beatriz G., and Karen Racine, eds. *The Human Tradition in the Black Atlantic, 1500–2000*. Lanham, MD: Rowman and Littlefield, 2010.

Northrup, David. *Africa's Discovery of Europe, 1450–1850*. 3rd ed. New York: Oxford University Press, 2014.

## Chapter 1

Brett, Michael. *Approaching African History*. Woodbridge, UK: James Currey, 2013.

Mitchell, Peter, and Paul Lane, eds. *The Oxford Handbook of African Archaeology*. Oxford: Oxford University Press, 2013.

Philips, John Edward, ed. *Writing African History*. Rochester, NY: University of Rochester Press, 2005.

Christian, David, ed. *The Cambridge World History*. Vol. 1, *Introducing World History, to 10,000 BCE*. Cambridge: Cambridge University Press, 2015.

Garlake, Peter. *Early Art and Architecture of Africa* (Oxford History of Art). Oxford: Oxford University Press, 2002.

Hamdun, Said, and Noël King. *Ibn Battuta in Black Africa*. Princeton, NJ: Markus Wiener, 1994.

Hilliard, Constance, ed. *Intellectual Traditions of Pre-Colonial Africa*. New York: McGraw-Hill, 1998.

Insoll, Timothy. *The Archaeology of Islam in Sub-Saharan Africa*. Cambridge: Cambridge University Press, 2003.

Levtzion, N., and J. F. P. Hopkins, eds. *Corpus of Early Arabic Sources for West African History*. Princeton, NJ: Markus Wiener, 2000.

Mitchell, Peter. *The Archaeology of Southern Africa* (Cambridge World Archaeology). Cambridge: Cambridge University Press, 2002.

# Chapter 2

Beckingham, Charles F., and Bernard Hamilton eds. *Prester John, the Mongols and the Ten Lost Tribes.* Aldershot, UK: Variorum, 1996.

Harris, Joseph E. *African-American Reactions to War in Ethiopia, 1936–1941.* Baton Rouge: Louisiana State University Press, 1994.

Kaplan, Steven. *The Beta Israel (Falasha) in Ethiopia: Earliest Times to the Twentieth Century.* New York: New York University Press, 1992.

McLeod, Erin. *Visions of Zion: Ethiopians and Rastafari.* New York: New York University Press, 2014.

Meriwether, James H. *Proudly We Can Be Africans: Black Americans and Africa, 1935–1961.* Chapel Hill: University of North Carolina Press, 2002.

Pankhurst, Richard. *The Ethiopians: A History.* Oxford: Blackwell, 1998.

Quirin, James. *The Evolution of Ethiopian Jews: A History of the Beta Israel (Falasha) to 1920.* Philadelphia: University of Pennsylvania Press, 1992.

Salvadore, Matteo. *The African Prester John and the Birth of Ethiopian-European Relations, 1402–1555.* New York: Routledge, 2017.

# Chapter 3

Austen, Ralph. *Africa in Economic History: Internal Development and External Dependency.* London: James Currey, 1987.

Ehret, Christopher. *The Civilizations of Africa: A History to 1800.* Charlottesville: University of Virginia Press, 2002.

Northrup, David. *Africa's Discovery of Europe, 1450–1850.* 3rd ed. New York: Oxford University Press, 2014.

Northrup, David. "Africans, Early European Contacts, and the Emergent Diaspora." In *The Oxford Handbook of the Atlantic World, 1450–1850*, edited by Nicholas Canny and Philip Morgan. Oxford: Oxford University Press, 2011.

# Chapter 4

Behrendt, Stephen, A. J. H. Latham, and David Northrup. *The Diary of Antera Duke: An Eighteenth-Century Slave Trader.* New York: Oxford University Press, 2010.

Curtin, Philip D, ed. *Africa Remembered: Narratives by West Africans from the Era of the Slave Trade.* Madison: University of Wisconsin Press, 1967.

Eltis, David, and David Richardson, eds. *Extending the Frontiers: Essays on the New Transatlantic Slave Trade Database.* New Haven, CT: Yale University Press, 2008.

Manning, Patrick. *Slavery and African Life: Occidental, Oriental and African Slave Trades.* New York: Cambridge University Press, 1990.

Miller, Joseph C. *The Way of Death: Merchant Capitalism and the Angolan Slave Trade, 1730–1830.* Madison: University of Wisconsin Press, 1988.

Northrup, David. *Africa's Discovery of Europe, 1450–1850.* 3rd ed. New York: Oxford University Press, 2002.

Thornton, John. *Africa and Africans in the Making of the Atlantic World, 1400–1800.* 2nd ed. New York: Cambridge University Press, 1998.

## Chapter 5

Bascom, William, and Melville J. Herskovits, eds. *Continuity and Change in African Cultures.* Chicago: Phoenix Books, 1965.
Callinicos, Luli. *Working Life: Factories, Townships, and Popular Culture on the Rand, 1886–1940.* Braamfontein, South Africa: Raven Press, 1987.
Northrup, David. "Becoming African: Identity Formation among Liberated Slaves in Nineteenth-Century Sierra Leone." *Slavery and Abolition* 27 (April 2006): 1–21.
Peel, J. D. Y. *Religious Encounter and the Making of the Yoruba.* Bloomington: Indiana University Press, 2000.
Vail, Leroy, ed. *The Creation of Tribalism in Southern Africa.* Berkeley: University of California Press, 1989.

## Chapter 6

Blyden, Edward W. *Christianity, Islam and the Negro Race.* 2nd ed. London: W. B. Wittingham, 1888.
Crowder, Michael. *West Africa under Colonial Rule.* London: Hutchinson, 1968.
Gray, Richard. "Christianity." In *The Cambridge History of Africa*, vol. 7, *From 1905 to 1940*, edited by A. D. Roberts. Cambridge: Cambridge University Press, 1986.
Hastings, Adrian. *The Church in Africa, 1450–1950* (Oxford History of the Christian Church). Oxford: Clarendon Press, 1994.
Lapidus, Ira. *A History of Islamic Societies*, 2nd ed. Cambridge: Cambridge University Press, 2002.
Levtzion, Nehemia, and Randall Pouwels, eds. *The History of Islam in Africa.* Athens: Ohio University Press, 2000.
Lovejoy, Paul E. *Transformations in Slavery: A History of Slavery in Africa.* 2nd ed. Cambridge: Cambridge University Press, 2000.
Robinson, David. *Muslim Societies in African History.* Cambridge: Cambridge University Press, 2004.

## Chapter 7

Cooper, Frederick. *Africa since 1940: The Past of the Present.* Cambridge: Cambridge University Press, 2002.
Nugent, Paul. *Africa since Independence.* 2nd ed. New York: Palgrave Macmillan, 2012.

# Index

Trevor-Roper, Hugh, 1–3, 8
Tuareg, vii
Tukulor people, 92
Turé, Samori, 92
Turnbull, Colin, 96
Turner, Henry M., 34
Tuskegee Institute, 78–79, 101
Tutu, Desmond, 147

Uganda, 98, 115, 120, 122, 138, 143
Umar Tall, al-hajj, 113
United Nations, 136
United Negro Improvement Association, 36
United States, xxi, 89, 121, 135, 142; Africans in, xxii, 34, 133, 147–49; African Americans in, 77, 113; and Africa, 36–37, 108, 137; civil rights movement in, 61, 103–3; religions in, 121, 127; view of Africa in, 62, 81–82
universities. *See* education, African: university
urbanization, 98, 148
Usuman dan Fodio, 112

Vail, Leroy, 80, 85, 86
Venice, viii, 31, 46, 53
Virginia, 17, 53, 81
Volta River, 53

Wagadu, 49–51
Warri, 107
Washington, Booker T., 78–79, 101
West Africa, xviii, xviii, 13, 16–18, 32, 48, 76, 98, 99, 144, 148; Christianity

in, 107–8, 120, 124; ethnicity in (pre-colonial), 86–92; Islam in, 103–5, 109–14, 116–17, 147; nationalism in, 124, 128, 131; trade in, 4, 9, 48–57, 63, 65, 69, 71–72, 82
West Indies, 39, 62, 77, 82, 103
West-Central Africa, 19, 55, 75, 82, 86
Western Sudan, vi, viii, 4, 50, 52–53, 92, 109–10, 113, 116–17
Wolof kingdom, 119
women, 2, 10, 26, 52, 90, 98, 99, 125, 140; elite, 4, 27; enslaved, 53, 63, 70, 111; in agriculture, 15, 20, 140; Women's War, 94. *See also* Candice; Makeda; Sheba, queen of; Zawditu
World Bank, 143
Wright, Joseph, 65

Yoruba: culture and identity, 88, 90–92, 108, 116, 121–22, 149; kindgoms, 69, 83; in Cuba and Brazil, 90–92, 108; in Sierra Leone, 88, 90–92; in the slave trade, 69, 82–83, 88

Zagwé dynasty, 25, 27
Zambezi River, 19, 48, 55
Zambia, 143
Zanji, 111
Zanzibar, 115–17, 124, 126, 132, 134
Zawditu, Ethiopian empress, 35
Zeila, 45
Zimbabwe, 8, 46, 136–38, 142, 148
Zimbabwe African National Union, 136
Zimbabwean Plateau, 46
Zionism, African Christian, 121
Zulu, 14, 90, 92, 100, 121